Why do some privatisations apparently fail to produce expected positive results? Economic theory tells us that privatisation should improve efficiency, but this book suggests that political bargaining in the process of privatisation works against the results we expect to achieve. To gain a more adequate understanding of what privatisation is really about, one also needs to look at the issue of power at the level of organisations undergoing privatisation. Privatisation is a gradually unfolding, evolutionary process, often with defective corporate governance. Politicking can take priority over performance, attention is diverted from efficiency, and the firm drifts.

This is the first and only book on privatisation which focuses on micro-level behavioural issues and it uses exceptionally rich case evidence to illustrate that privatisation is more about politics than performance.

Privatisation, politics,
and economic performance
in Hungary

Privatisation, politics, and economic performance in Hungary

Zoltán Antal-Mokos
Budapest University of Economic Sciences

PUBLISHED BY THE PRESS SYNDICATE OF THE UNIVERSITY OF CAMBRIDGE
The Pitt Building, Trumpington Street, Cambridge, United Kingdom

CAMBRIDGE UNIVERSITY PRESS
The Edinburgh Building, Cambridge CB2 2RU, UK   http://www.cup.cam.ac.uk
40 West 20th Street, New York, NY 10011–4211, USA   http://www.cup.org
10 Stamford Road, Oakleigh, Melbourne 3166, Australia

First published 1998

Printed in the United Kingdom at the University Press, Cambridge

Typeset in Times 10/12 pt [CE]

A catalogue record for this book is available from the British Library

Library of Congress Cataloguing in Publication data

Antal-Mokos, Zoltán.
Privatisation, politics, and economic performance in
Hungary / Zoltán Antal-Mokos.
        p.   cm.
Includes bibliographical references and index.
ISBN 0 521 59339 5 hardback
1. Privatization.   2. Privatization – political aspects.
3. Economic development.   4. Government business enterprises.
I. Title.
HD3845.6.A58   1997
338.9 – dc21   97–15775   CIP

To Judit

Contents

Figures

Tables

Preface

For some time the advice has been 'Go East, young man!' This book should be the guide for those who take this advice, either in person or in thought as investors, managers, consultants, and researchers – also for those who wish to gain some insight into how people behave, how organisations adapt to new challenges, or fail to do so, and how institutions evolve in a unique period of political, social, and economic change.

This guide is unusual in that it does not attempt to recommend a way. That remains to be explored by the adventurous. While the destination is believed to be known, the path is being mapped right now.

This book aspires to assist in reading signposts for walking through unknown territories. The signposts themselves will be familiar: corporate governance, strategy, organisational politicking – and human behaviour behind them all. They shape our everyday life regardless of location, level of economic development, and institutional system.

Acknowledgements

While it is certainly true that the author bears sole responsibility for the final result, there have been a few mentors, many colleagues, and numerous friends whose support has made this work an enjoyable adventure.

My greatest thanks and praise go to Saul Estrin who, after joining the London Business School, carried me through three years and countless revisions. He was asked to read drafts and revised drafts (and revisions of revised drafts) in unreasonably short time. Comments duly came in the margin – legible or otherwise, but always astute. Under his second-to-none supervision, life was a series of thought-stimulating challenges. For some time, none of us knew exactly just what would come out of this research project. I hope the result now justifies the patience he sometimes demonstrated while I was trying to keep up with his tempo. Thank you Saul for the pleasant opportunity of working with you, and further special thanks for securing London Business School hospitality for me to finish and polish this book.

David Chambers shaped my early attempts to get a grip on what seemed to be an incomprehensibly diverse area. His trust in my abilities was a principal incentive for me. He also helped me acclimatise in a foreign culture; so too did his wife, Hilary, whose fingers crossed for me must have helped a lot. Thank you both.

I am particularly grateful for the helpful comments and encouragement I received from Jone Pearce, Mario Nuti, Mark Schaffer, and Saul Estrin as this work proceeded to completion.

The sessions with Alessandro Lomi and Costas Markides will be long-remembered exemplars of how to combine a demanding workload with intellectual reward in a Ph.D. course. I also gained much from Nigel Nicholson's witty introduction to the esoteric world of doing research.

The year 1991 witnessed the arrival of some special people at the School. I have greatly benefited from the friendship of Jonathan Levie.

Thank you for the long hours of intellectual debate and occasional relaxation in our 'outer office'. Many thanks and cheers go to an international bunch of friends, especially Mark Edward Bleackley, David Cannon, Douglas George Carrie, Oliver Hansch, and Luc Renneboog, whose companionship ensured that my London experience did not pass without fun. A word of appreciation to all members of the LBSPHDFC, diligently led by James Taylor. Finally, I thank Bette Laing, Sarah Todd, and Rose Trevelyan for their heroic attempts to improve my English.

I am indebted to Miklós Dobák, Sándor Kovács, and Ernő Zalai of the Budapest University of Economic Sciences for their contributions which made it possible for me to pursue my interest in working for a Ph.D. at the London Business School. I also thank all my colleagues at the Department of Management and Organisation for holding out while I was 'out of action'.

This work could not have been completed without support from a number of people at various business organisations and institutions. They provided the 'flesh and blood' substance for the alchemy of inducing a theory. They told me about their experiences and even personal failures; others provided me with documents to peruse; and some backed me so that I could have access to the first two groups. We shared the belief that an important, once-in-a-lifetime process was evolving which called for description and analysis. They furnished me with plenty of information, and I had the privilege to learn from them. Not having the opportunity to express my gratitude to them here individually, I thank them all for their invaluable co-operation.

I am most grateful for the grant I was awarded by the World Bank Graduate Scholarship Program, and for financial support from the Know-How Fund. An earlier version of section 5.1 of this book on Pluto's case was first published in 1997 by Blackwell Publishers under the title 'Politicking and Privatisation', *Business Strategy Review*, 8: 23–30 © London Business School.

Several people at Cambridge University Press provided significant editorial and production support at various stages of publication. I thank Patrick McCartan, Sophie Noël, and Ashwin Rattan not only for this support but also for their ongoing encouragement and trust in the success of this volume. My special thanks go to Chris Doubleday for his unsurpassed attention to the many flaws in my writing, and for all his suggestions.

Throughout my life I have been carefully guided by my parents whose intellectual and emotional endowments have helped me find a balanced state of being. Drága Apa és Óma, köszönöm.

My wife Judit listened when I needed an audience, chatted without expecting an answer when I needed inspiration for thoughts, encouraged me, and helped in numerous ways so that I could focus on my work. Thank you Judit for standing by me and sharing your amazingly unlimited energy.

1 Introduction

Privatisation fits nicely into the trend of creating better governance structures worldwide. It has been a government policy in various countries for more than a decade. It became a major issue in the USA and the UK in the eighties. In a second wave, privatisation of the public sector occurred around the world, including in several developing countries. Owing to the tremendous changes that have been taking place in the countries of the collapsed communist bloc, the nineties started as the period of mass privatisation in Central-Eastern Europe. In many countries privatisation is a central component of the historically unique endeavour of building market economies region-wide on the ruins of state controlled ones.

This sweeping fashion for privatisation has attracted considerable research attention. However, much of the research has tended to focus on privatisation in market economies dominated by private actors. Although there is now a burgeoning literature on 'transitional economics', the economics of transitional economies, applied theoretical frameworks are often derived from Western experience, largely without appropriate contextualisation, and with a tendency to focus on macro-level issues and policy options. For a more adequate understanding of what privatisation is about, one also needs to look at behavioural issues arising at the level of organisations undergoing privatisation. In this book we take this route: the helicopter view is disposed of; instead we offer the view from the ground.

Central-Eastern Europe has been in turbulence since 1989. New states have been emerging, political and economic systems have been undergoing transformation, interests have been overthrowing ideologies. In this context, local business organisations must face challenges with no precedent whatsoever. Among the more substantial challenges are 'going private', that is the *transfer of ownership* of the firm from a collapsed socialist state to an emerging private sector, and the need for developing *new patterns of behaviour* to cope with their dramatically altered environment. These two challenges are, in fact, related in that privatisation is generally assumed to bring about stronger incentives, hence improved management and better performance. It is believed to facilitate restructuring, and to encourage new, more efficient ways of doing business.

It is beyond our space, time, and resource limits to address an exhaustive set of issues regarding the assumed relationship between privatisation and firm behaviour. The scope of the study reported here has been confined in terms of issues and context. *Specifically, we explain the role that politics plays in privatisation and its effect on the performance of privatised state-owned enterprises in the context of national transition.* 'National' refers here to the various social, political, and economic aspects of systemic changes. Accepting common usage, we shall refer to the process that countries of the former communist bloc are undergoing as 'transition'. However, 'transformation' may better describe this process since 'the future stable state of an evolving system is *not* predictable from its unstable state' (Levie, 1993: 9, quoting Csányi's (1989) 'replicative' theory of biosocial evolution; see also Murrell, 1992).

The main empirical body of our research comes from the Hungarian privatisation experience. This country had introduced some elements of a market economy with its stop-go reforms starting in 1968. A few of the institutions of a market economy, therefore, had been established by the end of the 1980s, when the opportunity for the 'national transition' opened up. Yet, her 'road to the free economy' (Kornai, 1990b) has proved to be a rocky one, on which privatisation has become one of the most fiercely debated issues to be solved on the way.

Although the case evidence is taken from Hungary, some general conclusions can be formulated which are applicable not only to transitional countries undergoing political and economic changes, but also in any context of ineffective corporate governance and changing property rights. For example, the journey of Pluto, the subject of one of our cases, down the path of privatisation dragged out for several years. It was a 'struggling through' process rather than a consciously planned and implemented, straightforward business transaction. Extreme as it may be, it illustrates some general features. To one degree or another, almost all cases of privatisation are subject to forces similar to those which the case of Pluto illustrates in excess: forces which all too often are not explicitly considered by either academics or managers. Those who have been involved in the privatisation process in Britain and elsewhere will recognise some features of this and other cases.

One would expect that as a formerly state-owned enterprise goes private, it can no longer be effective without being efficient, and consequently it will develop a pattern of behaviour better suited to the incentives that the new, private owners impose on its management. In particular, in the case of a 'troubled' firm, facing competitive pressures and losing the cushion of a soft budget constraint (Kornai, 1980), this pattern of behaviour would show the characteristics of a turnaround strategy. It is this assumed relationship between privatisation and strategy that lies at the centre of the book.

This study utilises concepts and frameworks of both economic and organisation theories. It focuses not only on ownership changes as inputs and the resulting changes in firm behaviour and performance as outputs, but also on the process by which these changes unfold. In that, it advances a view of privatisation that is driven by organisation theory to complement the dominant economic framework based on agency theory. On the basis of theoretical considerations and an analysis of the policy context of privatisation in Hungary, we have developed a political bargaining framework for better understanding micro-level issues of privatisation and behaviour. Formally, our research sought to explore *the conditions under which privatisation indeed facilitates favourable changes (a turnaround) in firm behaviour and post-privatisation performance*. In other words, *why do some privatisations apparently fail to produce the expected positive results*? Soon the *process of privatisation itself* became an important target of research inquiry. In a sense, we started from basics by asking the decisive question: *What is going on here*? It took a four-year-long research project and a series of case studies to give enough depth to an emergent political bargaining framework.

In-depth longitudinal case studies were conducted to investigate whether there was a certain pattern in the privatisation process. What are the characteristics of the privatisation processes of individual firms? What are the factors that control the dynamics of the process? How do process characteristics of privatisation affect turnaround? These were the questions that guided our inquiry.

The dominant, agency-theory based approach would suggest that with privatisation comes effective corporate governance, managers will be disciplined, the performance of the firm will improve, and everyone will be better off. Our results suggest that it takes more fundamental factors to offer a chance for improved post-privatisation performance. We unearthed some general stories from an enormous body of detail. They revealed what we believe are not only empirically derived and plausible, but also fascinating, lessons. One is that process matters. It matters so much that a firm, if its process of privatisation is based on one of the worst scenarios, will enter its private life with such a handicap that it soon may become a target again. Pluto has changed owners twice already, not counting its first acquisition by private owners from the state. Another lesson points to the importance of politics during, and sometimes after, the privatisation process. In a political bargaining process, which privatisation often appears to be, much damage to the pie can happen by the time everyone gets his or her cut, as evinced by the experience of some other case subjects like Neptune and the Deimos subsidiary of Mars.

There are two aspects of politics apparent in privatisation processes: first, politicisation of the context in which the question of future ownership is resolved, and, second, the intensity of organisational politicking. Politics during the privatisation process was found to influence post-privatisation performance through strategy-making and strategy content. Saturn's case scores low on politics: its management was able to focus on achieving recovery and preparing the firm for its privatisation. Other cases show the opposite story.

Indeed, one can distil a few general stories, or scenarios, from the cases presented in this book. We have labelled them as 'going through', 'muddling through', and 'struggling through', depending on features of politics, strategy, and consequent performance during privatisation. When these scenarios are coupled with privatisation outcomes, especially with different corporate governance regimes and varying levels of resource replenishment, post-privatisation performance can be either 'turnaround success', the case that common wisdom would want to see after privatisation, 'turnaround failure', or 'turnaround handicapped' – by either process characteristics of privatisation or its outcome, or both.

The main relationships are as follows:

(1) Characteristics of the privatisation process, of which politicisation and politicking were explicitly considered and found to be inter-linked, have an effect on properties of strategy, of which conscious-ness of strategy-making and the coping pattern of strategy content were explicitly considered and, again, found to be interlinked. Low levels of both politicisation and politicking seem to facilitate focused strategy-making and recovery, whereas high politicisation and politicking produce vague strategy-making and make the firm drift.

(2) Consequently, performance of firms during the privatisation process varies between the extremes of sustained stability and decline (which may be cushioned by the benevolence of the firm's environment).

(3) Thus, we found that typical scenarios, as dynamic configurations of the privatisation process, strategy-making and strategy outcome, and performance during privatisation, are likely to occur in the transition period.

(4) These scenarios, coupled with different privatisation outcomes, are likely determinants of post-privatisation turnaround.

Our results support the proposition that goal conflicts and their resolution through the use of political means make the outcome of the privatisation process difficult to predict on the basis of the rational actor model. Privatisation can be regarded as a gradually unfolding, evolutionary process. In national transitions, defective corporate governance can permit politicking to take a priority over performance. In the long-drawn-out process of privatisation, attention is diverted from efficiency. This exacerbates the firm's drift, which further restricts the chances of privatisation. Owing to uncertainties in the privatisation process, managerial business decisions are built on vague assumptions about the likely outcome of privatisation and, if these assumptions prove false, the firm's strategy will turn out to be ineffective. Essentially, these propositions suggest that political bargaining in the process of privatisation works against the results that we expect to achieve from privatisation.

This book has been written for a wide range of readers. Country experts may find the structured review of the Hungarian privatisation policy until 1994 the most interesting aspect, and helpful in evaluating the effectiveness of that policy. We hope the book offers researchers of transitional economics a wealth of empirical evidence to further develop insights about privatisation and, moreover, closer links with organisational theorists working in related fields. For students of business policy and strategy the book provides a set of rich descriptions of the actual process of privatisation in six firms operating in an environment rarely dealt with in standard case studies. Scholars conducting research into organisational phenomena will probably be interested not only in the case material as a resource but also in the analysis of this material, which highlights and integrates the importance of politicking and weak governance. On the practical side, policy-makers devising and implementing privatisation schemes, and managers and consultants involved in privatisation processes are the main targets of the author's efforts in producing this volume. The results of our analysis can make a significant practical contribution to both public policy and to the deliberations of potential investors deciding whether or not to become involved in privatisation in the formerly communist countries. Acquisition specialists, orchestrators and targets of hostile takeovers may also find it interesting to study issues they encounter, now in some cases to an extreme extent. With this diverse audience in mind, we shall conclude this book by putting the results in a broader context and offering questions for further study.

Figure 1 presents an overview of the chapters and sections of this book, and indicates some of the iterations between different phases of the research process that produced this volume.

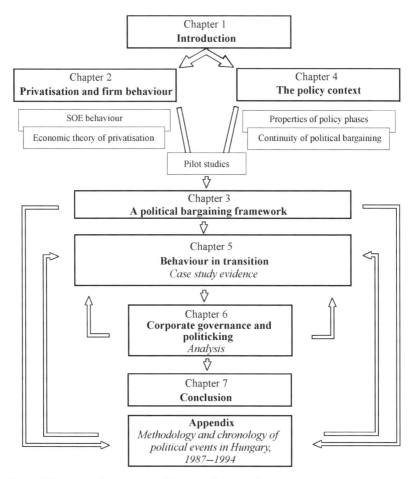

Fig. 1. The research process and layout of the book.

2 Privatisation and firm behaviour

Since the problems this research is concerned with have arisen only recently, it is not surprising that no coherent middle-range theory has yet been developed on how privatisation of formerly state-owned enterprises affects firms' behaviour patterns in transitional economies. There is, however, a considerable theoretical literature on closely related issues, partly in the field of economic theory and partly in organisation theory and strategic management, from which guidelines for this study were developed. Drawing on concepts from both economics and organisation theory in analysing patterns of firm behaviour corresponds with the contemporary development of strategy as a 'meeting-point' of the two disciplines (Williamson, 1990; see also *Strategic Management Journal*, February 1992, special issue devoted to the contribution of economics to strategy).

In particular, there appear to be two broad fields of study one could rely upon in addressing the research question. These are:
- behaviour of state-owned business organisations as viewed from public enterprise economics and the resource-dependence view of organisations, and
- the agency approach to privatisation and its presumed effects on firm performance.

2.1 Behaviour of state-owned enterprises

State-owned enterprise (SOE) behaviour has been a subject of interest in various disciplines. Most notably, public enterprise economists have developed a comprehensive explanation, but organisation theorists and strategy researchers have also contributed. In this section we explain state-oriented behaviour patterns with characteristics of the context within which strategic decision-making takes place. Special attention is paid to the vertical dependence of state-owned enterprises, their goal formation process, and the features of their external control. The discussion sheds light on why state-oriented strategies can be effective even at the expense of efficiency, and singles out bargaining as the dominant element of the behaviour patterns of state-owned enterprises.

It has been noted that state-owned enterprises often follow strategies in which managing the business is traded off against winning political support (Zif, 1981). Within the realms of two different disciplines, the resource-dependence view of organisations and public enterprise economics have contributed to the explanation of primarily state-oriented (as opposed to market- or business-oriented) behaviour of state-owned enterprises.

According to the resource-dependence view, organisational survival postulates interaction with those who control external resources (Pfeffer and Salancik, 1978). Since resources in the environment are unevenly distributed between different actors, organisations will direct their efforts to satisfying the needs of those environmental subsystems from which the critical resources can be acquired (Markóczy, 1989). In a market economy a private firm can obtain its critical resources above all from markets. A public enterprise may be able to compensate for the market resources that are not available to it because of poor performance with subsidies granted by politicians in return for meeting their needs (Schleifer and Vishny, 1994). A state-owned firm operating in a socialist economy faces an environment where economic resources are highly centralised, controlled and reallocated by the 'party-state', the symbiotic coalition of the Communist Party and the state authorities (Csanádi, 1987; Tsoukas, 1994). Resources, in a broad sense, may include direct financial subsidies from state funds as well as 'indirect' preferential regulatory treatment in terms of prices chargeable, wages payable, tax holidays granted, permission for hard currency import, etc. Table 1 illustrates the vertical, 'paternalistic' dependence of the socialist firm.

For the political system to be relevant for the organisation, it has to have an influence on organisational outcomes (Pfeffer and Salancik, 1978). In the context of state ownership and bureaucratic co-ordination of economic activities, the state dominates the economic payoff (Kornai and Matits, 1990). Managerial positions are often a political patronage prize. Firm behaviour shifts accordingly. In a state-controlled socialist economy – no matter whether it is a classic command economy, or a reforming one, governed via sophisticated indirect 'market-simulating' mechanisms, formal and informal 'expectations', and campaigns – the state regulatory and supervisory subsystems constitute the relevant sector in the firm's environment which organisational efforts must be directed to. In this setting, firms will develop a dominant competence to cope with

Table 1. *The socialist firm's vertical dependence*

Issue	Assessment
Entry	Bureaucracy decides on setting up new public firms, or permitting import competition or entry of private enterprise.
Exit	Winding up a firm is decided (rarely) by bureaucracy. No correlation with prior losses or insolvency.
Mergers and splits	May be initiated by firms, but last word remains with bureaucracy.
Appointment of leaders of firms	Bureaucracy decides or influences decisively the nomination and selection.
Output and input	No imposition, but 'pressures' from party and state organisations remain. Contractual disputes taken to authority, not court.
Exports/imports and foreign exchange	Interference via export assignments, import quotas, licensing procedure, and pressure.
Choice of technology and product development	Intervention via subsidy, credit facility, import licence, tied to the firm's choice.
Prices	Partial deregulation. Fixed prices influence free prices. Calculation methods prescribed. Protest pressure if price is thought 'unjustifiably high'. Highly distorted.
Wages and employment	Some state interference still present. For example, administrative ceiling, 'punitive tax' for high wage rise, informal pressure.
Taxes and subsidies	Tax system same for all in principle, easily tailor-made in practice. Extremely complex and often unpredictable. Concessions on amount and due date.
Extension of credit and loan repayment	Bureaucratic banking sector, as branch of the state. Soft budget constraint. Loan decisions are not based on economic rationality.
Investment	Partial deregulation, modest autonomy. Larger projects invariably need state funds.

Source: Based on Kornai (1992: 482–6).

their vertical dependence, while neglecting competence needed for managing horizontal dependencies (cf. McKelvey and Aldrich, 1983). Since competition is for resources from the state, 'strategic capabilities' and 'distinctive competencies' often imply political skills.

If state ownership and regulation induce an increased attention to the state in market economies, state orientation of the behaviour of socialist firms is probably further intensified not only by the high centralisation and reallocation of economic resources but also by the *political control* of the communist party-state. Following the works of DiMaggio and Powell (1983) and Tsoukas (1994), we regard political control as one of the coercive forces through which the state engenders 'behavioural isomorphism', the similarity of the behaviour patterns of state-owned firms. 'Structural isomorphism' has been explained similarly in a study of sixty large Hungarian industrial firms, in which Máriás *et al.* (1981) could attribute strikingly uniform organisational structures to the high level of vertical dependence on the state.

This does not mean that there is only one dominant behaviour model. In populations of firms that are less connected to the state (for example, private establishments in a so-called market socialist country), other models may become dominant. In addition, variants of the dominant model of state orientation may arise within the population of firms that are closely connected to the state (such as large state-owned industrial enterprises), since the state is not a unitary actor but is constituted of various bodies, each with its own preferred model of organisation (Carroll, Goodstein, and Gyenes, 1988). We return to this issue later in this section.

Public enterprise economics emphasises that the analysis of the behaviour of state-owned enterprises requires an understanding of the nature of objectives pursued by the management and the incentives and constraints it faces. Private and public firms differ significantly in both respects – therefore their strategies must also differ.

Positive research in economics has revealed that public enterprises usually do not aim at maximising profit; nor even do they, as the normative theory suggests they should be forced to, maximise social welfare (Aharoni, 1981; Bös, 1991). In fact, one of the most striking differences between the goal structures of private and public firms is that in the latter case a single objective function cannot be defined. State-owned enterprises are often expected to create employment, help develop certain geographical regions, hold down prices of certain goods, earn foreign exchange, develop technologies of 'national importance', etc. These objectives are also subject to frequent changes due to modifications in the priorities and power distribution of the political leadership. In short, public enterprises seem to follow multiple, and often contra-dictory, ill-defined or 'fuzzy' objectives which have emerged from a political process (Estrin and Pérotin, 1991).

In a situation like this, when what counts as good performance is virtually undefined, it often becomes impossible to monitor effectively the performance of public enterprises. Numerous and shifting targets make the term 'efficiency' blurred, and prone to being the subject of alternative interpretations. Governments, then, may feel it necessary to intervene in the operational activity of the firm rather than to monitor outcomes (Estrin and Pérotin, 1991). This makes the situation worse, since it may lead to passive, risk-averse and bureaucratic behaviour. Levy (1987) describes the trap of a downward spiral, in which intervention reduces management's effort and consequently firm performance, leading to an even tighter external control.

Government intervention, even if exercised indirectly through regula-tions, can also be used by the management as an argument against taking responsibility for poor performance. The management can always point out shared responsibility with some state or party agents with whom it has consulted before making major decisions, which also creates a mutual interest for the management and its superiors to disguise the poor results of the mistaken decision (Kornai, 1992). This suggests that strategy-making in the case of a state-owned, and particularly a socialist, enterprise can be conceived of as a process cutting across the blurred boundary between the enterprise and the government, and that the political relations of the management are of utmost importance (cf. Hafsi and Thomas, 1986).

These characteristics of goal formation open a wide space for *bargaining* between management and government. The phenomenon is not unknown in market economies (Aharoni, 1981; Birnbaum, 1985). In a socialist economy bargaining between the management and government is an ongoing process involving almost every possible issue (Kornai, 1986). In the Hungarian context in particular, the bargaining nature of the so-called market socialist economic mechanism, and the pre-eminent importance for a management team of managing relations with the state also received support from Carroll, Goodstein, and Gyenes (1988) and Kovács (1988) who found that managers spend much of their time on managing external relationships and participating in lobbies in order to 'move from one basket of ministerial preferences into another' (Kovács, 1988: 1285). This is what L. Antal (1985) described in rich detail and labelled 'regulation bargaining', as opposed to 'plan bargaining' of the classic command economy, where 'regulations' in the Hungarian eco-nomic jargon mean a constantly changing, hardly predictable, complex web of parameters (i.e. financial controls, targets, quotas, etc.) set by the superior organisations in order to regulate firms in the so-called indirect mechanism of economic management. The complex system of regulations also, by default, enabled creative accounting in order to camouflage poor performance and build up enough slack.

The bargaining process may result in the government being captured by the management owing to information asymmetry. In passing we note that capturing of controllers by those supposedly controlled may also happen in the course of privatisation. On the British privatisation, for example, Bishop and Kay (1988) and Vickers and Yarrow (1988) noted the importance of management's co-operation and support if the government's privatisation policy is to succeed, from which the political power of management results. As we shall see from the cases to follow, this applies even more in the transitional context of Central-Eastern Europe where the scope, size, and urgency of privatisation exceed the corresponding parameters of the British privatisation, heightening the need for the government to rely upon the managements of firms undergoing privatisation.

Furthermore, the state cannot be conceived of as a single principal but rather must be seen as a set of persons and organisations each with its own, often divergent, objectives and capabilities of influencing managers (Aharoni, 1981; Estrin and Pérotin, 1991; Kornai, 1992; Mintzberg, 1983). This may also permit managers of state-owned enterprises to ease away from the effects of external control by making alliances with some of the state controllers to play off against others. In other words, the fragmented state offers an opportunity for the organisation to turn to another state body for support if rebutted by one. This is a possibility even in the relations of the regulator and the regulated, even without assuming state ownership (Pfeffer and Salancik, 1978).

We can conclude, then, that in the context of state ownership, centralised and redistributed resources, numerous regulations, and political control, *bargaining* is likely to become the dominant property of firm behaviour patterns.

Compliance with, or orientation to, the strong state may not represent an *efficient* strategy; however, it may be an *effective* strategy in terms of satisfying the needs of the controllers of critical resources. The point that is being made here is that for evaluating the appropriateness of a strategy, effectiveness instead of efficiency is the criterion to be chosen, and these two criteria had been quite independent of each other under command and so-called market socialist economic regimes.

Multiplicity, internal inconsistency, political definition, and the changing nature of objectives define a task environment in which the management has much discretion in determining what actual objectives to follow. This corresponds to a seemingly paradoxical situation of both high environmental determinism *and* high organisational choice of strategy in which the management manoeuvres around external constraints and imposed prescriptions (Burgelman, 1983a, 1983b, 1991; Hrebiniak and Joyce, 1985; Levinthal, 1991). In its pursuit of objectives the management of a public firm usually does not have to observe so diligently the constraints that align the criteria of effectiveness and efficiency for its private counterpart. These constraints include product market competition or contestability, threats of takeover bids or bankruptcy, the managerial labour market, and effective monitoring by private shareholders (Estrin and Pérotin, 1991; Fama, 1980; Fama and Jensen, 1983; Kornai, 1980, 1986, 1990a,b; Walsh and Kosnik, 1993). For managers in socialist economies, however, these constraints were virtually non-existent, their place in the governance system taken by centralisation of economic resources and political control.

2.2   The economic theory of privatisation

The dominant theory on privatisation, particularly concerning its effect on firm behaviour, has been developed by economists in the principal–agent framework. It identifies significant changes in the context of the privatised firm, and offers these changes as an explanation for supposed changes in their behaviour. In this section we briefly present the concept of privatisation and the objectives that have been followed in countries embarking on privatisation. Then, turning to theory, we outline the contextual changes that are introduced by privatisation and to which changes in firm behaviour are attributed.

Although it has been studied for many years, the concept of privatisation still does not have an agreed definition (Hemming and Mansoor, 1988: 1, footnote; King, 1987: 18; Thiemeyer, 1986: 7–10). Undoubtedly, it denotes a shift from the public to the private sector, but this shift can take place in various forms. Which aspects of these forms are covered by the term 'privatisation' leads to differences between authors. Confusion about this word in the post-communist countries is further exacerbated when it is often used to denote commercialisation or corporatisation (or transformation, as it is often called in Hungary), labelling a firm as privatised even if it has only been converted into a commercial company form but is still wholly owned by the state.

Broad and *narrow* meanings of privatisation differ according to the ways through which the balance between the private and the public sectors alters. Swann (1988), for example, regards privatisation as a

Table 2. *A broad view of privatisation*

Broad policy options	Change in the ownership of an enterprise	Liberalisation or deregulation	Private supply with government's ultimate responsibility for the supply
Techniques	• sale of equity • sale of state-owned enterprise as entity • joint-venture • liquidation	• allowing entry into areas previously populated only by state-owned enterprises	• franchising • contracting-out • leasing of public assets

Source: Based on Cook and Kirkpatrick (1988: 3-4)

broad umbrella term: privatisation can take place without a change in ownership. Table 2 summarises various policy initiatives and techniques that are often gathered under the umbrella of privatisation.

Others use the term in a narrower sense, requiring *transfer of ownership* for the phenomenon to be called privatisation. In this book, the narrow meaning of privatisation is adopted. In our view, privatisation is about ownership. It refers to the transfer of ownership of a state-owned enterprise where entitlements to the residual profits from operating the enterprise are devolved to the private sector (Bös, 1991; Vickers and Yarrow, 1988). In this approach, privatisation and liberalisation, that is the transfer of ownership and the introduction of competitive forces to areas previously restricted to the public sector respectively, are two distinct concepts. This distinction, however, does not mean that the impact of privatisation on firm behaviour and performance, and that of liberalisation (or, rather, competition) can be analysed separately (Vickers and Yarrow, 1988).

Privatisation of state-owned enterprises can be partial or total, depending upon whether the state retains shares in the privatised company or not. It is hard to establish a criterion of when a firm with both private and state owners can be regarded as genuinely privatised. Even in cases where private owners acquire only a nominal minority holding in a state-owned firm, they may gain complete control over the firm. Similarly, the state in a minority position may have decisive influence on the behaviour of the privatised firm. Experience suggests that case-by-case study may be necessary to reach a verdict on this issue.

In the Central-Eastern European context, some authors also refer to 'hidden' or 'invisible' privatisation. 'Hidden privatisation' can take place through the depreciation system, leasing of assets, stock options of foreign investors, a bank's mortgages on state property, and other ways in which state property slips into private hands without being recorded in official accounts of privatisation (Matolcsy, 1991). In the Hungarian privatisation Canning and Hare (1994) noted 'invisible' privatisation taking place alongside 'official' privatisation when, for example, new private establishments lured away the intellectual capital and business contacts of a state enterprise. Although these are important channels of property transfer from the public to the private sector, in this book we focus on privatisation of going concerns initially owned by the state.

Privatisation in practice is of course not purely an economic concept but also a political and often ideological one. Governments pursue privatisation policies to achieve a political agenda. In the post-communist countries, where the development of democracy is so tightly coupled with economic reforms, especially privatisation, this holds even more strongly.

The improvement of industrial efficiency is by far the commonest *normative* criterion against which economists judge the success of privatisation. However, inducing a positive change in the efficiency of the privatised enterprises has not been the only *actual* aim of governments initiating privatisation policies around the world. For example, the principal aims (explicit as well as implicit) of the British privatisation programme included not only the efficiency motive but also, for example, decreasing the public sector borrowing requirement, reducing government involvement in enterprise decision-making, widening share ownership, and gaining political advantage (Marsh, 1991; Vickers and Yarrow, 1988). To judge by the experience of less developed countries, where, for example, capital markets may be absent or very small, additional goals can also be significant (Cook and Kirkpatrick, 1988; Ramanadham, 1989). Similarly, the economic, social, and political context of privatisation in the transitional countries of Central-Eastern Europe, and its vast difference from the privatisation context in Western Europe and the United States should also be noted (Estrin, 1991). From these differences it follows that privatisation is often intended to play significant roles in the development of capital markets and in strengthening product market competition.

Claims have been made that several positive effects of privatisation have been felt in practice, although some of these benefits may be attributed to liberalisation rather than privatisation *per se*. For example, students of British privatised enterprises, and often managers of these firms too, note that privatisation leads to major reorientation, a more business-like organisational culture, a change in the character of members of the management, less bureaucracy, more rational decision-making, rewards encouraging risk-taking, and structural changes of the organisation which facilitate measuring success and failure (Bishop and Kay, 1988; Brunnen, 1989; King, 1987; Morley, 1986). We now turn to economic theory for an explanation of these effects.

In the economic approach to privatisation, the basic assumption is that privatisation will lead to privatised state-owned firms behaving like any other private firm. In other words, they are expected to develop the same behaviour patterns, the same strategies that characterise business organisations in private ownership and are thoroughly described in various disciplines, including the whole strategy literature. Management is typically depicted as a rational actor acting under a set of external influences (Hammer, Hinterhuber, and Lorenz, 1989). Privatisation changes these influences, to which management reacts. This view is pushed further, to an admittedly extreme position, by Bös (1991) who asserts that, given the right incentives, bureaucrats' behaviour will copy that of the management of any private firm. In the remainder of this section we focus on incentives and constraints that change with privatisation. The discussion is built around the agency theory which appears to be the most frequently used approach for explaining the relationship between privatisation and firm behaviour, although an alternative has been offered in Haskel and Szymanski's (1990) bargaining theory of privatisation which derives efficiency improvement from changes in labour costs that are determined in a bargaining process. More recently, Boycko, Schleifer, and Vishny (1996) have presented a theory of privatisation, following their earlier work on corruption in relations between politicians and firms (Schleifer and Vishny, 1993, 1994). This theory offers a variant of the general economic approach to privatisation, focusing on excess employment of public enterprises due to political demand, and regarding privatisation as a strategy to separate the firm from politicians. However, it diverts from mainstream thinking in that this view regards the critical agency problem as being with politicians, not with managers.

Agency theory deals with a common situation of modern economic life, where ownership and management (decision control) are often separated (Fama and Jensen, 1983; Jensen and Meckling, 1976). An agency problem arises when a utility-maximising principal wants to induce a utility-maximising agent to act for the interest of the principal but they have different sets of objectives and information asymmetry exists. Assuming opportunistic behaviour, the argument goes, the agent may want to follow objectives – like prestige, power, growth at the expense of profit – that do not maximise those of the principal; therefore the latter has to establish incentives for the former. Since the principal is not able to collect and process all the information that would be needed in order to specify to the agent what to do under all circumstances, and he is not able to observe even the behaviour of the agent, a monitoring problem is also created. Now the principal's problem is how to design the best possible incentive scheme (contract) for the self-interested agent without full information on the environment and on the agent's behaviour, while taking monitoring costs into consideration.

Considering the two camps into which agency theory is split, positivist agency theory and principal–agent research, applications of the theory to privatisation seem closer to the first one, which deals with issues of ownership and control, and the disciplinary effects of incentive schemes, external labour markets and capital markets (Eisenhardt, 1989a; Nilakant and Rao, 1994: 650). In this approach, privatisation brings about a major change in the agency structure (Rees, 1988). It brings new principals with different objectives and monitoring systems, and corresponding incentives and constraints, into the principal–agent relationship. This is the reason why the allocation of property rights does matter with respect to firm behaviour and performance.

Following the structure of our earlier discussion of state enterprise behaviour, we group the major contextual changes due to privatisation under the headings of objectives, and the system of incentives and constraints. These are summarised in table 3 and briefly reviewed below. Not all these factors are conditional on privatisation. In particular, product market competition is often viewed as independent of the ownership arrangements, and also often considered to be more influential for firm behaviour than ownership. Regarding socialist countries, however, Kornai's (1990a) view on strong and weak linkages between different ownership and co-ordination regimes – with state ownership's strong linkage with bureaucratic co-ordination and weak linkage with market co-ordination – should be noted, suggesting that for product market competition to develop, privatisation may be a prerequisite.

Turning, then, to the goal formation process, multiplicity of objectives is expected to lessen as private owners are typically assumed by economic theory to have a single ultimate objective. This objective is that of profit maximisation which, giving the term 'performance' a specific meaning, allows the adoption of effective performance-related reward schemes, thus bringing closer the interest of the management to that of the owners. Improved managerial incentives, designed to serve private owners' profit-maximising objectives, then, will result in active management, searching for opportunities to increase profits. A clear specification of profit objectives by the owners not only simplifies the objectives to be followed by the enterprise management but also allows the establishment of a

Table 3. *Contextual changes due to privatisation*

Contextual changes in		
owners' objectives	incentives	constraints imposed by
• multiplicity and fluidity decreases • profit motive	• institutional barriers to state intervention, measurability of performance • externally well-defined incentives • performance-related rewards	• financial market discipline (threat of bankruptcy and takeover) • managerial labour market discipline • product market competition

lasting structure of priorities, a prerequisite for any consistent and stable behaviour pattern in the long term.

Governments may retain some influence over the behaviour of formerly state-owned enterprises; nevertheless privatisation always reduces state involvement in managers' decision-making. With unambiguous responsibilities and clearer boundaries between the state and the enterprise there remains less scope for bargaining and the management loses significant power to influence policy. The removal of government from business decision-making also has the advantage of shortening the decision processes by eliminating phases between the government and the management on the one hand, and by having a likely positive effect on intra-firm decision-making on the other. Hence it decreases bureaucracy which usually proves to be unsuitable in a turbulent business environment. Although, in principle, it is conceivable that the government keeps at arm's length from managerial decision-making of public enterprises, practice more often than not fails to prove this principle. It is privatisation that establishes solid institutional barriers to such an intervention, ensuring managerial autonomy in business decision-making.

Having been privatised, firms often become players in new environments, or, looked at from the other side, new environmental subsystems become relevant to the firms. Managements of formerly state-owned enterprises must face new pressures of a very different nature from those they were used to, including product market competition (Vickers and Yarrow, 1985, 1988), capital market discipline, (Aylen, 1988; Jarrell, Brickley, and Netter, 1988; Jensen and Meckling, 1976; Jensen and Ruback, 1983), and managerial market monitoring (Estrin and Pérotin, 1991; Fama, 1980). In the context of the transitional countries, these new constraints manifest themselves in liberalisation of imports, hardening of the budget constraint, and the possibility of investor-initiated privatisation.

There are, however, some conditions which are necessary for the assumed effects of privatisation on firm behaviour to be manifested. For example, certain ownership arrangements (dispersed ownership, or significant share retained by the state, for example) may impede effective monitoring. The size and structure of the business of the state-owned enterprise may hamper takeover attempts. In fact, some authors assert that the effects of privatisation cannot be predicted without taking into account a set of interrelated factors, namely ownership, competition, and regulation. All these factors determine managerial incentives, and the effect of changing one is dependent on the others (Estrin and Pérotin, 1991; Vickers and Yarrow, 1988).

3 A political bargaining framework

This chapter first looks at the question of how appropriate agency theory is when it is applied to privatisation in transitional economies. Since the answer is that it is less than sufficient for the purposes of our inquiry, we present a political bargaining framework focusing on politics, not to replace but to supplement the agency approach.

3.1 Principals, agents, and organisations

Economic perspectives, notably industrial organisation and transaction cost economics, have brought clear benefits to the study of organisations (Porter, 1980; Williamson, 1975, 1990). Recently, privatisation has become an issue where the contribution of economics is remarkable. In fact, representatives of no other discipline have as yet shown greater interest in the study of this subject. In this study of privatisation by economists, agency theory has received wide acceptance. In essence, the agency approach to privatisation asserts that, following privatisation and consequent on a number of changes in the context of managerial decision-making, firm behaviour will change and, ultimately, performance will improve. The question arises: is this theory appropriate in the transitional context of Central-Eastern Europe?

The agency approach provides important insights into the likely changes in firm behaviour due to privatisation, and aptly re-establishes self-interest and opportunism in organisational studies in contexts where goal conflicts are substantial, as in owner–management relationships (Eisenhardt, 1989a). However, we argue below that the study of privatisation can gain substantially from an approach driven by organisation theory. We discuss the weaknesses of the agency approach in this section, building the argument around three main issues, moving from the general to the specific. First, we identify general problems that arise when agency theory is employed in studies of organisations. Second, we examine questions that are related to the time span and the unit of analysis covered by privatisation studies. Third, we cast doubt on the validity of certain implicit assumptions when the agency approach to privatisation is employed in the transitional context of Central-Eastern Europe.

General problems in studies of organisations

For studying organisations in general, agency theory appears to have some limitations. By opening up the black box of the firm and putting the managers into the centre, agency theory makes a substantial step towards understanding the behaviour of the firm. By focusing on the relationship between senior managers and owners, however, it tends to ignore the existence of complex relationships within the organisation and restricts the notion of the environment to the incentives and constraints arising from the owners' objectives. In other words, agency theorists recognise goal conflict in the relationship between owners and management, but tend to consider single principal–single agent relationships and disregard goal conflict in intra-organisational relationships among the multiple agents. This is probably because in agency theory attention is focused outside the firm, and environmental determinism prevails: the organisation is seen as a rather passive subject, reacting to incentives and constraints, and serving first of all shareholders' interests. In contrast, an approach driven by organisation theory or strategic management would regard the environment not as a set of forces that eventually reigns over its constituent organisations, but as a set of opportunities and threats to be conquered by the organisations and the people who inhabit those organisations (Chakravarthy, 1982; Child, 1972; Eisenhardt, 1989a; Hirsch, Friedman and Koza, 1990; Hofer, 1975).

The agency approach assumes a great deal of rationality at the level of the organisation, ignoring possible goal conflicts within. We argue in favour of a *political* (or *power*) *model* of behaviour instead, where goal conflicts are resolved through the use of power mechanisms – bargaining, negotiation, and coalitions. Patterns of behaviour of the organisation (strategies) result from the action of individuals in the organisation (Mintzberg, 1978; Mintzberg and Waters, 1982). The chances for various members to influence the stream of action of an organisation are clearly different. Yet, it is not only the management which plays a part in shaping that stream. Organisational outcomes are affected by many. If we assume complete goal congruence, either by nature or by a probably rather sophisticated incentive scheme, for all the players who have some influence over organisational action, we arrive at the notion of the rational actor model which views 'events as purposive choices of consistent actors' (Allison, 1971: 11), consistent individually and consistent as a group. If, however, we accept the possibility of enduring goal conflicts, not to mention occasional erring of individual rationality, events appear as a *resultant* of 'compromise, conflict, and confusion of officials with diverse interests and unequal influence' (Allison, 1971: 162). In other words, firm behaviour is influenced by power and politics in and around organisations. Organisations are political systems, in which strategic decision-making is an interweaving of boundedly rational and political processes (Eisenhardt and Zbaracki, 1992; Mintzberg, 1983; Pfeffer, 1981). This perspective certainly does not imply that what results from conflicts and their political resolution will correspond with the preferences of any of the players. The power model of organisational strategic decision-making is also consistent with the resource-dependence perspective of firm behaviour as discussed in the previous chapter.

Problems in privatisation studies

We argue for the use of the *power model*, particularly in privatisation studies, because a consistent set of preferences at the level of the organisation, as the rational actor model assumes, could be expected only if goals of rational individuals were co-aligned by shared values or effective incentives and controls. These conditions, however, are unlikely to hold at times of systemic change. With the former external control mechanisms and dependencies of a transitional economy eroding and finally disappearing, the previous power structure is expected to unfreeze and then later reconfigure. One would say this is at the heart of the whole transition. Before reconfiguration, however, a wide space will probably open for diverse interests to be manifested. The context is vague, changing, and often volatile. Organisational outcomes, then, are likely to be largely influenced by internal politics, sometimes with a partisan kind of strategic decision process in which individual and group rationality towers over the organisation's global interests (Eisenhardt and Bourgeois, 1988; Hafsi and Thomas, 1986; Hannan and Freeman, 1984; Pennings, 1992).

For studying privatisation when the unit of analysis is the organisation, it is problematic that cause and effect in the relationship of privatisation and strategy appears unidirectional from an agency theory perspective. At the level of individual organisations, however, the relationship may be more complex. For example, it is not always obvious whether a privatised firm performs better than non-privatised firms because it was privatised, or it was privatised in the first place because it had better prospects of performing well.

Agency theory focuses on improved corporate governance following privatisation, at the expense of explicit attention being devoted to the importance of resources, skills, and capabilities for a successful turnaround. An approach driven by organisation theory would suggest that effective corporate governance in itself may indeed facilitate strategic turnaround, but only to the extent that it provides an adequate resource base and helps replace old dominant competences of privatised firms with new ones which increase their survival ability in the dramatically altered environment. In the terminology of organisational learning, one might formulate an assumption in terms of privatisation's contribution to organisational oblivion as well as to organisational learning. If, for some reason, privatisation fails to overcome inertial forces, to break the competence trap, and to support the development of new, appropriate skills and capabilities, it may even reduce the survival ability of the privatised firm.

Agency theory, as applied to privatisation, appears to employ an underlying logic of comparing the distinct states of 'before privatisation' and 'after privatisation' while ignoring the path in between, as if privatisation were not a process but a one-moment event whose presumed effects are immediate. This may be an appropriate way of looking at mass privatisation in the long run, but is misleading for short-term issues at the level of the firm. Transition of formerly communist countries is certainly not happening overnight. It is important to chart the changes in the behaviour of firms which privatisation encourages *during* this systemic transition. While the agency approach aptly directs attention to the importance of external economic incentives and constraints, i.e. selective forces that will inevitably reign in the long term, an approach driven by organisation theory could highlight the role and importance of voice, adaptation, influence tactics, and politics during the process of privatisation.

Similarly, in terms of an input-process-output model (Van de Ven and Huber, 1990), the agency approach seems to focus on the input and outcome of organisational change. Applied to the problem under study, the input (independent variable) would be the change in ownership (along with changes in incentives and constraints), and the output (dependent variable) would be some observed change in firm behaviour (or managerial decision-making, or, directly, firm performance). The explanation would then require a variance theory, and statistical analysis of variations in some outcome criterion, taking the traditional form of 'an increase in X is related to an increase in Y', but it would not capture the dynamic aspects of the process of privatisation (cf. Monge, 1990). We are interested not only in input and output, but also in the process by which changes of firm behaviour unfold. This interest requires a process theory, to complement variance theory, explaining the sequence of events based on a historical narrative. In return, understanding the process also requires a grasp of initial conditions and eventual outcomes (Abbott, 1990; Van de Ven and Huber, 1990). This study takes a micro-perspective by placing organisations in the centre, regarding process, power, and politics as important, and viewing the privatisation process as organisational change – sometimes as upheaval as cases will demonstrate. In this sense this book is about organisational change.

Problems in the Central-Eastern European context

When applied to privatisation in the Central-Eastern European context, some of the underlying assumptions of the agency approach to privatisation as it has been developed in the Western context require careful consideration. The assumptions we consider here pertain to initial ownership rights, institutional stability, and the range of possible firm behaviour patterns.

Initial *de facto* property rights are often blurred in transitional economies, with many stakeholders assuming property entitlements, even in Russia (Schleifer and Vishny, 1992). In some smaller countries of Central-Eastern Europe, as in Hungary, managers fought for part of the right to control the firm under the system and ideology of self-governance (Kornai, 1992: ch. 20). While demanding greater autonomy in taking economic decisions, they were also successful in getting a share of the property rights.

Institutional stability appears to be one of the major assumptions held by the agency approach to privatisation. The transitional economies represent a considerably different context. It is a region emerging from almost half a century of state control, where an effective capital market is absent; evaluation of firms lacks the information that is present in a developed market economy; managements as well as employees of firms have long been cushioned from the effects of inefficiency; the size, scope, and speed of privatisation exceed any previous experience; enforcing private-sector discipline may seriously threaten social stability; and the economic transition takes place in a politically overheated environment. For privatisation and firm behaviour, this is an institutional context in a state of flux.

An example of the issue at hand is that of the disciplinary effect of an emerging managerial labour market. Following the propositions of Fama (1980) and Estrin and Pérotin (1991), let us consider an emerging management market that is common to the private and soon-to-be-privatised sectors. In line with the underlying assumptions of the agency approach, one could hypothesise that the behaviour of the managers of state-owned enterprises may be disciplined by such a market in the transition period in Central-Eastern Europe. If, however, one considers that it takes a long time for a new institutional arrangement to emerge and become effective, the hypothesis will have to be moderated, by taking into account how privatisation, or the so-called 'system transition' in general, is carried out. If there are no other types of effective control on managements to squeeze out resources from the firms (as was political control, for example, under the communist regime) then, assuming opportunistic behaviour, the disciplinary power of the emerging management market will be severely limited. To put it simply, managers of state-owned firms will hardly bother with being head-hunted by emerging private firms if they have the opportunity, in the process of system transition, to become head-hunters (as owner-managers) themselves.

Similarly, while privatisation may decrease information asymmetry between agents and principals as the latter change from a divided group of bureaucrats to private stockholders with essentially the same shared objective, to assume the same relationship to hold during the transition period would be to neglect the rather unsteady nature of institutional arrangements. One must also consider the rudimentary nature of market institutions, such as stock exchanges, that enhance the opportunity of private owners to be well informed. Therefore, during the transition period, when the firm is still in state ownership, information asymmetry may even increase as the existing, often informal and political, information channels break up without being replaced with effective new ones.

The range of possible behaviour patterns that are generally considered in the agency approach to privatisation seems to be limited. The variety of behaviour patterns that is sufficient to describe firms operating in established institutional systems provides an inappropriate framework to analyse strategy content during the transition period. It was argued that state-owned enterprise behaviour can be effective at the expense of efficiency. When resources are drying up, political control is weakening, and SOEs' vertical dependence is lessening, new strategies are called for. However, the emerging patterns of firm behaviour will not necessarily reflect properties of genuine market-oriented competitive strategies. Drift, survival without significant restructuring efforts, and consequent depletion of resources are counter-examples (cf. Matolcsy, 1991; Török, 1992). The cases in chapter 5 will provide ample evidence that in transition, ineffective corporate governance structures often result in 'perverse' strategies (Estrin, Gelb, and Singh, 1991; Kornai, 1990b; Mayhew and Seabright, 1992). Similarly, owners' objectives such as the increase in shareholder value *of the privatised SOE* seem to be taken for granted when the agency approach is applied to privatisation. This may not necessarily be the case. Consider the extreme example of a firm acquiring a state-owned enterprise so as to shut it down (or just to deplete its resources), thus reducing competition or minimising the threat of new entrants. Shareholders of the acquirer will probably be better off in the long run but the question of how privatisation affects the target's behaviour and performance simply becomes irrelevant.

In sum, a framework based solely on the agency approach to privatisation seems inappropriate for understanding the relationship between privatisation and firm behaviour at the level of the organisation in transition. It needs to be complemented with an approach based on the political model of organisations. Some major differences between these approaches are summarised in table 4. Yet, one should realise these are not rival theories. They are in fact complementary in that the first provides a general formal theory to explain long-term effects at an aggregate level, whereas the second attempts to deal with phenomena at the level of the firm in a shorter time span in order to yield a middle-range theory whose validity is limited by time and space conditions. The agency approach can also serve as a benchmark, reminding us of the eventual economic purpose of privatisation. It directs attention to the importance of the specific ownership arrangements and the effectiveness of corporate governance that evolve in the course of privatisation in a given case. Taking this perspective, it is our aim to explore the benefits of mutual reinforcement and complementarity that can be gained from a two-pronged approach – that of economics and organisation theory – in the study of privatisation.

3.2   Privatisation, politics, and strategy

A framework in this context means a set of variables, stated in the form of categories or concepts, and their assumed relationships, stated in the form of propositions, that are expected to produce a predicted outcome. Concepts are conceptual labels on discrete events or instances of an observed phenomenon; properties are attributes or characteristics of a concept; and dimensions are locations of properties along various continua (see Strauss and Corbin, 1990).

Our framework is built on theoretical and empirical foundations which are laid down in this book as follows:
- a discussion of state-owned firm behaviour as seen from the resource-dependence and the public enterprise economics perspectives (section 2.1)

Table 4. *Approaches to privatisation and firm behaviour*

Agency approach	Political bargaining framework
Privatisation seen as	
having a stable start- and end-state (state-owned versus privatised)	organisational change process
Pattern of firm behaviour (strategy) seen as	
determined by rational managerial decisions	'resultant' pattern of behaviour, shaped by political resolution of conflicts
Context seen as	
incentives and constraints	a range of external and internal factors
management has to align with context	management can influence context
Assumed relationship between behaviour and privatisation	
once privatised, profit-seeking behaviour	in the course of privatisation, 'perverse' patterns of behaviour are possible We don't know, so descriptive cases are an appropriate research tool
Research interest	
focus on two discrete 'equilibrium states'	focus on pre-conditions, outcomes, and 'disequilibrium process' in between
interested in difference in behaviour before and after the transfer of ownership	also interested in behaviour in the course of transfer of ownership

- a review of the existing theory on privatisation (section 2.2)
- issues derived from a review of privatisation policy and practice in Hungary (chapter 4)
- an analysis of several in-depth longitudinal cases (chapters 5 and 6).

The framework is thus informed by theory and grounded in empirical study. It is also influenced by general concepts and theories of strategic management (particularly those from the school built on organisation theory foundations) and corporate governance (Monks and Minow, 1995). On this basis, a set of concepts were derived as shown in table 5. The assumed relationships between these concepts are depicted in our process framework of privatisation, firm behaviour, and post-privatisation performance in figure 2. These are explained in more detail below.

Table 5. *Concepts, properties, and dimensions in the framework*

Category/concept	Property	Dimension
Dependent variable		
Performance post-privatisation	Turnaround attainment	failure ⟷ success
Independent variable		
Privatisation process	Politicisation of context	high ⟷ low
	Organisational politicking	high ⟷ low
Privatisation outcome	Governance effectiveness	defective ⟷ effective
	Resource replenishment	low ⟷ high
Mediating variable		
Strategy process	Consciousness	vague ⟷ focused
Strategy content	Coping pattern	
• post-privatisation		drift ⟷ turnaround
• during privatisation		drift ⟷ recovery
Performance in the process of privatisation	Trend in market share and financial position	decline ⟷ stability

Our dependent variable is a variant of firm performance. Post-privatisation performance is specified as 'turnaround attainment', which is defined by a dimension on which 'turnaround success' and 'turnaround failure' are the two extremes. This definition follows from the consideration that state-owned enterprises are likely to face serious challenges owing to increasing competition, trade liberalisation, and other reforms that are introduced in transitional economies parallel to privatisation. Comparatively, state-owned enterprises in transitional economies are usually resource-deficient, where resource deficiency means, to varying degrees, inappropriate finances, lack of modern technology, and a managerial know-how that, although appropriate at times of high vertical resource dependence and political control, probably falls short of the requirements of market competition and efficiency. In such a business environment, SOEs are likely to face unprecedented competitive challenges. Being resource-deficient and hit by shocks, their level of economic performance will suffer, particularly if their initial position was already poor. To survive, then, they will need to attain a substantial improvement, a turnaround.

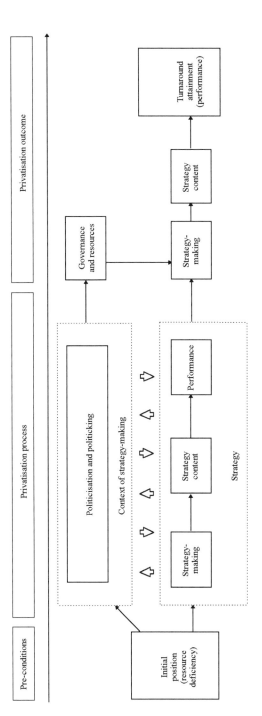

Fig. 2. Privatisation and behaviour: the process.

The independent variables include features of privatisation process and privatisation outcome. We clearly distinguish the process and the outcome of privatisation as two separate concepts. Privatisation process is defined as the flow or sequence of events (decisions and actions) that are taken to influence issues of future ownership. Turning points in this sequence are of special importance, and are defined as barometric events that cause the process to move forward and lead to a changed situation. Privatisation outcome denotes ownership arrangements and consequences that result from the privatisation process.

Two properties of the privatisation process are singled out in the framework, both revolving around the issue of politics. However, while macro-level politics is often discussed in relation to privatisation, it is rarely considered in specific cases at the level of the firm, while organisational politics has been largely ignored to date. To make an explicit distinction between these two, we shall use different labels to identify them. *Politicisation* denotes the extent to which circumstances of a political nature or, in the most direct case, decisions made on the basis of political preferences, influence the privatisation process. This property is again dimensionalised between high and low levels. In a case with high politicisation we should find evidence that political preferences had a significant effect on the privatisation process, probably marking a turning point in the flow of events. For low politicisation, where turning points are caused by genuine economic factors only, we should observe the lack of the effect of political preferences, or even resistance of decision-makers to political influence. We have already noted the political aspect of privatisation: governments pursuing privatisation always have a political agenda. The privatisation policies in the transitional economies suggest that politicisation is important. Case study evidence shows that it is important in different cases to different degrees. *Organisational politicking* is an umbrella term that combines properties of processes within and around the organisation. We dimensionalise this concept according to its intensity, between the extremes of high and low. In the case of high politicking, we should observe (1) sharp internal organisational conflicts in the privatisation process which are resolved through the use of politics, and/or (2) evidence that the privatisation of a given firm becomes subject of politicking among players external to the given organisation. Note that politicking is not exercised *against* privatisation, as Schipke (1994) assumes on the part of the old *nomenklatura*, but for a *different* outcome of the privatisation process in terms of winners and losers.

The outcome of privatisation is considered from two aspects. First, *governance effectiveness* is considered through ownership composition and concentration, where employee and/or state ownership, and dispersed ownership are both associated with weak owners and defective corporate governance, whereas external and concentrated private ownership is associated with strong owners and effective corporate governance. Second, *resource replenishment*, that is the level of additional resources brought in by privatisation (either directly by the new owners or from other sources that became available to the firm owing to it having been privatised), is taken into account. We emphasise again that resources may take various forms, from new finance through a tax holiday granted because of foreign ownership to the transfer of managerial skills. Resource replenishment can also be conceived of as a proxy for the new owners' capacity and intent to improve the target's resource base. Resource-deficient owners, with strict borrowing limits, as, for example, employee organisations in our cases, will not make a resource-abundant firm. Neither will owners whose objective is to siphon off resources from the target.

The basic assumption of our framework is that turnaround attainment is dependent not only on the outcome of privatisation but also on its process. In other words, it is not only the result of privatisation that matters. For post-privatisation performance, it also matters by what kind of process a firm has been privatised. In figure 2, this basic insight is developed a little further by providing a possible mechanism through which the assumed effect of the independent variables on the dependent one is played out. This mechanism is the firm's strategy-making process (its outcome being strategy content), and the firm's subsequent performance during the process of privatisation, which are regarded here as mediating variables for their role in linking the independent and dependent variables.

Following Mintzberg (1978) and Mintzberg and Waters (1982), we define strategy as *the pattern in a stream of organisational action* that reflects a certain *relationship between an organisation and its broadly defined environment*. We formulate the definition at a considerably high level of generalisation so that it can be applied to state-owned enterprises in non-market economies and, of course, to enterprises operating in a transitional economy. As depicted in figure 3, we distinguish between process and content ('making' versus 'outcome' of processes), and between idea and action (what is intended to be done versus what has been done).

Firm behaviour, in which changes due to privatisation are expected, is identified with realised strategy (or *strategy* for short) which, in turn, is the outcome of the process of strategy formation (*strategy-making*). While these concepts depict the organisation itself, intended strategy and

Strategy	Process	Content
Idea	Formulation of intended strategy	Intended strategy
Action	Formation of realised strategy	Realised strategy

Fig. 3. The conceptual strategy matrix. (*Source:* Adapted from Antal-Mokos 1990: 6, based on Mintzberg 1978 and Mintzberg and Waters 1985.)

its formulation are related to the management of the organisation. These are important distinctions for our topic since in this way it becomes apparent that aligning management's goals with those of the owners will not necessarily lead to corresponding changes in firm behaviour, as we have already noted in the previous section.

Strategy-making takes place with regard to a complex set of external and internal factors that are usually referred to as the *context*. It is the process of strategy-making through which context influences the behaviour pattern of an organisation, that is its strategy. External context is usually referred to as the environment of an organisation. In the agency approach to privatisation it is reflected in incentives and constraints. In the organisation-theory-driven view for which we have argued in section 3.1, internal factors – from which we single out organisational power and politics – are also considered.

The above definition of strategy emphasises a pattern of behavioural variables (Hambrick, 1983a, 1983b; Hambrick and Schecter, 1983; Porter, 1980). It also suggests that strategy is a dynamic concept (Galbraith and Schendel, 1983; Miller and Friesen, 1984; Mintzberg and Waters, 1982). It implies a pattern in a sequence of events. In particular, studies of *turnaround strategies* explicitly address the dynamic nature of the strategy concept since their major concern is precisely a change in the pattern over time that leads to improved and sustainable performance (Hofer, 1980; Stopford and Baden-Fuller, 1990). Turnaround strategies are often viewed as consisting of phases, of which we identify two, *recovery* and *capability enhancement* (cf. Arogyaswamy, Barker, and Yasai-Ardekani, 1995; Barker and Mone, 1994; Robbins and Pearce, 1992; Slatter, 1984; Stopford and Baden-Fuller, 1990). Recovery is more concerned with efficiency and emphasises the financial dimensions, and often includes retrenchment and downsizing. Capability enhancement goes further to create the foundation for future growth by developing skills. The empirical literature provides ample examples of specific behaviour that characterises these stages of the overall turnaround process, which can help in recognising recovery and/or capability enhancement in the behaviour of soon-to-be-privatised firms, if there is any. In the light of our cases, a particularly important finding is presented by Stopford and Baden-Fuller (1990) who found that in successful rejuvenation the chief executive plays an essential role by looking beyond the immediate, mostly financial, problems, triggering lasting changes in the way the firm operates, and acting as a teacher. In transitions where the legitimacy of the chief executive is questioned within and around the organisation, such roles can hardly be expected to be played well by them.

Consciousness is the only property of the strategy process that we explicitly consider in the framework. It refers to the extent to which the dominant coalition of an organisation perceives the situation as one requiring turnaround, and deliberately attempts to cope with it. Simply put, the issue this property looks at is whether those capable of influencing firm behaviour are aware of the difficulties and want to do something about it. This definition is reflected by the way this property is dimensionalised. *Focused* strategy process denotes awareness of the turnaround situation, recognition of the need of a turnaround, and an effort to implement such a strategy. *Vague* strategy-making, conversely, signifies lack of awareness and effort.

Strategy content is specified as the *coping pattern* of an organisation; that is the pattern of its behaviour *vis-à-vis* environmental challenges. The coping pattern is labelled *turnaround* if activities of recovery, followed by capability enhancement, are carried out, although during the process of privatisation, we expect firms to exhibit recovery at best. *Drift* is the label we attach to firm behaviour if no consistent pattern of activities of recovery and capability enhancement is revealed; this is similar to Glueck's (1972) passive, Miles and Snow's (1978) reactor, Porter's (1980) stuck-in-the-middle strategies, and Hrebiniak and Joyce's (1985) adaptation by chance.

Finally, we examine the *performance* of the state-owned enterprise *while it is in the process of privatisation* along a dimension with the extremes of decline and stability.

In this framework, the privatisation process affects turnaround attainment in two ways. First, it may result in a privatisation outcome that is either favourable or unfavourable to turnaround attainment by providing resources either sufficient or insufficient to realise such a strategy, and/or by implementing either effective or defective corporate governance. Second, process characteristics of privatisation are assumed to have an effect on strategy-making which, then, may produce strategy content that is either favourable or unfavourable to turnaround attainment. Interaction between players is assumed to take place in inter- and intra-organisational bargaining. It is in this sense that our approach can be considered as *a political bargaining framework of privatisation*.

Outcome / Process	1 effective corporate governance high resource replenishment	2 effective corporate governance low resource replenishment	3 defective corporate governance high resource replenishment	4 defective corporate governance low resource replenishment
1 low politicisation low politicking	1.1 turnaround success			1.4 turnaround handicapped (by outcome)
2 high politicisation low politicking				
3 low politicisation high politicking				
4 high politicisation high politicking	4.1 turnaround handicapped (by process)			4.4 turnaround failure

Fig. 4. Turnaround scenarios by privatisation process and outcome.

We further specify this framework by formulating a few propositions. In order to emphasise temporal dynamics, we present propositions that suggest relationships between various concepts in the form of likely *scenarios of privatisation, behaviour, and performance*. These propositions can later serve as signposts for understanding and analysing the cases in a disciplined and systematic way. In figure 4 a set of conditions results from juxtaposing the concepts that qualify the process and outcome of privatisation. Within this set of conditions, certain hypothesised relationships are expected to hold.

The conditional matrix yields sixteen scenarios for turnaround to succeed or fail. For purposes of illustration, the four extreme scenarios are described in some detail below.

Scenario 1.1. *Low politicisation and low politicking of the privatisation process, effective governance and high resource replenishment after privatisation: turnaround success.*

In this scenario, the ailing firm is acquired by a resourceful, more often strategic as opposed to financial, investor in a calm process. The expected result is turnaround success. The low politicisation and low politicking of the privatisation process allow for focused strategy-making during the privatisation process. The management is aware of the firm's difficulties and, in the absence of politicking, exerts collective effort to remedy the situation. In the absence of adequate resources, it focuses on recovery and, at the same time, facilitates privatisation on the basis of expected strategic benefits, from which it hopes to gain resources for building new capabilities. In this scenario, turnaround begins (in its first, recovery, phase) even before privatisation ends.

At the end of the privatisation process, the new private owners who acquire a majority holding indeed bring in fresh capital, management skills, and technology, and access to market channels. The firm can thus enjoy the benefits of high resource replenishment coupled with effective governance. Recovery can now be followed by the second phase of a turnaround strategy, capability enhancement and skill-building.

It is this scenario that appears most often in everyday expectations. Furthermore, this scenario seems to fit best with the agency approach to privatisation. In fact, a study which compares firms at two distant points of time, before and after privatisation, may well conclude that this is the only scenario, given that the dates of observation are distant enough to let cases of failure either disappear from the population because of selective forces or turn into success in subsequent takeovers. By taking a process view and charting firms' paths through their privatisation histories, we shall reveal other possible scenarios.

Scenario 4.1. *Highly politicised privatisation process with intensive politicking, effective governance and high resource replenishment after privatisation: turnaround handicapped by process.*

The firm is in a difficult position initially or soon after the beginning of transition and, therefore, it needs a turnaround strategy and adequate resources. Eventually, privatisation brings about both. However, in this scenario politicisation and politicking prolong the process and the firm becomes a political arena in which conflicts and their political resolution are dominant.

This results in significant delays in making necessary responses to environmental changes in a period when quick action should be taken to stop further deterioration of the firm's position. Possibilities for focused strategy-making are limited owing to the organisation being torn apart by internal politicking. Management feels paralysed by uncertainties that surround politicised privatisation, and thus strategy-making becomes subordinated to privatisation. Management may even view the privatisation process as an opportunity to obtain personal benefits (not necessarily by acquiring ownership) and not as an opportunity to enhance organisational capabilities, in which case business decisions are made by constantly considering their likely effect on the attainment of personal or group interests in privatisation.

As a consequence, the firm is drifting, and its position is deteriorating further. Once the firm is privatised, turnaround may still happen but it is expected to be seriously handicapped by process. Owing to losses in the course of privatisation, relatively higher levels of resource replenishment (including the replacement of the top management) may be necessary for a turnaround to be successfully implemented.

Scenario 1.4. *Low politicisation and low politicking of privatisation process, defective corporate governance and low resource replenishment after privatisation: turnaround handicapped by outcome.*

As in scenario 4.1, the expected result here is again handicapped turnaround. In this case, however, turnaround success is jeopardised by the outcome of privatisation. The transfer of ownership occurs in a smooth process. Focused strategy-making is not hindered by organisational politicking, and attempts may be made to achieve recovery. Privatisation, however, results in the firm being acquired by private owners who are deficient in resources to facilitate capability enhancement and weak in exercising effective governance at a time when management may prefer organisational peace to making hard decisions for recovery. The firm may still try to pursue a turnaround strategy, but its implementation will be at an obvious disadvantage.

Scenario 4.4. *Highly politicised privatisation process with intensive politicking, defective corporate governance and low resource replenishment after privatisation: turnaround failure.*

In this scenario, the firm is again one which badly needs turnaround strategy. For that, it also needs resources and a determined management to take those often tough measures that are necessary to keep the firm afloat. Instead, what the firm gets at the end of a long-drawn-out and highly politicised privatisation process are weak owners with no resources. By this time, the firm's position will probably be even worse owing to a high level of uncertainty and fierce politicking in the privatisation process. The expected outcome is, first, turnaround failure and, second, a possible subsequent takeover.

Other hypothetical scenarios shown in the table but not described above are expected to result in turnaround partially handicapped by both process and outcome to differing degrees.

These propositions suggest that long-drawn-out and political privatisation processes are less successful from the perspective of the firm involved. Furthermore, the fewer the additional resources brought in and the less effective the corporate governance resulting from privatisation, the less chance there remains for a firm to achieve a successful turnaround.

Whether a privatisation process is short or long does not *per se* seem to be a useful approach to evaluating the process. Instead, we introduce the concept of *procrastination* and define it as the ratio between the length of the actual process and the time span in which the firm could have been (and, considering the poor or rapidly deteriorating position of the firm involved, should have been) privatised with a satisfying result. In other words, what has been done is compared to what could have reasonably been achieved. The *optimal* privatisation point in this context takes its meaning accordingly. It is the point when the opportunity to conclude the deal satisfactorily is missed and the process becomes procrastinated. In the case of a procrastinated privatisation the defined ratio is greater than one. However, the ratio may also be less than one when the process concludes with premature hastiness in a deal that results in a less than satisfactory match of owner(s) and firm. In fact, we may assume that some privatisation processes become procrastinated in an effort by the decision-makers to prevent premature hasty deals from happening. It is important to emphasise that a satisfying result is considered here from the perspective of both the state and the organisation itself.

4   The policy context

This chapter provides an overview of the Hungarian privatisation process from about 1987 until 1994. It is not intended to give a complete account of privatisation in this period, let alone a record of all the aspects of the whole transition process. (For more details, see the references below in this chapter.) Our purpose is, first, to offer a guide for understanding the cases that follow (which themselves present much of the details about the context), by introducing the main players and reviewing the rules and the results to date. Second, by establishing a few main characteristics of the Hungarian privatisation process this chapter contributes to the political bargaining framework of privatisation, already discussed in the previous chapter.

We begin with a summary of economic reforms in the last twenty years of the communist regime. This background is followed by a discussion of the so-called spontaneous privatisation that was taking place from about 1987 until the freely elected government took control of the privatisation process in 1990. We then discuss two main phases of privatisation policy in Hungary in the period 1990–94, the first being characterised by an emphasis on centralisation and revenues to the state, and the second, by contrast, witnessing the use of decentralised methods and the influence of political considerations. We conclude this overview by highlighting a few major issues.

In order to provide a more comprehensive background for the discussion of privatisation policy phases in Hungary, selected economic indicators and exchange rates are summarised in tables 6 and 7, while the main political events and some economic developments are listed in an appendix.

4.1   Pre-transition reforms

The first debates on reforming the classic Soviet-type command economy began in Hungary as early as the early 1950s. Yet, Kornai's (1957)

Table 6. *Hungary fact-sheet*

Population, millions		GNP per capita, US dollars	
mid-1994	10.3	1994	3,840
GDP annual growth rate, per cent		Inflation, average annual rate, per cent	
1971–80 average	4.9		
1980–89 average	1.9		
1990	−2.5	1990	29.0
1991	−7.7	1991	34.2
1992	−4.3	1992	22.9
1993	−2.3	1993	22.5
1994	2.5	1994	19.0

Note: For background information on Hungary and the region, see also
http://www.worldbank.org/html/extdr/eca.htm.
Source: World Bank, *World Development Report 1996 From Plan to Market*,
appendix.

Table 7. *Exchange rates, 31 December 1989–94*

(Medium rate in forints, for one unit)

Currency	1989	1990	1991	1992	1993	1994
US dollar	62.54	61.45	75.62	83.97	100.70	110.69
Deutsche mark	36.87	40.47	49.83	51.96	58.06	71.47
British pound	100.23	116.58	141.48	127.03	148.90	173.11

Source: Adapted from Hungarian National Bank, *Annual Report 1994*, annex
B/III/2.

seminal work on 'The over-centralisation of economic administration'
was in practice followed in the early sixties by a centralisation campaign
that created large vertical conglomerates, in many instances by merging a
whole industry into a single trust.

It was only in 1968 that significant reforms were introduced with the
New Economic Mechanism, which attempted to increase enterprise
autonomy, market co-ordination, and the importance of the profit
motive. Many of the central controls were kept in place, however, and
around 1972 a new recentralisation took place, cutting back firms' short-
lived rights to make quasi-autonomous business decisions. An investment
and consumption boom, financed from borrowed Western funds and
coupled with foreign trade overwhelmingly oriented to the Soviet Union
and CMEA (Council of Mutual Economic Assistance), or COMECON
(the trade bloc of then communist countries) led to a serious crisis in the

balance of payments by the end of the seventies. Restrictive measures on the one hand, and decentralising reforms on the other, including breaking up some of the industry-wide trusts created twenty years earlier, were effected to revitalise the economy, but to no avail.

In 1984, state-owned enterprises were in principle given considerable autonomy with the introduction of the so-called self-governed forms of these enterprises. In about 70 per cent of the industrial firms (representing about 50 per cent in terms of output, although with significant variation in different sectors), the Enterprise Councils became the top decision-making body, in principle with the right of hiring and firing the general manager and making strategic decisions. Enterprise councils were made up of workers' delegates (50 per cent of the seats), managers (33 per cent), and the ministry's representative (1 person), the rest being appointed by the general director (the usual title of the chief executive of a state-owned enterprise). Although the composition of the councils *per se* may suggest otherwise, effective decision-making power was assumed by the management, with the councils either acting simply as a rubber-stamp on managerial decisions, or representing a body with which to reach a compromise by way of accommodating the workers' interest in wages. In other, normally smaller firms, the role of the self-governing body was played by the General Assembly of Employees, while public utilities, mines, and some other, generally large and for some reason distinguished, firms were kept under direct state (ministerial) control.

The basic idea of the Hungarian economic reforms had always been to increase enterprises' decision-making autonomy (Crane, 1991; Hare, 1991). These reforms, however, had only transformed the economy into one which was still centralised in terms of control over economic resources, although administered by the centre using indirect controls and regulations instead of direct commands (L. Antal, 1985). Organisations with poor performance had been bailed out with resources taken from organisations with high performance, suggesting that obtaining a tax concession, a firm- or industry-specific subsidy from the state officials may have been just as effective a strategy as cost-cutting, product differentiation, etc. In addition to the ways in which a firm could increase its chance to move upwards to a better final profitability position through fiscal redistribution, bargaining over output and input prices and other tactics could also improve original profitability.

The middle of the 1980s saw an unsuccessful attempt made by the communist party-state to boost economic growth which resulted in an even more serious balance-of-payments crisis. More substantial reforms followed, including a two-tier bank system, a taxation system which resembled its Western counterparts, and a bankruptcy law, to name just a few. Many of these reforms were effected in the period approaching the political turnaround, which seemed inevitable to many, but were still devised and brought about by communist governments.

For our purposes, the most important items of legislation enacted in this period were the ones which directly affected ownership, namely the Company Act of 1988, the Foriegn Investment Act, also of 1988, and the so-called Transformation Act of 1989. Thus, by the end of the eighties, a reasonably well-developed legislative framework for privatisation in Hungary was already in place (Boone, 1994). On the other hand, the process of gradually increasing enterprise autonomy, which culminated in these Acts, eventually resulted in blurred ownership rights, involving sharing between various bodies of the state and enterprise managers (Sajó, 1990; Szakadát, 1993).

By the end of the eighties, many of the constraints that had fulfilled the functions of corporate governance in the communist regime had been eroded, partly because of more or less continuous reforms increasing managers' decision-making autonomy from the economic centre, partly because of a depletion of resources that this centre could redistribute, and finally because of political changes that had seriously curtailed the Communist Party hierarchy's ability (and perhaps intent) to keep managers under control. We should note that almost a year before the 1990 election, opposition parties had already gained seats in the parliament, and in September 1989 an agreement had been reached on holding multi-party elections. Therefore, the incumbent government's legitimacy had already been diminishing. Sárközy (1993; English edition 1994), in his admittedly simplified example, portrays changes in corporate governance by 1989, asserting that self-interested abuses of state assets by managers were prevented primarily by political control. Ministries, party committees at various levels, and trade unions all monitored enterprise managers. In addition, the chief of personnel and the security guard of the organisation – positions often filled by people suspected of being informers – kept an eye on management, as did a wide range of informers of the Ministry of Home Affairs. By the summer of 1989, however, this network had dissipated, while new and effective mechanisms of external control and corporate governance were not yet in place. The appendix provides a chronological list of major political events in Hungary from 1987 to 1994.

4.2   Spontaneous privatisation

The term 'spontaneous privatisation' is usually employed to denote a process which started in about 1987 when the managements of state-owned enterprises (at first, only a few) discovered legal loopholes allowing the creation of subsidiaries capitalised with a proportion of the assets of the state-owned enterprise. It is a somewhat misleading label for what was taking place in Hungary and some other countries in the region in the late eighties with respect to ownership changes. In the strict legal sense of the word, it was not privatisation, and it was certainly not spontaneous. Yet, no thorough analysis of the Hungarian privatisation could possibly avoid a discussion of the phenomenon that has come to be known as spontaneous privatisation (Canning and Hare, 1994; Matolcsy, 1991; Sárközy 1993; Voszka, 1993).

On the one hand, spontaneous privatisation cannot be regarded as privatisation in the strict sense of the word since the state enterprises with majority holdings in the subsidiary companies still remained in state ownership. Minority owners were often other state enterprises and state-owned banks. Nevertheless, in the system of ill-defined ownership rights and ineffective corporate governance at the time, top managers of these holding enterprises could indeed assume quasi-ownership entitlements and play the roles of owners with respect to the management of the companies they created.

On the other hand, while spontaneous privatisation may seem unintentional from the standpoint of the state, it was clearly a deliberate action on the part of the managers (Voszka, 1993). As far as the state was concerned, state organs could, and indeed did, actively influence the process in general, even if not on the case-by-case basis that was to become the main approach to privatisation in Hungary. Among its means to encourage spontaneous privatisation were the increasing pressure on enterprises through tight credit and reduced subsidies, the tax concessions granted to every new company (later limited only to joint ventures with foreign capital), and the abolition of strict wage controls for companies, but not for state-owned enterprises. A ministry representative always attended meetings of enterprise councils, so enterprise plans for (partial) transformation could not be kept concealed. In many cases, concealment was not even the intention of managers, since they often voluntarily consulted with state administration, whose attitude 'seems to have been one of benign neglect', as Canning and Hare (1994: 213, n. 13) put it.

According to various reports (see, for example, the case collection in I. Antal, 1989; a case study analysis in Branyiczki, Bakacsi, and Pearce, 1992; and further analyses by close observers such as Matolcsy, 1990, 1991; Sárközy, 1993; Voszka, 1993), the motives of state enterprises were manifold, but it seems convenient to sort them into five categories. These are: easing financial pressure; reducing uncertainty; resolving organisational conflict; pursuing independence from the state; and acquiring personal wealth. While these objectives appear to have been present at the same time within a single enterprise, it is possible to treat them separately for analytical purposes.

Easing financial pressure. Large firms in poor financial condition rushed to exploit the newly discovered opportunity since it allowed them to forestall the effects of the new Company Act whose drafts they had found more severe than the old trade law (Sárközy, 1993). There seems to be a widely held view that spontaneous privatisation was the response of very different enterprises to common problems, of which the most important was their severely deteriorated financial position (in many cases due to forced commercial credits, often discussed in literature on the region under the label of 'financial queuing'). This, coupled with a loss of Soviet and/or CMEA markets, called for immediate action. Converting some of the assets of the state enterprise could contribute to alleviating the problem in several ways. First, the companies could be established virtually debt-free, thus opening new credit lines, with all liabilities kept with the state-owned holding enterprise which could go bankrupt without risking the existence of the companies. Between 1988 and 1991, every newly founded company, including those created with state assets, enjoyed substantial reduction in profit tax for a period of three years. Creative accounting also helped. Fixed assets could be re-evaluated when contributing them in kind to the company; obsolete stock could be written off. By creating many subsidiaries, relationships with banks could be optimised since the new companies usually dealt with different banks. Banks were sometimes also willing to convert a part of the debts to equity. Finally, in the case of outside investors, new capital could also be brought in.

Reducing uncertainty. When some of the stock of the new company was subscribed to by the founder's business partners, including most importantly banks but also suppliers and buyers, these partners became more closely tied to a network whose members could count upon mutual favours, such as price bargains or commercial credit. Mutual favour very often meant subscription to stock in companies founded by partners, thus resulting in a web of cross-ownership. Investments were made on the basis of reciprocity and courtesy rather than pure financial rationality (Matolcsy, 1991: 182). By subscribing to some stock in the new companies, suppliers and buyers often complied with the request of the management that wanted ownership to be dispersed amongst many shareholders. Managers had an interest in dispersed ownership not only because of the standard argument that typically relates it to less effective monitoring of managerial action, but also because dispersed ownership *amongst business partners* was expected to reduce uncertainty. The argument is similar to that of Schoorman, Bazerman and Atkin (1981) who, in the context of market economies, consider interlocking directorates as a strategy for reducing environmental uncertainty (but, for an alternative view, see Zajac, 1988). Spontaneous privatisation was also seen by some as a process of converting 'network capital' into physical (financial) capital in order to shield against uncertainty, thus reinforcing network relations (cf. Czakó and Sík, 1995; Stark, 1990, 1994a,b).

Resolving organisational conflict.   Breaking up the state enterprise into several independent companies was also a way to reach a compromise between headquarters (often located in the capital) and discontented plant managers (often in the countryside). The latter could thus take advantage of new career routes that were created by the establishment of companies, enjoy greater decision-making autonomy regarding the operation of their units, and probably enhance their prestige in the local community. The former, on the other hand, could retain strategic decision-making rights over the individual companies, and continue to exercise the function of internal resource allocation, now reinforced by ownership ties instead of the former administrative links between headquarters and subsidiaries. By law, a plant could initiate with the state supervisory board the process of separating from a large state enterprise and re-establishing itself as an independent company. For the headquarters, converting plants into companies was also a way of preventing them from going entirely independent in that way. Thus, the establishment of companies and converting the headquarters into an empty shell served the interests of the top manager (general director) by preserving his or her position, those of the staff of the headquarters by maintaining, albeit in a reorganised structure, internal resource allocation, and those of the plant managers by increasing their decision-making powers.

Pursuing independence from the state.   Spontaneous privatisation was also a defensive manoeuvre motivated by a desire for protection against state intervention. As the establishment of companies prevented plants from initiating independence, it also made it more difficult for state bodies to separate them from the state enterprise for any reason, for example in efforts to break up monopolies, or to sell units to investors, since by law only a state-owned enterprise, and not a company, could be drawn under direct state supervision (ministerial control).

Acquiring personal wealth. Another group of motives behind spontaneous privatisation was, of course, simple vested interest. The establishment of companies brought about new sources of personal wealth: the new companies had boards of directors and supervisory boards to which managers of the headquarters as well as those of co-owners could delegate their representatives. More importantly, managers could obtain ownership, even if minor, in the companies, not only diverting state assets to their own control, but often acquiring at least partial, legally recognised ownership.

The 1988 Act on Business Societies, Associations, Companies, and Ventures (the Company Act for short) came into force in January 1989. It provided the managers with a firm legal basis for continuing spontaneous privatisation by formally entrusting the enterprise councils of self-governed state enterprises to establish new corporate entities on the basis of the assets of the state enterprises. As Earle, Frydman, and Rapaczynski (1993: 5) point out, the Company Act was a major step on the path in which insiders attempted to convert their assumed quasi-ownership rights into formal rights. There is also anecdotal evidence on siphoning off resources from state-owned enterprises by transferring them through commercial contracts from state enterprises to private companies established following the Company Act.

The Act on Foreign Investments of 1988 also came into force in January 1989, allowing foreign investors to set up a business in Hungary without any special permission (except for some sectors, such as banking and financial services) and to repatriate their profits. Foreign ownership of land still remained subject to restrictions. Joint ventures with at least 30 per cent foreign ownership and meeting a couple of other requirements were entitled to significant tax privileges (in some cases an absolute tax exemption for five years and further allowances afterwards, again for five years).

With the Company Act and the Foreign Investment Act, it became possible for self-governed state enterprises to transfer state property into joint ventures with foreign co-owners whose mere presence was a further safeguard against state intervention. We should also note the January 1989 amendment to the Company Act which granted tax concessions for joint ventures with foreign capital of at least 5 million Hungarian forints (HUF; about US$80,000). Note that in the late eighties, according to a few well-publicised cases, top managers of state enterprises drew large bonuses of the order of millions of forints per year.

The Act on the Transformation of State Enterprises regulated corporatisation, or transformation as it is referred to in Hungary. A state enterprise could transform either to a limited liability company or a joint stock company limited by shares. Technically, the firm's Deed of Foundation – originally issued by a ministry when the state-owned enterprise was established – was modified, and separate Articles of Association were prepared which also established the division of the state-owned enterprise's 'own capital' between 'registered capital' and 'capital reserve'. Whereas the use of the provisions of the Company Act resulted in only partial conversion of state assets into corporate forms, the Transformation Act regulated the conversion of the whole state enterprise. The successor company of a state enterprise converted according to the Transformation Act also inherited the predecessor's liabilities. On the other hand, this act opened new ways of appropriation by enterprise insiders who became entitled to acquire newly issued shares in their firm at a discount of up to 90 per cent of par. A powerful incentive existed therefore to undervalue the assets of the state enterprise to be transformed in a period when state control of this corporatisation did not prevail.

The Transformation Act stipulated that 80 per cent of the proceeds from the sale of shares in a transformed firm should go to the state property management organisation (not established yet), while 20 per cent should be transferred back to the firm itself as capital reserve, from which issuance of employee shares (as prescribed in the Company Act) could be financed.

A self-governing state enterprise that had transferred more than 50 per cent of its assets at book value into companies was required to wholly transform within two years. In exceptional cases, it was made legally possible to draw self-governing state enterprises (but not companies) under direct state (ministerial) control.

On the extent of spontaneous privatisation we can provide only estimates. Csanádi (1991) analysed balance sheet data of about sixty state enterprises that were the first to found companies with their assets. This only appears significant if we note that most of these firms were certainly large ones, representing a greater proportion of state assets than the number would suggest. Mizsei, Móra, and Csáki (1994: 45) assert that estimates have been exaggerated, and believe that only 11 per cent of state property had been converted into corporate structure by 1989. Unfortunately, the authors do not reveal which sectors of industry they considered in their estimate. A similar figure is given by Gatsios (1992). Voszka (1993: 96), on the other hand, maintains that hundreds of spontaneous privatisation deals had been struck by the time the State Property Agency (SPA) was established in March 1990. In most cases, only a minor part of state assets was contributed in kind to the companies; in several dozen other cases, however, only a small state-owned enterprise was left behind to carry out the function of asset management over a range of individual companies established on the basis of production plants as well as administrative departments.

4.3   Centralised privatisation for cash

The Hungarian privatisation policy between 1990 and 1994 is usually considered to consist of two main phases (Canning and Hare, 1994; Csillag, 1994). The first phase, analysed in this section, started with the state's attempt to put a stop to the, assumed or real, abuses of spontaneous privatisation, which culminated in a centralised and revenue-centred policy. The second phase, discussed in the subsequent section, was that of changing priorities on both counts, and giving way to a more decentralised and politically motivated approach.

Privatisation monitored by the state

After the elections in May 1990, the new centre-right government, led by the late Dr József Antall, was supported by a three-party coalition composed of the Hungarian Democratic Forum (HDF), the Smallholder Party and the Christian Democratic Party, together controlling about 58 per cent of the seats in the single-chamber parliament.

The declared privatisation policy of the government ruled out cross-ownership and giveaway methods, and indicated an intent to service foreign debts from privatisation revenues. The exclusion of the cross-ownership solution that had been favoured by many in the era of spontaneous privatisation followed from the new government's critique of previous abuses and its apparent conflict with the management of state-owned enterprises. The policy of debt service from privatisation revenues was in line with the expectations of international financial institutions and a consequence of Hungary's high hard-currency debt. At a time when the government wanted to attract foreign capital, it was not considered a viable option to withhold due payments, which could send a deterring signal to foreign investors who might feel their investments to be insecure in a country that stops servicing its debts. Such a decision would also have had detrimental effects on the relationship with the International Monetary Fund, whose credit policy towards the country was also a factor considered by investors.

The Antall government declared that it wanted to reduce the share of state-owned assets in the so-called competitive sector to about 50 per cent by the end of its term in 1994, and to develop the institutional framework of a market economy. It envisaged a rapid privatisation process in order to achieve this objective, and a transparent one so that transactions could be justified to the public and accusations of squandering state property could be fended off.

Following public outcry over the abuses of spontaneous privatisation, an attempt had been made to reinforce the ownership rights of the state with the creation of the State Property Agency (SPA) in March 1990 by the Act on the State Property Agency and on the Management of State Property in State Enterprises. Other relevant legislation included the Act on the Protection of State Property Entrusted to State Enterprises, the Act on Privatisation of Properties of the State in the Retail Trade, Catering, and Consumption Services (the Pre-Privatisation Act which targeted mainly small business and was intended to precede large-scale privatisation), and the Property Policy Guidelines on the priorities of privatisation and on the use of the proceeds from it. The Property Policy Guidelines placed the reduction of state debts at the top of the list of priorities, which also included transparency and objective asset valuation. The State Property Agency staff were encouraged to achieve the highest price by incentives tied to revenues from transactions.

The first Property Policy Guidelines were passed by parliament as 'temporary' in March 1990, to be renewed in October for 1991, yet they remained in force until the end of 1992 by way of extension. In October 1991, however, the legislature decided against the proposal of the government to extend the guidelines again, and deferred the matter until the discussion of a new package of privatisation law scheduled for the first months of 1992. Thus, for a period of several months there were no valid Property Policy Guidelines, which made the SPA the *de facto* policy-maker, although even in this period policy-making by the SPA was certainly influenced by the same political and economic considerations that shaped the Property Policy Guidelines. In this context, and with due attention to the political developments (see appendix), note Schleifer and Vishny's (1993) assertion that a weak and divided government with ineffective control over its agencies will probably see a high level of corruption. This line of research inquiry will not be followed in this book.

Although the State Property Agency was created as some sort of government bureau, it was headed by a board of directors consisting of eleven members who initially represented the parliamentary parties and various government organs. The SPA was first charged with the supervision of the process of transformation and privatisation. With respect to those firms already transformed into companies, it held the shares not yet sold. It also personified the state as owner for firms still in a state enterprise status. Over these firms the SPA exercised the functions of corporate governance, most importantly by appointing or approving (if proposed by others, including state organs and the firm itself) members of their boards of directors and supervisory boards, by confirming – or replacing – management, and by approving decisions involving the divestment of state property of significant value. In the first few months of its operation, the SPA struggled with having only a small staff – later the main problem was rapid turnover – and had to establish its position as the organisation personifying the state as owner with respect not only to state enterprises, but also *vis-à-vis* other state bodies.

With the legislation of 1990, rules of a state-controlled but essentially decentralised privatisation were laid out, in which the primary initiative rested with the managers, and the state, as personified by the SPA, was to oversee the process and make sure that the relevant law was adhered to. This short period did not produce spectacular results in terms of the proportion of state assets already sold, since the SPA's main concern at the time was to take control of the process and to develop its own organisation.

Centrally managed sale of state property

From the end of summer 1990, state-controlled decentralised privatisation was gradually replaced with a state-governed, centralised approach. The government attempted to centralise decision-making power on transformation and privatisation of state enterprises.

After a few months during which the SPA was operating under the supervision of parliament, it was drawn under the government's control with an amendment to the law on the SPA, enacted in July 1990. Its first managing director, appointed before the elections, was also replaced, signalling the government's intent to exercise tighter control over the privatisation process. The possibility of appealing against the decisions of the SPA in court was revoked. Party representatives were gradually replaced on the SPA's board of directors. The eleven members of the board were appointed for five years, and could be dismissed, by the Prime Minister. According to the law the board had final, undivided (that is, between its members) responsibility to make decisions, and it could delegate its authority to a management committee in cases not exceeding certain limits in terms of value and number of employees concerned. On certain issues, the SPA's managing director and the directors (and later the newly created Privatisation Branch Committee that acted as a preliminary filter before issues were submitted to the management committee and the board) could make decisions.

Parallel to the increase in the SPA's authority, the government also attempted to curtail state enterprise managers' acquired powers with a decree on re-elections of enterprise councils. Motivated by experiences of spontaneous privatisation as well as by political considerations, the government ordered the enterprise councils to be re-elected until 15 September 1990, and the renewed enterprise councils were required to re-elect the general director with a two-thirds majority within fifteen days. That the government's decree was directed clearly against the managers was apparent, since in most of the enterprises, enterprise councils had just been renewed after fulfilling their five-year mandate (as specified in the 1984 legislation). In the summer, however, only slightly modified enterprise councils were elected, which relieved only a few top managers of their positions. The secret ballots held in September had similar results, contrary to the expectations of many politicians. According to Matolcsy (1991) and Sárközy (1993) (who were both close observers, the first holding government office at the time, the other being regarded as the 'father of the Company Act'), apart from just a few dozen cases the enterprise councils were re-elected with no substantial change in their membership, and the existing general directors came out of this challenge reconfirmed in their positions. Another government decree that illustrates the government's anti-management position, curtailed the possibility for state enterprise managers to hold positions in the management bodies of companies.

Also in autumn 1990 the governing coalition, whose popularity had been declining almost throughout its term, failed dramatically at the local elections where not only the opposition but also former local council leaders, now entering elections as independent candidates, collected most of the votes. Since municipalities were entitled to shares in privatised companies according to the value of land in each municipality in use by the firm relative to its total asset value, one could expect that politics would play a role in debates between municipalities and the privatisation agency on the exact share to be allotted.

This was the general climate when the SPA launched its central privatisation programmes, which are described in the following paragraphs.

Pre-privatisation. This programme, on the basis of the Pre-Privatisation Act passed in September 1990, targeted small shops in the retail, catering, and consumer services sectors. The programme was expected to proceed fast enough to justify its name, but within a short time administrative problems and political conflict were impeding progress (Canning and Hare, 1994). Many of the shops and retail outlets belonged to large state enterprises that acted as middlemen and their existence was threatened by the programme, which intended to privatise individual shops by open auctions. These enterprises could be expected to proceed with auctioning their shops, as the law required them to do, with little interest. This programme, also called 'small privatisation' in other Central-Eastern European countries, is not a subject of our study (Earle *et al.*, 1994). However, outlets that belonged to a chain of stores were excluded from pre-privatisation. Some enterprises, as illustrated by Mercury's case in the next chapter, could argue that their shops actually constituted a chain, thus exempting themselves from the programme and placing their transformation and privatisation under the procedures of 'large privatisation'.

Active privatisation programmes. The First Privatisation Programme was launched in September 1990 and involved twenty large enterprises which it was believed, on the basis of their relatively favourable economic conditions and of earlier discussions with potential investors, would be sold quickly (Canning and Hare, 1994). Note that in some cases, enterprises were requested by the SPA to participate in the First Privatisation Programme, while in others the firms themselves asked the SPA to allow their entry into the programme (Branyiczki, Bakacsi, and Pearce, 1992). The Second Privatisation Programme aimed at empty shells that had transferred more than 51 per cent of their assets to companies or joint ventures. Other active programmes targeted special sectors, such as historic vineyards, the construction industry, and those severely hit by the collapse of Soviet and CMEA markets.

Investor-initiated privatisation. In an attempt to speed up privatisation, the SPA introduced the investor-initiated programme in February 1991. Outside investors could submit proposals to the SPA for partial or full acquisition of state enterprises. Typically, the SPA made an open call for bids in order to obtain competitive proposals in the spirit of state revenue maximisation.

Asset protection procedure. Following provisions of the Act on the Protection of State-Owned Assets of 1990, state-owned enterprises were obliged to seek the SPA's approval in cases where the value of state assets sold without involving transformation of the whole enterprise itself exceeded a certain limit. These assets could be the enterprise's own nursery school or even a whole production plant. In some cases, for example where a subsidiary or a plant of a state-owned enterprise was contributed in kind to a joint venture, a transaction under the asset protection procedure might result in the establishment of a new company.

Supplementary methods. Combined with the aforementioned programmes, some additional methods of divesting state assets were also in use. Property transfers to the church, social security funds, and other beneficiaries are beyond the scope of this book. Here we emphasise only two groups that were active in acquisition of shares: the employees and the local governments.

Employees had two preferential ways of acquiring shares. They could purchase employee shares, tradable only among employees and pensioners of a given firm, issued to the extent of 10 per cent of the firm's registered capital, at 90 per cent discount, which was covered from the firm's capital reserve. This capital reserve was created from the 20 per cent of the privatisation proceeds that the privatised firm was entitled to, while 80 per cent of the proceeds was the net revenue of the SPA. Managers and workers could also acquire common shares at a discount, in the SPA's practice at 50 per cent of par. The total allowances to which employees were entitled had a ceiling in terms of a percentage of the firm's asset value or its wage level.

Municipalities were also beneficiaries of share transfers from the SPA upon transformation, according to the value of land where the self-governing firm and its plants, shops etc. were located. However, before September 1991, when state enterprises under direct state (ministerial) control were transformed into a company form, municipalities were not granted any shares.

The various programmes of centrally selecting and privatising packages of firms were generally perceived as failures, and in many cases, indeed, did not bring the expected results for various reasons. Delays were caused by the claims of municipalities, the time required to select outside consulting and investment firms from several hundred applicants, and the time required by those selected to proceed with their complex task.

The introduction of investor-initiated privatisation also failed to accelerate the process as it turned out that foreign investors were rather unwilling to enter competition by submitting tenders. One might assume that among the reasons for this reluctance was their realisation that as the state-owned enterprise's market share was eroding, there was less need for a potential investor to team up with the firm to be privatised. Instead, greenfield investment and developing an own distribution network may have become preferred alternatives. In addition, the deteriorating financial position of many state-owned companies may have suggested that investors could acquire necessary assets more cheaply in a liquidation sale, with the additional advantage of bypassing the SPA's bureaucracy and dealing directly with commercial banks (as recommended by Price Waterhouse; see Frydman *et al.*, 1993: 117). Both assumptions gain support from cases in the next chapter.

Perhaps the most important cause of perceived failure of privatisation, however, was the SPA's high asking price for the firms involved. This was certainly a consequence of the country's international debts and was encouraged by the SPA staff's incentive being tied to sales revenue. In addition, at least in part, it was due to the political sensitivity of the issue: following the heated public debate on spontaneous privatisation, deals had to be protected against accusations of selling off the family silver (Canning and Hare, 1994; Frydman *et al.*, 1993).

Under pressure of continuous criticism for being slow, bureaucratic, and unsuccessful in accelerating and properly controlling the privatisation process, the SPA introduced some elements of a decentralised approach to privatisation. This is where the end of the first phase and the beginning of the second phase of the Hungarian privatisation policy is usually located.

4.4   Decentralisation and politicisation

From the second half of 1991 and particularly in 1992 the Hungarian privatisation policy took a turn. Two major trends were characteristic of this policy shift. First, direct state (SPA) control over privatisation was relaxed. Second, privatisation became more and more influenced by the aim of enhancing the opportunities for domestic investors and employees to participate in the privatisation process.

Self-privatisation

Owing to the perceived failure of centralised programmes, and because of the realisation that, even in the first phase, enterprise initiative had played an important role, the so-called self-privatisation was introduced in the middle of 1991. The SPA invited proposals from consulting firms which then could effectively play the role of the SPA on the basis of a framework contract that specified the basic rules. The SPA's direct involvement was reduced to intervening only if the law was not adhered to. First, state enterprises with less than 300 employees and an annual turnover of less than HUF 300 million (about US$ 4 million) were included in this programme. In the second round, launched in May 1992, the ceiling was lifted to 1000 employees and a turnover of HUF 1 billion (US$ 13.3 million).

Since most of the enterprises included in this programme do not meet our selection criteria for case studies (see the methodology section in the appendix), we refer to Canning and Hare (1994: 192–4). It is important to note, however, that the introduction of self-privatisation was a departure from the first principle of previous policy, that is centralisation. Speed, even if concerning only a certain group of enterprises, took priority over control. In effect, we can consider self-privatisation a special case of enterprise-initiated, or spontaneous, privatisation. Enterprise initiatives that had been suspended for a while during the government's efforts to centralise the privatisation process were revived around spring 1991, when it became apparent that the new government could not proceed with privatisation without relying upon the management (Matolcsy, 1991). For a certain group of firms, by summer 1991, spontaneous privatisation was dead, but it soon recovered, disguised as self-privatisation. The SPA terminated self-privatisation at the end of 1993.

A few tables summarising privatisation results until the end of 1992 in Hungary are presented. Table 8 presents the number of complete transformations of state enterprises initiated, or in the case of enterprise initiatives, approved or rejected by the SPA, as well as the value of assets involved, at book value and revised value as approved by the SPA upon transformation.

Table 9 gives similar data on the so-called asset protection transactions, that is on divestitures of assets of state enterprises without the transformation of the state-owned enterprise itself. Both tables cover only 1990–92 since data for later years were not available in a compatible format. It may be indicative that the kind of data published in *Privinfo*, the primary public source of privatisation data, tended to change in line with the shift of the declared policy. After 1992, separate tables and charts were prepared and published on 'techniques for encouraging domestic investors'.

We can draw a number of conclusions from the data presented in these tables. Table 8 seems to support the view that even in the first phase of privatisation policy, said to have been characterised by centralisation, the initiative came mostly from the management. At least in terms of the number of transformations, the data support Voszka's (1993) remark that spontaneous privatisation continued under the SPA's monitoring. Managements were then seeking the SPA's approval and all the issues related to the state-owned enterprise's transformation and subsequent privatisation became subject to bargaining. In this period, emphasis was more on corporatisation than genuine privatisation, partly because of the SPA's effort to control the process and forestall any possible deals pre-arranged by managers and investors by overseeing transformation prior to privatisation (Frydman *et al.*, 1993). In the bargaining process, the SPA could obtain information and influence asset valuation. In principle,

Table 8. *Transformations and asset value involved by type of initiation, 1990–92 (HUF billion)*

	1990	1991		1992	
		increment	cumulative	increment	cumulative
Self-privatisation					
Number of transformations	0	20	20	237	257
Book value of assets	0	1.15	1.15	27.35	28.50
Revised value of assets	0	1.56	1.56	24.74	26.30
Management and/or investor initiated					
Number of transformations	27	153	180	116	296
Book value of assets	26.19	167.30	193.49	216.51	410.00
Revised value of assets	41.47	240.01	281.48	129.66	411.14[a]
State initiated					
Number of transformations	0	18	18	31	49
Book value of assets	0	150.43	150.43	215.57	366.00
Revised value of assets	0	182.16	182.16	744.84	927.00
Total approved					
Number of transformations	27	191	218	384	602[b]
Book value of assets	26.19	318.88	345.07	459.43	804.50[c]
Revised value of assets	41.47	423.73	465.20	899.24	1364.44
Rejected					
Number of transformations[d]	8	3	11	4	15
Book value of assets	3.99	1.05	5.04	1.95	6.99

Notes: [a] Not given in source. Calculated from available data.
[b] According to a later issue of the same source, 690; calculated sum is shown.
[c] In source, given as 645.54; calculated sum is shown.
[d] Without those rejected earlier but approved or in progress since then.
Amounts stated in Hungarian currency can be converted with exchange rates given in table 7.
Source: Adapted from *Privinfo*, 1(1):5, 1(10):17, 2(3):24, 2(12):18, and own calculations.

Table 9. *Asset protection transactions and asset value involved, 1990–92 (HUF billion)*

	1990	1991		1992	
		increment	cumulative	increment	cumulative
Establishments of companies: total					
Number of transactions	46	80	126	46	172
Book value of assets	11.50	9.84	21.34	1.86	23.20
Revised value of assets	19.45	17.85	37.30	7.50	44.80
Establishments of companies with domestic partner					
Number of transactions	18	52	70	29	99
Book value of assets	1.51	2.22	3.73	1.57	5.30
Revised value of assets	2.07	7.03	9.10	4.30	13.40
Establishments of companies with foreign partner					
Number of transactions	28	28	56	17	73
Book value of assets	9.99	7.62	17.61	0.29	17.90
Revised value of assets	17.38	10.82	28.20	3.20	31.40
Rejected					
Number of transactions	12	3	15	2	17
Book value of assets	0.49	0.22	0.71	0.33	1.04
Asset sales related to establishment of companies					
Number of transactions	0	17	17	0	17
Book value of assets	0	5.17	5.17	0	5.17
Revised value of assets	0	7.00	7.00	0	7.00
Approved other transactions (sale of individual assets, etc.)					
Number of transactions	38	169	207	244	451
Book value of assets	1.86	6.73	8.59	5.80	14.39
Revised value of assets	3.96	13.15	17.11	12.24	29.35
Rejected other transactions					
Number of transactions	11	5	16	3	19
Book value of assets	0.92	0.94	1.86	88.94	90.80

Note: Amounts stated in Hungarian currency can be converted with exchange rates given in table 7.

Source: Adapted from *Privinfo*, 1(1):5–6, 1(10):18, 1(13):29, 2(3):24, 2(12):19.

the enterprise councils had the right to decide upon transformation, but these decisions were subject to the SPA's approval or possible veto. The small proportion of transformations rejected by the SPA indicates that in most cases the SPA preferred bargaining to vetoing management's proposals. Thus, just as the 'spontaneous' label did not fit perfectly, the 'centralised' period was not exactly what its label would suggest either.

In terms of asset value involved, however, the state continued to dominate the initiation of transformations, even if we assume that all asset protection transactions shown in table 9 were initiated by the management. The data also indicate a shift to self-privatisation, again in terms of the number of transactions.

Both table 8 and table 9 show significant differences between the book values of assets involved in transformations and asset protection transactions and their revised values as reappraised and approved by the SPA at the time of the transaction. We may reasonably assume, as our case studies in the next chapter indeed show, that in the absence of appropriate capital market institutions, reappraised asset values result from a bargaining process. The right of final approval rested with the SPA which, again instead of rejecting a transformation initiated by the management at the outset, apparently preferred exercising control in the course of this bargaining process. Thus, the distinction (originally devised by the SPA) between state-initiated and management-initiated processes might be less relevant than the fact of who has control over the evolving process, to what extent, and by what means that control is exercised. An analysis of the cases presented in the next chapter will shed some light on these questions.

Politicised privatisation

The introduction of self-privatisation was followed by changes that made the year 1992 a milestone in Hungarian privatisation policy. These changes indicate that the second principle that had governed privatisation policy to date, that is maximisation of revenues, lost its overwhelming importance and gave way to other considerations.

The legislation and institutions of privatisation and state asset management changed. In January 1992, a new minister without portfolio in charge of privatisation (privatisation minister for short) had been appointed, whose 'strategy for breakthrough in privatisation' laid out new priorities for the Hungarian privatisation. A new package of privatisation law was enacted. The institutional framework that provided support for privatisation was further developed (credit schemes, Guarantee Fund, etc.). Even the formal organisational rules of conduct of the

SPA, which had already been in existence for two years, were eventually prepared. In October 1992 the State Asset Management Company (SAMCo) was established under the rationale of separating privatisation and long-term management of state assets. SAMCo and the firms under its authority are outside the scope of this book since we are interested in privatisation rather than the management of assets in long-term state ownership (Canning and Hare, 1994: 203–7; Voszka, 1995). The establishment of SAMCo curtailed the powers of the SPA over state assets.

The possibilities for domestic investors to finance acquisitions of state property were expanded. Interest rates on the so-called Existence Loans (or E-loan), launched in March 1991 specifically to encourage domestic investors, were decreased from 75 to 60 per cent of the central bank's base rate, and the ceiling on the amount one could borrow was abolished. Also note that in many cases as little as 2 per cent 'own capital' was required to take an Existence Loan with two years' deferment of capital and interest repayments and an eight year loan period. Applications for E-loans were evaluated by commercial banks according to standard criteria; the risk to banks was practically eliminated by a state-owned Guarantee Fund.

The first 'compensation notes' appeared on the market in early 1992, and started trading on the Stock Exchange a few months later. As we have already noted, the new government rejected in-kind restitution. Instead, owners or their direct heirs whose property had been confiscated by the communist state and those who had suffered injustice for political reasons were given tradable securities called compensation notes up to HUF 5 million (about US$ 60,000). The notes were quoted on the Stock Exchange, bore an annual interest of 17 per cent, and could be used to acquire state property, including housing and land, or to obtain a fixed life annuity. In cases where stock offered for sale by tender could be paid for in compensation notes, the SPA accepted them at 'nominal value', defined as the face value increased by accumulated fixed rate interest, although the compensation notes were quoted at a steadily decreasing price (January 1993: 80 per cent of face value; January 1994: 60 per cent; January 1995: 40 per cent. *Figyelő*, 17 August 1995, p. 24). This was attributed by many to an insufficient supply of state property to be bought in exchange for compensation notes. The Ministry of Finance originally estimated that claims would be submitted to the National Office for Compensation and Settlement of Damages in the amount of about HUF 60 billion (US$ 720 million). Eventually, the number of claims submitted under various Compensation Acts reached more than two million, and the total face value of compensation notes issued reached more than twice as much as expected (which is almost four times as much as nominal value; *Privinfo*, 1995, 4(15): 37), thus creating a substantial demand for state property.

Other methods that gave priority to domestic investors with limited resources were soon introduced. For cases where two calls for bids were unsuccessful, privatisation by leasing was made possible. Payment in instalments on terms and conditions not worse than those of an Existence Loan became accepted. Also in this line of measures was the Small Investors Share Purchasing Programme, a scheme allowing citizens to purchase, on credit, stock in privatised state-owned companies up to a limit of HUF 100,000 (around US$ 1,000; for exchange rates refer to table 7). This programme was under consideration for a long time and was eventually introduced, involving only two firms, only a couple of months before the end of the government's term in 1994.

In June 1992 the Parliament passed the Act on Employee Partial Ownership Programme (often referred to as MRP, the Hungarian abbreviation, or, as here, ESOP, following common usage in the West). With this, a new scheme for employee ownership was introduced in addition to earlier opportunities (which involved employee shares and preferential purchase of common shares, as specified by provisions in the Company Act and the Property Policy Guidelines, supplemented from late 1991 by the giving of priority to competitive employee bids, other conditions being equal). Following this Act, a new organised player entered the bargaining game: the firm-level ESOP Organising Committee, which received its mandate from employees who wished to participate in an ESOP acquisition of shares. ESOP organising committees were required to submit a feasibility study. If the SPA approved it, most often with modifications resulting from bargaining, an ESOP Organisation was established to represent the employee-owners. Often, the ESOP acquisitions were financed from loans with guarantees provided by the company whose shares the employees acquired.

Table 10 shows revenues of the state from privatisation in the period 1990–94, clearly indicating the policy shift discussed in this section.

These data indicate that the percentage of cash revenues relative to the value of compensation notes accepted for acquiring state property dramatically decreased in the second half of the government's term. (A similar trend appears in data on sales by SAMCo.) Amongst the possible reasons for the policy shift, political motives (winning the electorate's favour, offering concessions to various political groups) are usually considered to be significant. Hence, most observers agree that the year 1992 divided privatisation policy in Hungary into two markedly different phases, where the second phase is seen as typically 'political' (Csillag, 1994), or 'populist' (Canning and Hare, 1994). As Canning and Hare

Table 10. *Revenues of the state from sale of state property by the SPA, 1990–94 (HUF billion)*

Form of payment	1990[a]	1991	1992	1993	1994
HUF cash	0.14	4.82	17.51	15.30	14.10
Foreign currency cash	0.53	24.61	40.98	25.50	6.10
Total cash	0.67	29.43	58.49	40.80	20.20
Loans[b]	–	1.01	9.07	21.70	30.23
Compensation notes	–	0.00	2.52	16.90	44.88
Dividend, rent and others	–	0.94	4.74	2.40	1.96
Total non-cash	–	1.95	16.33	41.00	76.07
Total revenues	0.67	31.38	74.82	81.8	97.27

Notes: [a] From March, when the SPA came into operation.
 [b] Mainly Existence Loans. From 1994, payments in instalments are also included.
Amounts stated in Hungarian currency can be converted with exchange rates given in table 7.
Source: Adapted from *Privinfo* 1(1):6, 1(10):18, 1(13):30, 2(3):24, 3(5):34, 3(13):36–7, 4(6):25, 4(9):6–8.

point out, however, the departure from the revenue-centred approach may also be attributed to the possible lack of sufficient interest from foreign investors who may have already acquired most of the firms for which they were willing to pay cash. Yet, *privatisare necesse est*, and the observed shift may have also served the purpose of keeping the privatisation process going.

4.5   The continuity of political bargaining

We end this chapter by highlighting major issues. Four questions are singled out: the legacy of the past, the effect of the use of 'cheap money', the role of insiders and networks, and politics and bargaining in the privatisation process. These issues will be demonstrated in the next chapter where we present six cases from the Hungarian privatisation.

Legacy of the past

It is important to realise that privatisation in Hungary was not introduced out of the blue but in a specific social, political, and economic situation, and it is this concrete historical context and not an abstract discussion of social justice or economic rationality that determines many aspects of the process. In accordance with this view, several authors interested in privatisation in Hungary have pointed out that policy options had been considerably restricted by the time the freely elected government took control in summer 1990 (Canning and Hare, 1994; Earle, Frydman, and Rapaczynski, 1993).

We briefly recapitulate here the factors surrounding privatisation – factors that appear to determine many features of the declared, and actually followed, privatisation policy of the government – by grouping them in three categories. These are economic conditions, property rights/ corporate governance, and political considerations.

Economic conditions. Consideration of mass privatisation by free distribution was precluded by the highest foreign (hard-currency) debts in per capita terms in the region, combined with apparent pressure by international financial organisations, most notably the International Monetary Fund, and the government's firm commitment to repaying all due debts in an era of recession, decreasing gross domestic product, and decreasing exports. The question whether to sell or give away state property did not actually mean there were real choices. The debate on full in-kind 're-privatisation' (restitution), that is the transfer of state assets to their former owners, also seems to have been resolved by the pressing need to generate income from privatisation, leading to 'compensation' instead.

Property rights and corporate governance. We have already noted that earlier reforms, aimed at increasing enterprise autonomy, had resulted in blurred property rights. Managers had assumed quasi-ownership entitlements, leaving the state in a relatively weak position. Thus, although the government was firmly against insider privatisation, managers were bound to play an important role due to the property-rights legacy and lack of effective corporate governance.

Political considerations. Privatisation to insiders was unacceptable for the new coalition. The common view held by many among its ranks that state enterprise managers were members of the old *nomenklatura* who should not be allowed to convert their managerial powers into those of owners, and the public outcry over the abuses during spontaneous privatisation, made it impossible to adopt such an approach. However, even if full re-privatisation was rejected, some sort of compensation of former owners clearly followed from the political values held by the coalition, which considered it a priority to create a wide middle class and cultivated good relations with Christian churches that claimed back their confiscated property.

The effect of 'cheap money'

Regardless of the motives behind the policy shift in 1992, with the appearance of various forms of preferential payment two types of currency became accepted in privatisation deals, 'real money' and 'cheap money', the latter including soft loans, compensation notes, and instalment payments. The implications of the two currencies are important.

First, an investment offer financed from an E-loan was worth only about half of an up-front cash bid, allowing for the state subsidy provided with an E-loan. Second, a similar argument applies to the compensation note, traded on the Stock Exchange at increasingly less than its face value but accepted by the SPA at nominal value, calculated as the face value plus accumulated interest. Thus, someone who could use compensation notes could offer a purchase price approximately three times that of a cash-paying bidder. Third, in some cases several options – such as compensation notes and paying in instalments, not to mention various incentives for employee ownership – could be used in combination, further increasing the gap between 'real money' and 'cheap money'. Thus, in cases where payments were allowed to be made in 'cheap money', those who were entitled to take advantage of its use could artificially increase their bidding power.

It may appear that this group first of all includes resource-deficient, mainly domestic, would-be owners such as employees and original recipients of compensation notes, in accordance with the declared policy shift as laid out in the government's 'Strategy for breakthrough in privatisation'. However, before prematurely jumping to the conclusion that from 1992, resourceful (mainly foreign, but also a few domestic) cash bidders were necessarily bound to lose in bidding contests, two caveats have to be noted. First, note that it was the SPA that had authority to decide upon the structure of different forms of payment acceptable in a bidding process. One could assume that permitted forms of payments might be specified in the tender announcements in accordance with the seller's preference with respect to the eventual winner. Second, cash bidders, domestic and foreign alike, were often able to find ways of circumventing their exclusion from the use of 'cheap money'. This was the case when the SPA accepted compensation notes from anyone, and not only from those who had received them as the victims of economic or political reprimands under the communist regime. Cash bidders could also make an agreement with those entitled to various price concessions to acquire shares from them subsequent to privatisation and share the benefits of state subsidies.

Insiders and networks

Insiders' roles in the Hungarian privatisation process have been prominent. It was apparently decisive in the era of spontaneous privatisation. Insiders' influence remained relevant even in the so-called centralised phase of privatisation policy.

The ability of insiders to influence privatisation is rooted above all in quasi-ownership entitlements acquired during earlier reforms. However, it is reinforced by a number of other reasons including, for example, an obvious information asymmetry which creates an enormous monitoring problem and renders corporate governance ineffective. In addition, there is a trade-off between transparency and other considerations, such as speed, and it is transparency that has lost priority in the Hungarian privatisation process. Finally, the bargaining nature of the process certainly created more latitude for managerial influence.

In several cases insiders were successful in creating a web of cross-ownership, thus strengthening a network based on mutual favours as well as business relationships. As Canning and Hare (1994) point out, cross-ownership developed further even after the era of spontaneous privatisation, in part because of widespread debt–equity swaps which in turn could be attributed to strict bankruptcy legislation since 1992.

The importance of network, or relational, capital in the Hungarian transition has been emphasised by Matolcsy (1991) who argued that mutual favours had no longer been directed only at consumption in order to obtain scarce goods, but also, and more importantly, at accumulation of physical capital. Networks comprise both insiders (e.g. managers) and outsiders (e.g. officials of party and state bureaucracies). Following Bourdieuesque traditions of sociology (Bourdieu, 1978) and utilising Granovetter's (1985) theory of embeddedness of economic behaviour, Stark (1990, 1994a,b) and Czakó and Sík (1995) also emphasise the role of networks and network capital in Hungary before and, increasingly, after the political turnaround. However, they focus on small entrepreneurs rather than large enterprises. The role that networks play in the privatisation process therefore remains as a subject for further study.

Politics and bargaining

Politics. The role that politics can play in privatisation has been studied from various angles. One possibility is to look at the legislature's politically motivated decisions that have consequences on general privatisation policy, as did a study by Urbán (1993). In a similar approach, Boycko, Schleifer, and Vishny (1994) assert that privatisation policy choices are determined by politics. Considering political objectives of privatisation, Brabant (1992) singles out strengthening of democracy and social stability, restriction of the role of the state, and breaking of the politically appointed managerial structures. Estrin (1994) emphasises securing of the irreversibility of the reform process, and directs focus on how different privatisation policies separate losers and winners. Batt (1994) appears to be more interested in general issues of political legitimacy. Others discuss the political economy of privatisation, placing special emphasis on political considerations surrounding debates on, implementation of, and obstacles to privatisation policies (Rausser and Simon, 1992; Schipke, 1994; Winiecki, 1992). In a speech, Stone (1994) went further when he defined privatisation as 'being in essence a transfer of power', and 'a political act'. What is common in most of these treatments of the subject is the recognition of policy choices on various issues related to privatisation as choices that affect the distribution of wealth and, eventually, power. Indeed, the Hungarian privatisation seems to have been inextricably interwoven with politics. We have noted political considerations as factors affecting the government's declared privatisation policy in 1990. They also played a role in the subsequent implementation of the Hungarian privatisation, as indicated by our review of particularly the second, politicised phase. In this phase, decisions, motivated at least in part by political considerations, determined to a great extent who was allowed to the bargaining table by increasing domestic players' ability to enter bargaining even if their initial bargaining power based on economic resources was weak.

What has almost entirely been neglected in these discussions of privatisation and politics is *politicking* (i.e. organisational politics). While the effect of politics on general privatisation policy choices has been given considerable attention, politicking at the level of and within individual organisations, particularly the state-owned enterprise that is subject to privatisation, appears to have been ignored by scholars.

Bargaining. The gradual and evolutionary nature of the Hungarian reforms has been noted. Authors usually point out Hungary's pragmatism and case-by-case approach in selecting and applying privatisation techniques (Canning and Hare, 1994; Frydman *et al.*, 1993; Mizsei, 1993; Urbán, 1993). However, what appears as gradualism and pragmatism may have only been a continuation of the bargaining system that had characterised Hungary for decades and had gained increasing importance since the 1968 reforms. Following reforms, bargaining upon state directives, production plans and the like had been replaced by bargaining on regulatory controls, prices, wages, etc. At about the end of the communist regime, and even more apparently after the political turn-around in 1990, players and their relative bargaining powers did change, of course, just as the stake in the bargaining did, but the primarily bargaining nature of the allocation processes remained. This should come as no surprise, considering Rausser and Simon's (1992) argument that ill-defined economic rights will naturally lead to the rise of a bargaining problem. To simplify: from lack of rules, bargaining follows. More precisely, existing rules and policies could be interpreted and applied in different ways, providing only a framework for bargaining.

One could infer that drawing general lessons about the Hungarian privatisation is next to impossible. Indeed, Frydman *et al.* (1993) conclude that this case-by-case, bargaining approach makes it extremely difficult to generalise about the Hungarian privatisation. In our view, however, this *is* precisely the generalisable pattern that characterises the privatisation process, which itself can be seen as part of the legacy discussed above. Privatisation policy in Hungary may seem hectic if one focuses on the wide range of techniques used in the process; yet, by focusing on preferences granted to different groups of possible owners, markedly different phases can be discerned, in which otherwise excluded groups were allowed to enter the bargaining process. Furthermore, by noting underlying mechanisms of conflict resolution, bargaining and politics appear to have been remarkably constant characteristics regard-less of the phases (which themselves seem to have been induced in part by political considerations). In simplifying words: policy may change, bargaining remains.

5 Behaviour in transition

This chapter charts the path to privatisation of six Hungarian firms. The cases underline the fact that privatisation in Central and Eastern Europe (and elsewhere) needs to be considered in the context of a political view of organisations, as a complement to the dominant economic model based on agency theory.

The appendix to this book presents a section on methodology, arguing for the case study design and presenting details on case selection, access to information, methods of case analysis, and disguise techniques.

All cases were taken from the consumer goods sector. Five are manufacturing firms, one is a trader. Each case begins with a brief introduction to the firm and its industry (the 'stage'), followed by a narrative of the privatisation process (the 'play'). 'Actors' who appear in all or most of the cases are listed in table 11. Persons are given expressive pseudonyms according to their titles, ranks or positions; organisations take a pseudonym based on a characteristic feature. These pseudonyms, of both persons and organisations, are used as proper names and thus are capitalised. Actors appearing with the same pseudonym in different cases may or may not be the same, unless their identity is distinctly stated.

We present the privatisation processes in chronological order so that we can focus on links between successive events. From distinct events, phases of the process are distinguished and organised under subheadings that are indicative of the main theme of the specific phase.

The cases present some quantitative information, but only to the extent necessary to indicate the firm's size, its performance level, and the value of planned or actual privatisation deals. The appendix describes the tactics employed to disguise numerical data. Quotations in the cases are taken from both interviews and documents (see also the appendix).

Table 11. *Actors appearing in all or most of the cases*

Insiders
The *Company* concerned; its *General Director* and other members of the management team; the *Enterprise Council* and its Chairman; the *Board of Directors* and the *Supervisory Board* once the firm has been transformed (corporatised); the *ESOP Organising Committee*; the ESOP once it has been established; its Leader and Trustees; the local labour union.

The state
State Property Agency (SPA); *Responsible Politicians*: political appointees (at least to some extent) who are likely to transmit political considerations (any of the ministers in charge of privatisation, or the chairman of the SPA's Board of Directors, or a distinguished member of this board, or some other official); *decision-makers*: any decision-making body or person with high authority, such as the SPA Board of Directors, the SPA Management Committee comprising top and senior executives, the SPA Privatisation Branch Committee comprising SPA officers and representatives of other state agents; an *SPA Executive*: any one of the SPA's managing director, his deputies, a director or a deputy director; *SPA officials, administrators, and staff members*: officials of various rank, *directly* dealing with the case concerned; *other SPA officials*: usually support staff, legal experts, or auditors; the *Ministry* which the firm concerned belongs to; *Ministry officials*: any of the rank of Minister, State Secretary, Deputy State Secretary, or Head of Department; the *Competition Office*: overseeing adherence to rules of fair competition.

Outsiders
The *Bank* (with initial always capitalised): the main bank of the firm concerned – usually the largest creditor, and may also be the provider of an Existence Loan for a management/employee acquisition; the *Advisor* to the State Property Agency; the *Consultant* who advises the management and/or the ESOP organisation – may also advise an investor or the SPA; the *Auditor* of the firm concerned.

Also appearing
Investors (who may become bidders), other banks, various domestic and foreign institutions, party politicians, national union leaders, lawyers, etc.

5.1 Pluto: Struggling through

'Pluto', a relatively large firm with almost 1,000 employees and a net asset value of more than HUF 1 billion (about US$ 15 million), operated in an industry with a handful of major suppliers, all having licence agreements with Western firms. For Pluto, brands licensed from its

Western 'Licenser' accounted for more than a third of sales and profits. Prices were fully liberalised in 1989. Demand rose until 1991, but later declined sharply. Four competitors had already been privatised by 1991, with foreign companies holding majority stakes in each.

When the process of Pluto's privatisation began, it was the third largest supplier of its products in Hungary; it was also an important local employer and a significant taxpayer. Since 1985, Pluto had operated as a self-governed enterprise under the general management of an Enterprise Council. For Pluto, privatisation was a long, complicated, and high profile journey. We pick up the story in March 1989.

The spontaneous start-up

This was the era of so-called spontaneous privatisation. In March 1989 the Enterprise Council authorised Pluto's General Director to explore the possibilities of establishing a joint venture with Licenser. By November 1989, negotiations had led to an offer. In order to inject finance, the Licenser would acquire a 35 per cent equity stake; benefits were promised for managers and employees. The necessary legislation was already in place, and interest was shown by both parties. So Pluto's privatisation could have been concluded relatively quickly and smoothly.

As it turned out, the journey had only just begun. After preliminary talks with government officials, an Expatriate Investor (Hungarian by birth, representing a firm with headquarters in a remote tax haven) also submitted a formal offer. He met the General Director to present two alternatives: he would either purchase 100 per cent of Pluto's assets, or acquire 50 per cent of the equity by putting in finance of an amount equal to Pluto's asset value. Promises were made to modernise equipment, to keep the incumbent top management, and to increase wages.

In effect, the meeting of the Enterprise Council in early December 1989 settled the future for Pluto. It was presided over by the Enterprise Council Chairman, himself a top manager and a mechanic by profession with no higher education, who was understood to be an associate of Pluto's General Director. Six issues had been discussed before the General Director reported on the talks he had had with possible investors. In his comments he favoured Expatriate Investor's offer. He appealed for the members' 'good decision', adding that 'I can state with full responsibility that this management is not committed to anyone, only to the Enterprise Council, and to all the employees of the firm.' The Licenser's offer was rejected with the result that the choice was reduced to accepting one of the Expatriate Investor's alternatives. The Enterprise Council voted for the second one.

The Expatriate Investor was pleased to learn about the Enterprise Council's decision, but only thirty-six hours later he asked that the first alternative be accepted instead. He reasoned that 'it seems much simpler [and] the final outcome is the same' since he, eventually, wanted to own 100 per cent in any case. Another Enterprise Council meeting was called at unlawfully short notice. This modified the previous resolution. One of the interviewees for this case history believed the Enterprise Council members 'could not differentiate between the alternatives'.

High-level government officials also committed themselves to the Expatriate Investor's offer. One official assured Expatriate Investor that he would 'intercede with the responsible ministers in order that the necessary permissions be issued ahead of their turn'. As the 'quickest and least difficult' way of getting the transaction done, an assistant minister proposed that Pluto be drawn under ministerial control, turned into a limited liability company with the state as the sole owner, and sold to the Expatriate Investor. This procedure, he argued, would give the foreigner assurance, and at the same time would be public and would provide protection against an accusation of 'squandering' (i.e. 'selling the family silver for peanuts'). Another proposal argued that only privatisation in this way could ensure Pluto's development. At this time the Expatriate Investor sought an option for six months, pointing out that he could not responsibly mobilise finances until his position as a purchaser was secure.

Young Turks' game

What happened next was a variant of the young Turks' game (Mintzberg, 1983). This is depicted in academic research on organisational power as a zero-sum game fought for all or nothing, reaching deep into the organisation. It is usually initiated by a small but critical group from within the organisation which needs to seek dominant external influencers (Mintzberg, 1983). In Pluto's case, the coup was initiated by a few middle managers and eventually resulted in the blocking of this 'ethically challenged' (Mahoney, 1994: 13) acquisition attempt. 'It was a period of big fights, internal strife, ... external supports [lobbying]', remembered the Leader of the soon-to-be-established Independent Union, a middle manager himself. 'The management did not give much attention to the firm, because everybody was engaged in these internal problems. This was a very baleful, stormy period.'

The General Director stated that 'my personality is the guarantee that I have always represented and will represent the interest of Pluto's working collective'. Not everyone was impressed by this assurance. A small group of 'rebels' protested against the planned deal, challenging the legitimacy of the incumbent top management. Their fight, which seemed like Don Quixote's tilting at the windmill, subsequently developed into a micro-level movement of social resistance. They argued in a letter to a member of parliament (MP) that assets had been undervalued, the Expatriate Investor's financial background was questionable, the sale would solve the problem of 'some missing stock', etc. The young Turks started a fight against what they saw as fraud and bleak prospects for Pluto. They believed that a fulfilment of all the promises made by the prospective acquirer, coupled with his need to tap Pluto's cash flow in order to repay debts, would suck out resources and lead to an eventual collapse.

They were accumulating support from within and below, and from 'outside influencers'. Tactics used to enlist external support included further letters that were sent to another MP, to the county chief police commissioner, the county public prosecutor, the supervising Ministry, the State Audit Office and, when established, the State Property Agency (SPA, created in March 1990 to oversee privatisation and represent the state as owner, replacing the ministries in this role). Five members of the Enterprise Council entered an action in court, requesting that the Enterprise Council's resolution be declared null and void since 'management deliberately misled the Council'. A press campaign began. One day the General Director called the incipient resistance a 'manifestation of resentment, increasing desire for power, weakness of mind and character'; on the next day a heated public demonstration was held. The young Turks were out and vocal.

But to no avail: the firm was drawn under ministerial control. The authorities' earlier commitment was cemented in a letter from the Ministry, promising that a closed call for bids would be announced, and the Expatriate Investor would be granted a right of first refusal. He was also assured that the SPA, once it came into operation, would regard the outcome of the negotiations with the Ministry as binding.

These developments might have daunted Pluto's rebels. On the contrary: they redirected their efforts towards the newly formed SPA. However, the SPA first had to establish its own authority against other state agents. The Ministry argued that the Expatriate Investor's offer was the best possible, and favoured a closed (invitational) tender. The SPA suggested an open call for bids, 'according to the rules, contrary to prior government-level (or seemingly government-level) commitments', and stated: 'It is the SPA's right to make a decision', while itself seeking support from an MP.

Only a couple of weeks before the 1990 general election, an open call for bids was advertised, albeit in a somewhat low-key brief announcement, letting it be known that 'purchase of the whole firm will be favoured'. The deadline for submitting offers was two weeks ahead.

Only two bids were submitted: both the Licenser and the Expatriate Investor confirmed their earlier offers. The Ministry proposed that the Expatriate Investor be given an option, strongly arguing in favour of Expatriate Investor's offer and referring to earlier commitments. The price difference between the two offers, as presented by the Ministry official, reflected a direct comparison of differently structured deals. In fact, in relative terms the Licenser's offer valued Pluto significantly higher than that of the Expatriate Investor, and the Licenser was prepared to pay a better relative price even for a minority stake. Yet, the presentation of the offers as set out in the Ministry official's argument suggested quite the opposite. In other words, a case for the Licenser's offer could have been made just as strongly if the Ministry had so wished. In any case, an official was soon able to inform the Expatriate Investor in a handwritten letter that he 'managed to contact [the highest government level] and I assure you your option is firm and will be honoured'.

The Expatriate Investor was given an option for six months. He promptly became involved in decision-making at Pluto. For example, he mediated a purchase of imported used equipment. This deal was presented to the SPA by the General Director as exceptionally favourable. Middle managers later attacked the purchase as a waste of money on junk. At about this time the county police terminated an investigation into allegations of missing stock. To keep the story simple, we pass over police and tax authority investigations, public prosecution, and investigations ordered by the Ministry into the firm's operations (there were a couple of these during the year, without any 'serious' outcome).

The young Turks, growing in number and fortified by increasing employee support, kept pressing. In a letter to an MP they attacked the General Director, the Expatriate Investor and, now that the option had been given, the SPA as well. Gossip had it that the Expatriate Investor conducted 'most of his negotiations in weekends, or after working hours, at the General Director's apartment or his [wine] cellar'. Critics pointed out the remarkable speed with which state bureaucracy had made commitments in late December and early January 1989–90: 'it seems the point in all this was only that the transaction could still be managed by the old Government'.

Although the Expatriate Investor was portrayed in his own letters and [according to] some other documents as a potential investor having ample resources, he was in fact engaged in a vain search for money and bank guarantees. It was at this point that the Independent Union was founded with a membership of eighty-five, although only some forty turned up at the founding meeting. 'Forty-five did not dare to come', said its Leader. 'On the next day we were up to two hundred', and membership kept increasing, and was soon to exceed that of the old union which appeared to support the General Director. Following the election, new leaders were appointed at the Ministry and the SPA. Alerted by objections raised by representatives of the largest party in the new Hungarian coalition who had been contacted by middle managers, Ministry officials became concerned about the deal. In concert with the SPA, however, they decided to wait since 'it would not be advisable, in the interest of good foreign perception of Hungarian economic conduct,' to withdraw the Expatriate Investor's option.

As a preparation for the sale, Pluto was transformed into a limited liability company with the SPA as its sole owner. Timing was of the essence here. Pluto's operating profits were at a peak when the transformation (corporatisation) occurred. Pluto had to pay tax on its peak-level profits as of the day of transformation. Later it turned out that the outstanding results of the period were considerably lower when properly offset by tax arrears and irrecoverable debts.

One of the core young Turks was appointed to the Supervisory Board on the proposal of the General Director himself. This move was later described by the person concerned as an attempt to satisfy the quarrelsome, which itself was only part of an 'if you cannot beat them, try to enlist them' tactic. This proved to be a mistake in the game, since it meant that the challenged was himself responsible for allowing the challengers to get close to information: they obtained the data to make a reasoned case. Other efforts by the General Director to placate the opposition, again mistaken, included 'incentive trips' and promises of promotion. Some of the General Director's close associates became uncertain whether it was worth remaining loyal; after all, it was their positions that the General Director was promising to his opponents.

As the option period was about to expire, the Expatriate Investor and the SPA signed a sale contract on option terms. Payment was due in twenty-five days, and the deadline was extended twice. But the Expatriate Investor failed to line up funds. This provided the young Turks with ammunition for a final attack. They pointed out that what they had said was now proved true: the emperor had no clothes. They had also by now enlisted to their side the deputy mayor of the town where Pluto was located and one of the General Director's deputies. The time had come to increase pressure on the SPA. 'The control over [this] privatisation has fallen out of your hands', wrote the Independent Union Leader, threatening to call a strike. Some parts of this letter became public knowledge via the press – an additional pressure on the SPA.

The SPA abandoned the sale contract because the Expatriate Investor missed the very last deadline. He continued to ask for more time in a personal letter to a high-level state bureaucrat, expressing his appreciation of 'your abilities and the grasp you have of complicated situations and the high standard at which you operate to protect the interests you represent'. Similarly, he hoped that 'you have a reasonable estimation of my standards and what I have to offer'. But by this stage all this elicited was an even firmer rejection.

For the young Turks, the problem was no longer the Expatriate Investor but the General Director. The Leader of the Independent Union demanded his replacement in a letter carrying the signatures of hundreds who were prepared to strike. Pluto's contract with a business partner was said to serve the self-interest of the General Director, who sat on the partner's board.

The General Director set about defending himself. But his eroded legitimacy meant he had no chance to mobilise backers as influential as those of the young Turks. Instead, he orchestrated an inflow of supportive letters from customers, and attempted to cover an unfavourable purchase of used equipment with an expert's technical report. It was all too late. The SPA suspended him from his position. Allegedly, he was then moving documents in cardboard boxes out of the firm. Middle managers described him in a report to the SPA as 'old fashioned, building on his network, keeping everybody around him in a state of being intimidated, following only his self-interest'. As even the traditional union's leader acknowledged, 'The trust in the General Director has crumbled.' The General Director went on sick leave and after his recovery was allowed to take early retirement.

Having won a job tender against an outsider, the leader of the young Turks was soon appointed Managing Director. In a restructuring programme, management ranks were completely reorganised within a few weeks. A new position of General Deputy was created for the closest associate of the new Managing Director.

Meanwhile the Expatriate Investor was fighting an endgame, claiming that the SPA was acting under pressure from Pluto's 'troublemakers'. He sought justice for himself – from both domestic and foreign high-level politicians – which triggered some correspondence between ministries and embassies. Referring to 'a most reliable source' in a pleading letter, he accused middle managers of colluding with the Licenser to block the deal with him, and claimed that they had intervened at the Hungarian bank involved so as to stop it from providing a guarantee. Articles in a press campaign took up positions on both sides. Some pictured a palace revolution led by power-seeking middle managers. The Expatriate

Investor was portrayed as a victim, cornered by the SPA with require-ments that were impossible to meet. Others presented the opposite story, claiming that the members of the Enterprise Council had been worked on well in advance by the coalition of the General Director and the Expatriate Investor. The Expatriate Investor also published his version in a paid full-page advertisement. At this time he was described as 'a swindler with a gift of the gab but with no money' in a letter which prompted inter-office correspondence within government but whose sender and his address turned out to be non-existent.

These actions had no effect on what was to come. The SPA Board of Directors reviewed the case once more and kept up its rejection. The firm had already gone a long way down the privatisation path. But it was still only half the journey.

Time is passing

After all the scandals came slow progress and meticulous adherence to rules. In April 1991 the SPA selected an advisor and a valuation report was ready by September. The advisor's Sales Recommendations were prepared and approved by the SPA in late November. The condition that 'special attention must be paid so that the Licenser-relationship does not have a negative influence on sales opportunities' was presciently included in the privatisation strategy for Pluto.

A dozen major firms were interested in the acquisition, including foreign owners of other Hungarian firms directly competing with Pluto. The firm's bitter experience was that the owner of one of its competitors used due diligence, granted for all who bought the information memor-andum from the SPA, only to get confidential business information without ever wanting to submit an acquisition offer.

The year 1991 ended with Pluto's transformation into a joint stock company limited by shares – an attempt to ease the sale procedure. We now enter the fourth year of Pluto's privatisation process.

Pluto slowly goes private

Of the seventeen companies invited, only one submitted a bid – so much for the competitive bidding that the SPA was hoping for. This was a Consortium led by the Licenser. The SPA rejected it because it offered insufficient cash proceeds and because the Consortium demanded cancel-lation of debt and tax arrears. Nevertheless, talks began. The SPA emphasised Pluto's strategic prospects; the Consortium pointed at its current financial and market difficulties.

Pluto's management and employees (M&E) themselves put in a bid.

The buy-out vehicle was structured so that Pluto's directors and board members controlled an interest of about 30 per cent, the rest being widely spread. Around this time national privatisation policy shifted, which may have signalled to management how to present their bid. The M&E buy-out proposal emphasised the importance of 'the emergence of a group of Hungarian owners [which] could also be welcomed politically'. The idea of a pure management buy-out without employee participation had been dropped: 'The press would have jumped on us immediately, saying that the previous managers wanted to squander [the company], and now the new ones want to steal it for themselves.'

The SPA and the Bank were supportive to the M&E buy-out idea. The Bank's help was essential since M&E could line up only limited funds. Their proposal included a statement of intent to draw in external capital after the privatisation, which the management was confident it could do better than the SPA. According to the SPA's advisor, the Licenser was playing for a liquidation sale while deterring other potential bidders. The Consortium's revised offer was still conditional – on a debt–equity swap – which the Bank was reluctant to accept. The tender was declared unsuccessful, and the parties entered into negotiations freed from binding tender rules.

Although the SPA advisor proposed a different financial structure for the deal and favoured equity-raising being managed by the SPA instead of being attempted by M&E after privatisation, the SPA decided to sell 80 per cent of the shares to M&E. Payment was made mostly with a loan from the Bank. It was only a formality to sell the remaining shares for so-called compensation notes a few months later. M&E assumed all debts of Pluto and there were no conditions, making the deal look better than a sale to the Consortium. However, the form in which the privatisation was structured brought no new resources and created the need for M&E to tap Pluto's resources so as to repay its debts to the Bank; and it secured none of the tax concessions available to firms with at least 30 per cent foreign ownership (like all but one of Pluto's competitors).

Pluto was at last 100 per cent privately owned. The privatisation process might at this stage have been considered complete. However, the new story which begins here about a private firm's efforts to solve the problems of a critical financial situation, and still to retain majority ownership for M&E, was largely dependent on the nature of the privatisation process which had gone before.

The search for an investor

Optimism was prevalent in interviews conducted at about this time. However, this proved to be a false dawn. Pluto's management was seeking investors, but opportunities were missed or, rather, mismanaged. A promising offer was obtained from a major foreign company. Partly because management attempted to avoid becoming subordinated to that company's other Hungarian acquisition, and partly because they may have been going for the big win, another offer was also obtained. It was hoped that the two potential investors would engage in competitive bidding.

Market demand continued declining in 1993; competitors backed by foreign investors made the market a tough place to live in. Commercial depots that had been separated as independent limited liability companies were abusing Pluto's resources. There was tension in management ranks between those in top positions who were in charge of negotiations with potential investors, and those who remained middle managers and represented some several hundred employees as co-owners. As Pluto's financial and market position worsened further, one of the potential investors lowered its offer and raised conditions to the point that management terminated negotiations. Meanwhile, Licenser took away its brand from Pluto and switched to one of Pluto's competitors while denying that it did so because of Pluto's talks with investors. The other potential investor soon announced loss of its interest in the acquisition, denying that it did so because Pluto had lost the licence. Acquiring Pluto in Hungary was only a minor fight in the backyard in the battle that foreign companies fought against each other.

For a while, management dropped the whole idea of getting a foreign investor on board. They hoped that later they might have a better position to negotiate, or even an opportunity not simply to 'stay upright' but to 'stand on our own two feet'. They succeeded in finding a replacement for the Licenser, but on worse terms. The Bank was getting impatient and started tightening control over the firm. The Managing Director was reported to be 'not worried'. Yet, news about possible layoffs leaked out as the Bank demanded that the management take 'every necessary step without delay and with appropriate firmness', pointing to the example of some competitors. Privatisation of the last two firms still in state ownership was also to be completed soon. Both were sold to foreign investors, and thus obtained funds to repay debts, qualified for tax benefits and immediately started restructuring. All of Pluto's competitors were able to take advantage not only of additional resources but also of owners coming from outside the firm's dominant coalition and having the power to break any existing coalition if necessary in order to improve efficiency. But how could Pluto's management make a couple of hundred people – proud owners themselves – redundant when they had reached the top with the support of the very same people?

Decisions made on the basis of mutual favours and interpersonal commitments do not necessarily reflect economic rationality.

Forced sell-out

The Bank submitted an ultimatum to management: unless certain targets (increased sales volume and successful capital-raising) were achieved, it would take over the shares at an 'acceptable price'. It became more and more urgent to attract foreign capital into the firm so that it would be entitled to tax concessions. There was no investor in sight. Instead, management was taught a lesson by a potential acquirer who, having conducted due diligence examinations of the target, elaborated on managerial mistakes and inadequacies in a long letter which ended with its withdrawal from any possible acquisition.

Management intended to cover the amount of M&E's debt to the Bank from Pluto's resources. The Bank would not tolerate further delay in stemming the losses and objected to the tapping of Pluto's resources. So Pluto was taken over by a Domestic Investment Group brought in by the Bank. If the takeover had been rejected, the Bank would have simply discontinued loans to Pluto. At a speed which suggests thorough preparations beforehand, the new owners sold slightly more than 30 per cent of the shares to an offshore company in only two weeks, thus qualifying the company for tax benefits.

Management knew it had no choice. Some argument within its ranks arose: the top management was accused of mismanaging the search for investors and neglecting the business itself. As a member of the young Turks (still a middle manager) commented: 'We made a big fuss three years ago but the team has now entirely fallen apart. There should have been teamwork in the running of Pluto, but unfortunately there was no sign of it.'

Restructured, then sold again

In the first half of 1994 the new owners drastically restructured Pluto. The former top management was retained in second-level positions; some others were fired. They introduced tight financial control, sold some of the assets, completely renewed the managerial information system, and re-established Pluto's control over distribution. The Bank converted some debt to equity and extended the deadline for debt repayments. The owners, enjoying substantial support from the Bank, managed to re-negotiate arrears with the tax authority. By May 1994 an information memorandum for investors had been prepared, and in the summer Pluto was once again sold. The buyer was a large foreign firm that had already made a large acquisition in Hungary but had never formally bid for Pluto. Its two Hungarian acquisitions combined to create the largest player in the industry. A major capital expenditure programme was launched, while the workforce was substantially reduced.

5.2   Mercury: Family silver somewhat tarnished

'Mercury' was a retail chain operator with many shops around the country, and employed several hundred people in late-1990. By 1992 the number of employees had decreased by more than a fifth, partly because of the divestment of some shops (see below), and partly because of the decrease in central administration as part of a streamlining effort.

Until the early 1970s, Mercury had enjoyed a monopoly position. A few small firms were established later, mainly in the countryside, without really challenging Mercury. In 1988 the firm still dominated the market. From 1988, trading constraints were gradually relaxed; by the end of 1989, domestic trade was fully liberalised. Several hundred retailers entered the market. In addition, the 'black market' (with an estimated market share of 30 per cent) and, because of liberalised hard-currency allotments, 'tourist imports' hit the firm. 'The monopoly situation collapsed in a minute', said an interviewee, although as a chain, Mercury still remained the largest firm. Even in 1990, it could claim about 40 per cent market share. At this time Mercury developed a wholesale business. Foreign trade, at least in one of Mercury's two main businesses, was entirely liberalised in 1989. In this business, Mercury's product mix mainly consisted of cheap Eastern brands, and its stock was losing value every time a new competitor offering attractive Western brands entered the market. Mercury then placed an emphasis on keeping a wide range of high quality goods in its shops, which increased its reliance on short-term credit to finance the stock. Its short-term liabilities increased by 50 per cent in the first two years of the 1990s, becoming equal to the firm's 'own capital'. At the same time the firm's market share reached its nadir with about 25–30 per cent.

Mercury was run by the General Director who had graduated in 1976 in economics and was appointed in 1990 after a job tender. His Deputy in charge of economic matters, who was later to become the ESOP Leader, came from a bank where he had specialised in privatisation matters. He joined Mercury after the beginning of the privatisation process, essentially for the purpose of managing it. The deputy in charge of trade had earlier spent several years at the Ministry which the firm belonged to. The management saw its task as pursuing a turnaround strategy, 'preparing for getting out of the crisis' that it faced due to increasing competition and shrinking domestic demand.

The first investment tender

From early 1990 the management was already formulating clear objectives for the firm, including broadening the business domain by establishing manufacturing capacity, shifting emphasis towards foreign trade and, in the long term, turning the firm into a trading house. They intended to modernise the retail chain by developing a unified corporate image, to establish an up-to-date information system, and to develop sales methods by adjusting the product range to increasingly differentiated demand. Increasing advertising efforts, introducing sales by catalogue, and enlarging the agent network were all on the agenda. The management also set out to streamline central administration, and placed an emphasis on the education of the workforce (e.g. in languages).

The management estimated the amount that would be needed in order to ensure long-term stability and carry out their intended business strategy. They longed for an investor who would increase capital, thus acquiring at least a 35 per cent shareholding, who would not repatriate profits but reinvest them, who would provide long-term professional partnership, whose contribution would be cash in hard currency and in-kind provision of technology (i.e. not merchandise and know-how), who would secure export markets, and who would actively promote the development of the company into a trading house acting as a European distributor. These were included in the tender as requirements to be met by a potential investor for 'a successful marriage'.

In March 1990, Mercury's Enterprise Council authorised the management to initiate transformation and privatisation. In the spirit of 'spontaneous privatisation', the management invited investment bids from its foreign partners and advertised an open tender. They also submitted their transformation plan to the SPA. In September 1990, Mercury's Consultant could inform the SPA that there had been two firms interested in the investment.

At about that time, however, the Pre-Privatisation Act was passed, and Mercury was considered to be subject to this Act, implying that its outlets would be auctioned one by one. The very existence of the firm was put at risk.

As required by the Pre-Privatisation Act, the management named those shops that met the criteria for auctioning (e.g. according to size and number of employees). At the same time, they requested the SPA to be allowed to transform Mercury into a company form while keeping the remaining outlets. The SPA accepted their request, but further increased the number of shops to be auctioned. This was an issue in negotiations with a Ministry official in charge of the matter. The management sought to convince him that Mercury's shops represented an integrated chain and thus should not be subjected to the Pre-Privatisation Act. In these talks it must have helped that an executive had worked for the Ministry. The management also attempted to convince the SPA that the proceeds from selling Mercury as one entity would be higher than what would be raised from auctioning shops individually. As with several other firms in the same situation at the time, Mercury could only achieve a compromise. Auctioning of the selected fifty shops was then implemented. Without following this line of the story, we should note that Mercury gave every support to the managers and employees of these shops so that they could acquire the outlets. In return, these shops were then supplied by Mercury (as wholesaler) under long-term contracts.

In late 1990 the SPA authorised Mercury's management to negotiate conditions of privatisation with potential investors, but the final agreement had to be approved by SPA. The management informed those who had earlier expressed interest in an investment about the changes in Mercury's asset base, i.e. the losses of some of its shops, due to the Pre-Privatisation Act.

By early 1991, two foreign firms had confirmed their interest: a French Trader and its Partners (FTP), and an American Department Store Operator. FTP saw the situation as one that called for drastic restructuring. It noted that it had recently restructured itself and gained experience; it wanted full management control regardless of minority ownership; it did not specify either the proportion they would acquire, or the amount to be paid; and its investment would mainly take the form of know-how and non-pecuniary contributions. The American firm took a more partner-like approach and aimed at 'building a profitable business' jointly with the Hungarian party. It wanted 'to move at deliberate speed in the next several weeks to identify outstanding issues, and put together an itinerary of our next visit'.

The General Director and his two deputies, the Chairman of the Enterprise Council and their Consultant regarded FTP's offer as demonstrating low commitment; their emphasis on drastic restructuring was a black mark. They objected that Mercury would be subordinated to the minority owner, and regarded FTP's business plan as being contrary to Mercury's own strategic objectives. The offer from the American Department Store Operator was well received: it did not want to terminate Mercury's independence and immediately repatriate profits. Its considerable size and capabilities were appreciated, and the fact that it had no other interests in Europe was also noted. The SPA approved this evaluation of the offers, but held the right to approve the buyer, and wanted to have the final say in determining the price for a part of Mercury. On the issue of the sale price, tenders were to be invited.

In April 1991 the American company withdrew from any possible investment. Mercury's management believed this was due to the fact that the American firm itself was going through a major downsizing programme and was completely giving up plans to expand in Central-Eastern Europe.

Mercury's management again submitted a transformation plan to the SPA with updated information. (This 'transformation concept' actually did not take the form of the Transformation Plan required by the Transformation Act; rather, it served as a basis for negotiations between the management and the SPA.) The firm, including the chain of the remaining retail outlets, would transform into a joint stock company limited by shares. The management emphasised again that they wanted to keep the shops, since at this time there was still a danger of being further truncated. It was hoped that a strategic investor, i.e. an investor involved in the same business, would make a considerable investment in order to obtain a majority position; other requirements included at least partial reinvestment of profits, the securing of export markets, a commitment to capital expenditure programmes, and support of partial employee ownership.

In a rather impatiently worded letter, FTP attempted to speed up the process. It then visited Mercury and the SPA and outlined its offer, now indicating a price and a possible ownership split, and specifying various conditions. FTP's offer was far from the requirements of the firm, and even further from the SPA's expectations although these were not formally specified at the time. FTP urged the SPA to speed up asset valuation and, on that basis, specify in writing the expected price, indicating that it would withdraw if an agreement could not be reached soon. They pointed out Mercury's rapid loss of market share to increasing competition, and remarked that they were also involved in investment discussions in a neighbouring country. In spite of its low commitment offer, FTP apparently assumed that the SPA would just be glad to sell Mercury quickly.

In June 1990 the SPA specified the requirements to be met by a potential investor. A stake of 51 per cent could be sold to 'professional' (as opposed to financial or institutional) investor(s) in a closed (invitational) tender. Of the total investment, 40 per cent was to be paid for SPA shares, the rest could be spent on equity raising. Conditions of partial employee ownership were also stated. Mercury appears to have waived the 20 per cent of the proceeds from the share sale which it would be entitled to. According to an interviewee, this gesture was to make sure that, in return, the SPA would approve transformation 'one-to-one', without cutting off further shops.

Second privatisation tender

Invitations to fourteen potential bidders resulted in three offers in September 1991. An Italian Manufacturing Firm was rejected owing to not meeting formal requirements, leaving a Middle East Company (MEC) and FTP to choose from.

MEC's offer for a stake of 55.5 per cent included cash for the SPA shares and an equity increase, but both were subject to adjustments, reducing the amount by at least 20 per cent. It developed an argument around different methods of valuing Mercury. While the SPA considered the firm's assets and liabilities as the basis for valuation, MEC wanted to base its appraisal on future cash flow, and was willing to accept the SPA's view only if no reputation or goodwill for Mercury was to be taken into account, and every item of the assets was to be reappraised. 'If the new value assigned to an item is less than the value set forth in the Appraisal in the Tender, the new value will apply. However, if the new value of an item is greater than the value in the said Appraisal, the value in the Appraisal will apply.' MEC also proposed that the thus reappraised value of Mercury should be factored by 79.68 per cent, which represents the ratio between the value MEC placed on Mercury and Mercury's asset value as given in the tender documents. The offered amounts would be adjusted accordingly. That is, even if the new asset valuation (by MEC's rules) confirmed the previous one, the amounts actually paid would be 20 per cent less than said in the offer. This offer was also made conditional on various incentives and guarantees from the Hungarian government: for example, the proceeds to the SPA were to be spent in part on repaying Mercury's loans. MEC also wanted to be the main supplier of Mercury, and its exclusive purchaser of third party merchandise. The SPA was to guarantee that municipalities would only raise the rental payments for the properties that are leased by Mercury within limits.

FTP's offer for a stake of 51 per cent included a much lower amount for the SPA shares and equity raising. It still placed much emphasis on restructuring, arguing that 'if we act quickly, the good name of Mercury can be saved and [it can] remain a trustworthy, important company in Hungary'. Its investments would be put into machinery for a production unit. Its offer also included conditions, most importantly complete management control and the status of purchasing and selling agent for

Mercury. If one or several requirements were not strictly fulfilled, the SPA was to pay a penalty of several million forints in addition to a refund of any amount already invested and in addition to expenses. FTP also claimed to have acquired rights as a result of its earlier offer; almost questioned the lawfulness of the current tender procedure, and 'reserve[d] all legal steps in this matter'.

There was no bid from 'Expander', although it had approached the SPA at the time of the call for tenders. Expander was a fast-growing, diversified Hungarian firm, also with interests in retail, that operated under the majority ownership of its leader, the 'Empire Builder'. A large proportion of Expander's shares were owned by foreign investors.

MEC's offer was ranked first by an evaluation committee (management, Enterprise Council, Labour Union, Consultant). FTP's low-price proposal and claim to have acquired rights was not welcomed. Mercury's General Director asked SPA to authorise the management to conduct negotiations, and to reconsider the possibility of issuing new employee shares, since 'the firm has waived its entitlement to the 20 per cent of the proceeds from the sale of state-owned shares'.

Although the SPA and the Consultant prepared draft replies to bidders assuming that the tender would be declared successful, the SPA later thought otherwise. It declared the tender unsuccessful, but left open the possibility of talks with MEC, probably to allow free negotiations without having to follow the binding rules of the tendering process.

The talks between the SPA and MEC were going on from October 1991, often about issues not within SPA's authority to decide. The management and the SPA suggested a compromise in November. They were willing to accept in advance the final results of an asset valuation, if it was carried out by an internationally recognised appraising firm, and if MEC also accepted its results. One of the Big Six accounting firms was proposed. Some other claims, such as the devaluation of the company by a ratio set by MEC, were rejected. The SPA considered the offered price 'close to our prior expectations', but MEC's proposals on guarantees to be provided by the SPA were seen as 'exaggerated'. MEC withdrew from further negotiations in the following month. A Mercury executive explained: 'MEC found out the conditions [business environment within which Mercury was operating]; they could not understand how the firm was still in business.'

Transformation and offer off-tender

During the negotiations with MEC, preparations for transforming Mercury into a company form were under way. Focusing on transformation also meant that the relative importance and urgency of 'genuine' privatisation decreased. This may have come as a benefit to the management by keeping privatisation in suspense until favourable opportunities of managerial and employee ownership (already in the pipeline) opened.

Following reconciliation with the Ministry, the union, the municipalities that were entitled to some shares in Mercury, and the Bank (Mercury's main creditor), which was willing to consider acquisition of some shares, the Enterprise Council approved the Transformation Plan, in which the management and employees aspired to manage the SPA stock in the 'transitional period until the sale of the state-owned shares', and wanted the right of first refusal.

In early 1992, before the transformation was approved by the SPA, a new potential investor appeared on the scene: the 'Emerging Investment Group' (EIG) and its partners wanted to acquire between 51–82 per cent of the shares, 'assuming that the management of Mercury will support this effort'. They were said to be backed by a number of foreign strategic investors. EIG Leader wrote they were 'most impressed by the present management of Mercury' and their investment group was 'particularly excited about the growth potential for this company', adding that their interest was strongly based on two factors: 'first, the present management led by General Director must commit itself to continue its effective leadership. Second, this purchase must be concluded on a rapid basis in no more than sixty days.' In a fax sent from EIG's office, Mercury's management asked the SPA to approve the appointment of EIG as Mercury's privatisation advisor, emphasising EIG's earlier achievements in attracting foreign capital into Expander. The possibility of creating 'at least 120 new jobs' was anticipated, and a speedy privatisation process was urged.

When the SPA approved Mercury's transformation – and a political protégé on its Board – it also prescribed that the buyer of the SPA shares was to be chosen by open tender. Since EIG wished to acquire more than 51 per cent of the shares, it was necessary to remove the ceiling set earlier up to which stock could be sold. In the event of an unsuccessful tender, Mercury was to be given into asset management, again by way of open tender, a procedure which was requested by, and would probably create an opportunity for, the management. Finally, the SPA declared that Mercury could keep the rest of its shops, and stated that 'employee shares could be issued in accordance with the Transformation Act', that is, against 20 per cent of the proceeds from the sale of state-owned shares (which the firm once waived). The resolution did not explicitly mention the firm's other proposal regarding the sale of SPA shares to employees at a discount but referred to the 'highest permissible amount and form', which can be understood as meaning the discount provided by the Transformation Act would exhaust the permissible limit.

The SPA official dealing with the Mercury case notified the management of the resolution, and at the same time specified its ambiguous wording on employee ownership. He presented two channels for acquiring ownership: first, under the Transformation Act, new employee shares could be issued, and, second, parallel to outside investment, a certain amount of stock could be sold to employees at 50 per cent of the price the external investor paid. This interpretation of the SPA resolution was later codified in Mercury's Deed of Foundation. Mercury was soon converted into a joint stock company limited by shares, with the SPA and municipalities among its owners.

At the time of the transformation, the SPA was involved in discussions with EIG. According to EIG Leader, Mercury's management had indicated strong support for their acquisition effort. Subject to no more than ninety days' due diligence, EIG was prepared to make an offer on behalf of an investor group to acquire a controlling interest. The identity of 'a number of leading strategic' investors remained undisclosed, but EIG Leader now emphasised his extensive experience in Mercury's business. EIG Leader still was 'most impressed by the present management', and 'particularly excited about the growth potential for this company' which would justify more than 200 new jobs in Hungary during the following three years. While paying due respect to the rules and procedures that the SPA had to follow under the law, in the context of this bright future EIG asked for preferential treatment. It argued that it had little interest in proceeding if its offer had once again to be subject to a long and drawn-out tendering process. In fact, EIG had submitted no bid in the previous tendering processes. The SPA regretfully informed EIG that it had to call an open tender.

Third investment tender

From the beginning of 1992, Mercury's management placed emphasis on streamlining the organisation. One layer in the hierarchy was eliminated, while a new unit was established specifically to deal with the shops. The marketing and finance functions were strengthened. Later in 1992, Mercury started slowly to regain some of its lost market share. Yet, after decades of profitable operations, Mercury ended 1992 with a loss. Not only competition, but the new Accounting Act also had a part in it. Earlier, Mercury could record a profit by simply moving stock between its wholesale warehouse and its retail chain, no matter whether or not the goods were actually sold. 'We could make profit as we wished.' From

1992, profit could be booked only after goods were actually sold. Its profit was also reduced owing to devaluation of outdated stock at the time of transformation.

In spring 1992, the SPA selected an Advisor by tender. A financial institution in which EIG Leader's family had a 12 per cent interest also applied, allegedly at the request of Mercury's management. According to the General Director's deputy who was to become ESOP Leader, the bank's reference to Mercury's request was only an attempt by EIG Leader to improve his position. Yet, General Director may have made such a request by himself, without letting his deputies know of it.

The call for bids was advertised in early summer. A controlling stock was offered for sale. Of the total investment, 80 per cent was to be spent on acquiring existing shares, with 20 per cent on increasing equity; bids in line with the goals and objectives laid down in Mercury's transformation plan were encouraged.

With the support of 80 per cent of the employees, an ESOP Organising Committee was established, including the two deputies to the General Director and a head of department who was also the local union secretary.

In September 1992, the SPA received two bids: one from a Consortium of EIG and its partners, another from Mercury's ESOP that had teamed up with the Bank (ESOP-Bank). The Consortium included the American retail firm where EIG Leader claimed to have been president. This firm was now represented by EIG Leader's father, who was also the chief executive officer of a corporation involved in retailing similar goods to Mercury's. They did not offer a specific amount to be spent on either raising equity or the acquisition of SPA shares. For the transfer of all the shares in Mercury, which was now described by the bidders (earlier excited about growth potential) as 'potentially viable', the SPA would get 25 per cent of Mercury's profits after tax for five years, and the total amount of after-tax profits from the sale of the current inventory of Mercury. A joint venture with Mercury and the company run by EIG Leader's father was planned.

It was noted that since receiving the call for tender, they had held several discussions with Mercury's management. They had assured the management that a significant employee ownership would be supported. Mercury's management, however, had informed them of their competing bid. Although the Consortium had made efforts to combine forces with Mercury's ESOP, the management and the employees teamed up with another partner.

The ESOP and the Bank offered 75 per cent (almost 100 per cent if Mercury's goodwill was valued at zero) of par value for existing shares, and undertook equity increase of a smaller amount. Of the existing shares, 80 per cent would be acquired by the ESOP from an E-loan, taken from the Bank. The employees also laid claim to further stock at a discount. On the rest of the SPA shares, not acquired in this tender, the bidders wanted to secure an option for three years. Flotation on the Stock Exchange within a few years was anticipated.

The selection of the Bank as their bidding partner was explained by company interviewees with previous experience of possible investors. Some of these were manufacturing firms, trying to find distribution opportunities. They thought it would be 'suicide to base our future mainly on products of only one manufacturer when the market needs variety'. They saw examples of such 'suicide' in other Hungarian retail businesses. Others were considered as 'speculators, interested only in the shops, and it was clear they would sell the chain one by one as ice-cream parlours or something'. Therefore, they had given up their original intention to find a foreign strategic investor. They organised the ESOP, with the support of a high-level state official who supplied them with information on expected changes in legislation. It was regarded as important to conclude privatisation quickly, because 'by 1992 the competition reached peak level, which required total effort, and not a torn, ragged and divided firm. [We] could not afford it that half of the management was privatising and tendering, instead of actual work [i.e. doing business], [at a time] when a strategy should have been formulated.' According to some, Mercury 'could have attained profitability even in 1992, regardless of the new Accounting Act, if we could have concentrated our forces better'. The ESOP alone, certainly without resources, had no chance of winning since an equity increase was required in the tender. It was the management who included this requirement 'two tenders earlier' so that Mercury's financial difficulties could be alleviated. Now they needed a partner who was able to meet this requirement. The Bank seemed an ideal co-owner, since it would thus commit itself to financing Mercury, and a promissory note (a necessary requirement for ESOP to bid) would also be granted.

The SPA's Advisor and an appointed expert regarded 75–78 per cent of the nominal value as a reasonable price. Evaluating the EIG-led Consortium's bid they pointed out that 25 per cent of the yearly profits for five years would give the SPA a very low income, even if a positive effect of the investors' activity on Mercury's performance was assumed. The SPA would receive almost nothing from the sale of the current stock, since even the bidder, as well as the management, considered the merchandise stock as overvalued, and in part outdated. From the ESOP-Bank deal the SPA would get a considerable and immediate income, and another sum would be paid on raising equity. According to the evaluators, there was no risk in accepting this offer, since a promissory note had been provided by the Bank. The evaluators apparently did not take notice of the Bank's condition that made the final decision upon the E-loan subject to the result of due diligence.

After the deadline for submitting the bids, but before any official announcement on the results, EIG Leader thought the time had come to substantiate their offer. He sent a letter to almost everyone at the SPA whom he thought had something to do with the Mercury privatisation. Most of the recipients promptly forwarded the letter to the one directorate which was, in fact, in charge. The bid was attached to each copy of the letter. In the last paragraph of their offer they had expressed the hope that their bid would receive confidential treatment 'according to normal professional norms'. Nevertheless, EIG Leader appeared to be quite well informed of the ESOP-Bank offer. His highly accurate estimates of the numerical data included in the ESOP-Bank bid are worth noting. Elsewhere he specifically referred to the ESOP bid. He argued that an ESOP would place too high a financial burden on the company, which was already rather indebted. In his view, the high cash amount to be paid to the SPA made the ESOP offer appear illusorily more advantageous, but it would undoubtedly lead to bankruptcy. He also pointed out that the state-owned Bank financing an ESOP acquisition 'only means that the money wanders from one pocket of the state to the other, while getting lost in the process'. EIG Leader assured the recipients of his letter 'that there will be no passive [e.i. non-strategic] investor who will be willing to invest in Mercury'. It remains an unanswered question whether this statement should be regarded as a forecast made on the basis of professional considerations, or as a warning from a financial mediator who had a wide network in the world of investors.

The idea of co-operation between the two bidding groups was again raised, which would have given employees a stake of 34 per cent. EIG Leader warned that a failure of Mercury's ESOP acquisition, which he believed was sure to happen, would discredit the whole ESOP programme and retard the development of employee ownership in Hungary. Some arguments referred to Mercury's internal communications, indicating a suspicion that the management had not allowed the employees to know of his 'let's team up' proposal. Had the management done so, he was 'almost sure ... [employees] would be in full agreement with us'. Finally, he judged the whole ESOP initiative as the management's 'irresponsible and manipulative attempt to use the ESOP programme to preserve their privileges even at the price of bringing the company to bankruptcy and thus plunging the employees into unemployment'.

According to a Mercury executive, EIG Leader had initiated a meeting with the ESOP representatives, and wanted to impel them ('with every means', 'by intimidating the management') either to withdraw the bid or to submit a joint offer. They did not give in.

It was now the ESOP Leader's turn to defend their case. The content of EIG Leader's letter did not remain unknown to him, and he too sent out letters to decision-makers. He argued that the Existence Loan was to be taken by the ESOP and not Mercury, although the ESOP organisation obviously wanted to pay back the debts from Mercury's future profits. As with EIG Leader's letter, this one too set out a politically loaded argument in that 'the firm would remain in dominantly indigenous ownership' and 'carrying out the already formulated strategy coupled with domestic ownership would also reduce prices' and 'increase employment (by establishing manufacturing capacity)'.

The understanding and mutual support that had seemingly characterised the relationship between the management and EIG apparently turned into confrontation. A partial explanation could be that even in early 1992, the relationship was only *seemingly* cloudless. First, it was only General Director who had had discussions with EIG. Second, EIG may have been supported by the management as an advisor and mediator (in these roles, EIG had indeed proved successful), but not as a possible owner.

The General Director reminded the SPA that it had approved giving the company back 20 per cent of the proceeds from the sale of the shares, from which the issuance of employee shares could be financed. This issue was still disputed between the company and the SPA. Although the company had already waived this amount, the SPA had indeed agreed to transfer it back to the firm.

The SPA declared the joint bid of the ESOP and the Bank the winner of the tender in October 1992, and specified the conditions on which an agreement with the winners was to be signed. No bid was declared second. Among the conditions, the SPA required Mercury to auction a further 25 per cent of its retail shops under the rules of the Pre-Privatisation Act, on top of those that had already been cut off from its chain (the 'new condition' hereinafter). This meant depriving Mercury of some of its assets as they had existed when the tender was announced.

On the basis of the SPA's decision, a draft agreement between the SPA and the ESOP-Bank consortium was prepared by SPA officials who included the new condition in the draft. Mercury's capital reserve was to be reduced by the amount equal to the asset value of the shops to be auctioned. The ESOP considered the new condition contrary to the conditions as specified in the call for tenders. The SPA's revised draft then specified that 'the *smaller* shops *up to* 25 per cent of the total' (emphasis added) were to be sold; there was no explicit reference as to what would happen with the income from the shop sale. The ESOP suggested, as a compromise, that the shop sale be carried out by Mercury 'under its own name and for its own good'. According to company executives, the SPA staff realised the new condition was 'not entirely lawful, but it was binding and had to be executed' one way or another. On the other hand, Mercury's management did not want the 'spotlight, which we would have certainly attracted' if they had insisted on keeping every shop.

The SPA management was in favour of accepting the proposal. They assumed that the new condition was to serve the purpose of increasing the privatisation supply and not the proceeds to the state. The compromise could serve this purpose. In addition, if they had insisted, it would have undermined Mercury's business plan prepared to service the debt for which the Bank made out the guarantee. This could have jeopardised the whole deal. The SPA staff's flexibility thus seemingly removed the last obstacle from concluding an agreement with the tender winners.

It takes two

The relationship between the Bank and the ESOP was twofold: that of creditor and debtor, and that of partners in investment and future ownership of Mercury. In addition, the Bank was the main creditor of the company itself. Accordingly, for providing the E-loan and for the investment by the Bank, a credit contract (with related security and guarantee contracts), and a syndicate agreement were to be made between the parties. The security contract was to state that the ESOP would put its shares under the Bank's charge until the E-loan was repaid, while the guarantee contract was to provide a guarantee by Mercury for the ESOP's debt. The syndicate agreement was to settle some issues regarding the partners' relative positions and voting behaviour as co-owners of Mercury.

The Bank proposed a syndicate agreement with the ESOP. Although having in principle only a minority position, it wanted to have more influence on Mercury. The Bank suggested that the ESOP should vote for the Bank's proposals at Board meetings, and required compensation for the ESOP's taking of resources from Mercury to repay its debts to the Bank itself. Another demand stated that, in the event of the SPA depriving Mercury of the proceeds from the sale of the shops, the 'Bank as a financial investor will suffer', for which it should be compensated with free stock transfer. The Bank also emphasised that it wished to sign the share sale agreement with the SPA and the other contracts with the ESOP at the same time, in one act. The ESOP objected to the Bank's claims. In their opinion, some of the claims were against the ESOP Act; they would suffer just as much from the consequences of the new condition as the Bank. Both the Bank and the ESOP seemed to regard asset deprivation as a possibility, although within the SPA it had already been approved that the proceeds from the shop sale should be left with the Company. Presumably, those concerned had not then been notified.

Despite the compromise that the ESOP offered to the Bank, they could not reach an agreement. This caused a delay in concluding their agreement with the SPA which, forced by its own procedural regulations to effect the sale within a month of the decision on the tender, urged the Bank to proceed. It pointed out that the Bank and the ESOP must have already reached an agreement before submitting their joint bid, since 'it had served as the basis for you to provide the guarantee'. That the guarantee had been made subject to due diligence was left unnoticed.

The ESOP Leader and other interviewees explained later that the Bank had granted its support at the time of the tender on the basis of their earlier relationship, without giving much thought to the matter. It was the Bank's first transaction of this kind, and the Existence Loan was apparently considered by the Bank's executives as a way by which the National Bank provided credit for ESOP organisations.

From January to May 1993 the debate dragged on. The Bank explained the delay to the SPA with various arguments, including legal subtleties, and the changed situation caused by the new condition (this falsely assumed hurdle was soon cleared). Throughout these months the SPA kept urging the Bank, threatening it would have to submit the issue of Mercury's privatisation before the decision-makers again. When promising negotiations indicated progress, the SPA accepted the Bank and the ESOP's joint request that the SPA extend the deadline to conclude an agreement with it. The Bank and the ESOP then confirmed that they had 'basically agreed' on the syndicate agreement, but 'unforeseeable, technical' problems had arisen: under the law, the agreement with the Bank 'may come into force only with the approval of the ESOP Assembly', and signing the share sale contract with the SPA could happen only after that. The syndicate agreement was indeed coming into shape, providing 79 per cent voting rights for the Bank. Yet, signing the contract with the SPA suffered delay again: the Bank had not yet approved the E-loan 'because the Bank's president and chief executive officer had been taken ill'. According to the ESOP Leader, 'the Bank has confirmed that [the loan] will be approved' in a few days. Instead, the Bank sent, for the first time, written draft contracts to the ESOP. The drafts, at least in the ESOP's opinion, included 'new elements' and 'obligations that are contrary to the ESOP Act'.

The SPA was starting to have enough of the delay. It put the blame on the Bank's exaggerated claims (according to a handwritten note, 'the Bank wanted to pillage the ESOP'), and considered the option of giving the ESOP a few months to find a new partner. Mercury and the ESOP again offered the Bank a compromise, and attempted to exercise pressure by hinting at the possible termination of business with the Bank: Mercury was understood to be an important account for the Bank. The Bank fought back: it said it was willing 'to finance the Company's operations for a year, but only if an agreement ... were reached', while holding the right to terminate its relationship with Mercury at any time, making it clear who was dependent on whom in their view. The ESOP made a further concession as a final compromise, while company executives approached high-level SPA officials who were considering dropping the Bank altogether and creating some other opportunity for the ESOP to finance the acquisition. There was no need to do so: in a few weeks the ESOP and the Bank eventually reached an agreement. The agreement with the SPA could now be concluded, although the signing ceremony did not take place until early June.

As the ESOP Leader explained later, they considered the Bank's requirements as 'one-sided blackmail' at the time; now the management is more appreciative of the Bank's priorities. Later the relationship between the ESOP and the Bank improved; although there were other issues of misunderstanding (for example, on management issues; see below), 'normal co-operation developed' slowly.

Change in top management

In May 1993, as the time of the Annual General Meeting of the share-holders was approaching, the ESOP Assembly voted for a change in Mercury's management. The voting eventually resulted in ESOP Leader's overwhelming support, while the members of the ESOP Organisation practically relieved the General Director of his position, although it could officially be effected only at Mercury's Annual General Meeting. Owing to the delay in signing the share sale contract with the SPA, however, the share price had not then been paid; therefore the shares, currently owned by the SPA, had not been endorsed to the new owners. Consequently, the ESOP was not in a position to vote at the shareholders' meeting. Now, how should the SPA vote just before stepping down as Mercury's majority owner?

The Bank suggested that the SPA should vote at the shareholders' meeting with the full stock. However, if the SPA did not attend the meeting, there would be no quorum and the meeting would have to be reconvened in fifteen days, which would allow for sorting out ownership rights. The SPA did not attend the meeting. It later argued that the person in charge had not received the invitation. In the meantime, the SPA had seen one of its internal reorganisations, the Mercury case had been taken over by another directorate, and the invitation must have been mislaid somewhere. The General Director sent the invitation and other documents again one day before the meeting, but there was obviously not enough time left for the SPA to prepare.

One of the ESOP Trustees suggested in his letter to the SPA a quick endorsement of the shares so that the ESOP could vote at the reconvened shareholders' meeting. He also asked for a personal meeting with the SPA management. According to the company bylaws, the election of the executives was an issue requiring qualified majority voting (75 per cent). He argued that the SPA with its remaining stake could have a decisive influence on the voting even after the share endorsement, and requested that the SPA support the ESOP's position. Paying tribute to the support shown by the SPA for the ESOP, in line with current government policy, he asked for further help. Referring to the ESOP's Assembly and the results of its voting procedure, he assured the SPA that there was no general management crisis at Mercury; only the trust in the incumbent General Director had been shaken, because the ESOP members considered the current business policy to be the main cause of decreasing sales. Besides, neither his lifestyle (supported from company resources) nor his leadership style were respected at a time when 'every participant in the ESOP has acknowledged that carrying out the ESOP programme requires sacrifice from everyone'. They thought this should apply to the General Director, too. He apparently had other ideas. The ESOP Trustee did not fail to hint at the possible negative press coverage, should the SPA decide not to support their case by voting.

The SPA's view was that it had better not 'get involved in debate on personal matters', which they saw as connected with the tension between the Bank and the ESOP. According to an interviewee, the Bank intended to 'cement the General Director in his position', regardless of the will of the ESOP members.

The reconvened shareholders' meeting took place after the ESOP and the Bank had paid for the shares and these had been endorsed from the SPA to them. The General Director proposed the Bank's representative as acting chairperson of the shareholders' meeting, but this was rejected by the ESOP and the SPA. Then an ESOP trustee was elected unanimously. The SPA's voting behaviour must have taken the Bank by surprise: when the SPA's representative announced he would abstain from voting on each point on the agenda, the Bank's representative questioned what that would mean. The SPA's representative only repeated 'it means that [the SPA] will abstain from voting on each point'. Thus, the number of exercised votes decreased, with the practical result that the SPA thus granted a qualified majority for the ESOP in terms of the exercised votes. Decisions taken at the ESOP Assembly could thus be effected.

The General Director was relieved of his position, and the ESOP Leader was appointed as Managing Director. The Bank gained veto power in major issues by increasing the level of the 'qualified majority' from 75 to 79 per cent so the Bank's minority interest would be enough (after the equity increase). To complete the transaction, the SPA transferred 20 per cent of the proceeds from the share sale back to Mercury soon after the shareholders' meeting.

Outstanding issues

Now that 'We [had] put a full stop at the end of a process, everyone [had] calmed down, [and] everyone was doing his/her job', as an interviewee reflected, the management continued streamlining and modernisation projects that had started about a year earlier. They developed Mercury's computerised management information system, started a shop refurbishment programme, carried out front-line education for shop staff, worked on improving the Mercury image, organised sales campaigns, etc. The Bank increased Mercury's equity later in 1993, in October, as undertaken in the bid.

After the 1994 election, the SPA prepared a detailed privatisation review for the acting Prime Minister and, eventually, for the new government. Following contractual requirements due to the new condition, some of the shops had been sold by this time in a way that did not seriously impair Mercury's chain; other outlets were still advertised. Just before the SPA closed its review, the Managing Director (once ESOP Leader) could have this result accepted by the SPA as a 'fulfilment of obligations under the agreement'.

Employee shares had not been issued yet. The amount from which these shares were to be financed was instead used by the company to ease financial strains. Since there was no deadline specified in the agreement in this respect, it was left to the management to decide when it would issue employee shares.

In May 1994, the Managing Director 'was wrestling', in his words, with the SPA over the acquisition of shares purchasable by the employees at a discount. Progress seemed to be blocked by political uncertainty, at which time 'the SPA was not really operational'. In June, however, Mercury was commissioned by the SPA to sell this stock to its employees on behalf of the SPA.

The last outstanding issue in June 1994 was that of the option of the buyers to acquire the remaining SPA shares at par. This seemed to have been put on hold for some time. One SPA staff member believed that the management would want to carry out a 'pure MBO', a management buy-out, and request the Bank to give up its option; the Managing Director did not confirm this assumption.

Modernisation projects continued in 1994. Mercury's executives characterised these projects as 'relatively risky' and 'strained', adding that 'there are really no resources to finance' them. There was some relief that the Bank had increased equity, and the SPA had transferred back 20 per cent of the sale price.

Flotation, planned by the ESOP and the Bank at the time of the bidding, has not occurred yet.

5.3   Saturn: Squeeze play

'Saturn' became independent of an industry-wide trust in the late eighties, and operated as a state-owned enterprise under direct ministerial control (i.e. there was no enterprise council). It was engaged in a consumer product industry, produced its own products, but also carried out commissioned business for other firms. It made modest profits on sales of more than a billion forints (US\$ 13 million) in 1991. Saturn had one site only, and employed several hundred people.

Saturn exported about half of its production, mainly to Western countries. In the Hungarian market it had about 15 per cent market share in its main product line. More than 80 per cent of its products had been produced for more than twenty years. From the early nineties, Saturn had to face decreasing domestic demand and growing competition. A sensitive point of the operations was the commissioned business, a highly profitable but volatile trade. The firm was run by a General Director, appointed in 1985 in his late thirties and confirmed in his position since then several times. He chose the other members of the management team.

The management's initiative

The management started preparatory discussions with the Ministry, the SPA, domestic business partners and foreign potential investors in 1990, but only in October 1991 did it submit a Transformation Plan with an (updated, then revised) asset valuation to the SPA. They planned to convert the firm into a joint stock company with shareholders including the SPA and the firm's business partners. 'There were examples that served as a pattern, but the Ministry profoundly objected to cross-ownership', explained the General Director. Transformation was planned to take place at the beginning of the next year, to be followed by a sale of shares to and an increase of the registered capital subscribed by foreigners, who would eventually hold a 30–40 per cent interest. Financial investors were preferred to 'strategic' ones, admittedly because they were thought to have no intention 'to influence the company's economic activity'. The management held firm views as to what they wanted to do with the new finance. The General Director stated at a workers' assembly that 'we shall use the capital provided by the foreigners to pay back short-term loans, to modernise and enlarge storage facilities, and to improve technology'. He also argued that 'When most of the country's enterprises are becoming joint ventures of mixed [domestic and foreign] ownership . . . , if we stay out of this process, that would necessarily lead to loss of markets.'

Further discussions with the SPA and the Ministry followed, and went on until February 1992, turning the original Transformation Plan upside down in a period that the General Director described as 'rhapsodic [i.e. erratic]'. It appeared that state agents intended to put recommendations of corporate governance textbooks into practice. Evaluating Saturn's Transformation Plan in March 1992, the Ministry could already refer to 'reconciliation in the meantime' which had resulted in giving up the 'debatable cross-ownership solution'. Instead, the SPA would have a 96.3 per cent interest and a municipality 3.7 per cent. At the same time the SPA determined that there should be only a three-strong Board, with two outsiders one of whom would be the Chairman, as opposed to the management's proposal of six board members that would have included the top management.

On the issue of 'real privatisation' in the second step, the Ministry supported a 40 per cent foreign interest 'only if the rest of the state-owned shares can indeed be sold to domestic owners. Besides employee ownership this can be achieved by shares–compensation notes swaps, and farmers' ownership'. The Ministry also suggested that a high proportion of the shares should be sold in return for compensation notes and that the maximum legally possible discount should be granted to the employees in order to create an indigenous 'owners class', and that 'in order to strengthen [export] market positions . . . strategic investors should be preferred to financial ones, contrary to the firm's proposal'.

The SPA passed a resolution on Saturn's transformation a few months later, prescribing that employee shares could be issued subsequent to the privatisation, and that 20 per cent of the SPA shares should be reserved for later sale in exchange for compensation notes (as specified by the provisions of the Compensation Act). The rest were to be offered for sale. When Saturn transformed into a joint stock company, its equity was divided between registered capital and capital reserve in a ratio of about 3:1.

At the time there already seemed to be interest in the firm. The Hungarian subsidiary of a foreign bank claimed that it could introduce a strategic investor, and requested the SPA to suspend the proceedings of Saturn's privatisation for three months while they prepared an offer, and urged the SPA to declare its position because 'our commissioner is becoming downhearted'. They also asked the SPA to help in obtaining information from the management. Two weeks later the foreign bank again urged the SPA to postpone the privatisation, this time at the top level of the hierarchy, and repeated the complaint that the management was not co-operative. The General Director suspected that the prospective buyers were only after information about Saturn because they had already made an acquisition in Hungary and were competitors. The foreign bank's request was refused on the ground that the SPA certainly could not delay the process for months and grant exclusive rights to the bank for mediating between the SPA and a potential investor.

First tender with no success

A tender for consultants attracted ten offers which Saturn's top management and its Board of Directors evaluated. The General Director argued that the offers were quite similar, and the decision could only be made on the basis of trust. It must have certainly helped that one bidder had been working with the company on the introduction of the TQM (total quality management) concept. It was also considered an important factor that a consultant should 'be able to carry out the privatisation by considering the management's concept', and 'the other important factor was the readiness to co-operate'. More than two months later the SPA approved the management's choice of a consultant. The Consultant prepared a draft call for investment tenders but had to revise it, since the SPA wished to emphasise in the tender announcement that bids from employees enjoying discount opportunities would be treated as equal to bids of 'external, or capital-strong investors'. It insisted on keeping the opportunity for a two-step tender procedure.

In a review of Saturn's situation at the time of the tender, the company's financial position was said to be 'balanced', with no delays in payments. In the second and third quarters of the year, however, some losses were made, casting doubt on the possibility of achieving the planned level of pre-tax profits. The management regarded the accomplishment of the profit target as top priority, not only because of the bank's judgement but also because of the forthcoming privatisation. They had introduced measures to improve the situation by restricting purchasing ('only if approved by top management'), monitoring revenues and costs item by item every week, and preparing weekly cash flow reports. Co-operation between marketing and production functions was improved. Yet, the decline of the industry whose products Saturn stored had caused severe problems. In terms of volume, this highly profitable business reduced to a fraction of what it had been in the previous year. In terms of profits, the effect was alarming. 'We must prepare for survival', the management declared. In addition, the Western export markets for Saturn's own products had posed larger than expected difficulties. This situation was certainly mirrored in the increased stock of finished products. To alleviate the difficulties, the management had launched sales promotion and cost-cutting programmes which previously had not been common practice. Buyers were monitored by making use of a computer program, and they were not serviced until outstanding payments had been settled. The proportion of cash sales in total sales increased; a successful campaign helped to clear stock at reduced prices. Maintenance works were delayed. The management also attempted to reduce social benefits. These measures brought some results, and the firm could record profits at the end of the year, although these were less than planned.

The call for bids was advertised towards the end of 1992. An ESOP Organising Committee had been established by then and was interested in acquiring a stake of 52 per cent. They calculated that the company would be profitable even after meeting obligations for the ESOP. They promised to prepare the ESOP feasibility study and submit a bid by the end of March 1993, and asked the SPA to consider their intent to bid later when evaluating submitted tenders.

There was no officially submitted tender; only the ESOP's announced, but informal interest could be entered in the minutes of the tender opening, although the Consultant had directly invited several firms. The foreign bank that had earlier seemed interested did not reply to the Consultant's enquiry. The SPA approved a second call for tenders but asked the Consultant to prepare a detailed report of the causes of lack of interest. The Consultant pointed out that the time period available to prepare bids had probably been too short, general considerations of country risk might have played a role, and investors who already knew the firm might have been deterred from bidding by the need to make large investments to update the company's technology to modern Western standards. In an interview, the General Director implied there was an additional reason, namely that the management had some discretion in how to present the firm to potential investors, and it could be done in a way that they would not want to make an acquisition. A foreign company that appeared to be planning substantial downsizing at Saturn was given such a discouraging impression.

On the eve of the second call for tender, the General Director informed the Board that the SPA supported the ESOP concept. They had asked four consulting firms to submit offers to assist in preparing the ESOP's bid. At this time they wished to acquire 51 per cent of the shares but also wanted to have a 30 per cent foreign interest in the company.

Second tender fails

Soon after the tender announcement the SPA and leaders of all the firms in Saturn's industry discussed how to speed up privatisation. The Ministry encouraged employee ownership through ESOPs but, at least in Saturn's case, the SPA firmly rejected it. It applied different principles to different companies in the industry. Specifically, 'Saturn was threatened, not in writing of course, that they would sell it to the Social Security Fund', recalled the General Director; this was the option which he was against since the firm needed a 'future-oriented', resourceful owner. For the same reason, the General Director personally did not particularly support the ESOP. Repaying the ESOP's debts and financing necessary developments seemed too demanding a pair of tasks to accomplish in parallel. Pondering on why other firms had, nevertheless, chosen this path to privatisation, he suspected personal factors, such as the number of years until retirement – implying that one can gain a lot before retirement and then leave the firm to its fate – and the possibility of a clandestine acquirer to which the ESOP could pass on the shares it acquired at discount.

As for Saturn's ESOP, its plans for the size of interest to be acquired changed several times. Only a few weeks after it intended to acquire the majority position, the business plan for 1993 envisaged only a minority one. The management's letter to the SPA also asserted that they favoured a foreign strategic investor's majority and capital increase, with additional employee ownership through an ESOP and other means. These changes in the ESOP's aspiration level admittedly resulted from bargaining with the SPA whose position appeared to change depending on how it regarded the chance of selling Saturn for cash to a resourceful buyer. In effect, the ESOP would be allowed to get what would to be left after a – hopefully successful – tender.

There was no bid submitted. However, two firms had indicated their interest to the Consultant. If nothing else, this could be entered in the minutes. A foreign company had announced a non-binding interest and required one or two months to prepare a bid. It intended to establish a store chain in Hungary, of which Saturn could be a supplier. They gave up their acquisition intent soon afterwards.

The other interested company was 'Mighty Multinational'. It first indicated interest in late March after a visit to Saturn, and asked the SPA to keep the tender for Saturn open for an additional eight weeks to give it the opportunity to investigate other factories in the industry. In another fax, sent only twenty minutes before the opening of tenders, Mighty Multinational announced that on the basis of its investigations Saturn seemed the best acquisition target in this industry, and asked the SPA again to extend the deadline to allow it to submit a formal bid within two months. It also indicated its objective to acquire all the shares in the firm, requesting the SPA to convince the minority-owner municipality to sell its shares. No possible employee ownership was considered.

Offers and negotiations off-tender

Saturn at this time appeared to be a target exhibiting relatively better performance in a drastically worsened business environment. According to a report to the Board, owing to new, active marketing methods, domestic sales had increased, but the commissioned business continued to decline drastically, causing serious damage to Saturn's return on sales. The devaluation of the pound had also hit the company. In export markets competition had intensified owing to low-cost producers. Saturn had been working on launching new products. The management had succeeded in reducing interest payments with a better credit policy, but the firm's indebtedness, partly inherited from the time when Saturn became an independent firm, remained a serious burden. Had the commissioned business brought in results such as those in 1991, profits would have risen, which indicates the management's success in its efforts to compensate for this lost opportunity. The firm's cash flow was said to have been very well managed. Organisational changes had also been made. Personnel of a whole department, dealing with suppliers, had been replaced. A new export department had been established. The ISO 9000 quality standards were being introduced at that time and their audit was scheduled for early June. All this was done by mutual agreement. 'It was not that I decided', explained the General Director. They had meetings and debates, then 'once we decided, everyone acted on that'. The members of the Supervisory Board and the Board of Directors were said to be 'people who did not go for personal gains but for the firm's interest'. The Supervisory Board stated at its first meeting that it intended to assist the management, and then it regularly reviewed the firm's situation and provided feedback to the management.

Mighty Multinational paid a visit to Saturn and again requested that the deadline be extended, now until the end of May. Just as in earlier correspondence with the SPA and the Consultant, its letter started by emphasising how important a company the potential acquirer was. It was not only one of the largest world wide companies in consumer goods with leading positions providing very strong financial resources but it was also a strong presence in Hungary already. It intended to invest a large amount in Saturn, which would be managed as a division of Mighty Multinational Hungary, in order to upgrade it to its own requirements. Ambitious plans were outlined for quality improvements, exports, technology and know-how in the technical and marketing areas. Making an offer was subject to satisfactory due diligence and the possibility of the acquisition of all the shares, among other conditions. The SPA wanted Mighty Multinational to make a binding offer. Until the issue of ownership was resolved, the management saw their main objectives as 'to ensure the viability of the company and to facilitate privatisation' in a very unfavourable environment.

The Annual General Meeting of the shareholders affirmed that the company had made achievements: it was still profitable and financially stable, although short of resources to invest. No dividend was distributed, but profits were to be spent on new equipment.

The SPA at this time considered the possibility of a new tender for Saturn. Alternatively, it could just wait for Mighty Multinational's offer. The law permitted the privatisation of state-owned assets by leasing after two unsuccessful tendering processes. This possibility was also contemplated, and the management had earlier expressed its interest in it in case there was no other solution, but the SPA expected that Mighty Multinational would submit a binding offer even before the alternative of privatisation by leasing was fully examined.

Not knowing what would eventually happen, the employees' representatives must have felt it important to secure the benefits they were entitled to under the law. The local Union Leader's letter to the SPA simply confirmed that they wanted to take the opportunity of acquiring some shares at a 90 per cent discount, as stated in one of the SPA's earlier decisions.

Instead of a binding offer, Mighty Multinational again requested an extension of the deadline. Then it did submit an offer for 100 per cent of the shares, but explicitly stated that it was a non-binding one. It did not wish to share ownership with either the employees or any third party. In case shares had later to be sold to employees, the difference between the price of their shares and the value of their shares was, of course, required to be met by the SPA. The prospective acquirer again introduced itself at considerable length, emphasising not only its mighty size and resourcefulness but also its already considerable importance in foreign direct investment and employment in Hungary. It placed a value of several hundred million forints on Saturn, but more than half of this was to be deducted because of debts. Thus, the cash price offered was only a couple of hundred millions, and even that was to be reduced by any losses that might have occurred in the working capital value between 31 December 1992 and the date of transfer. On the other hand, planned investment was substantial. The transfer of know-how and the use of Mighty Multinational trade marks were to be the subject of separate service agreements. Mighty Multinational would source locally and intended to boost Saturn's existing exports. It did not fail to emphasise how beneficial this would be to the country's trade balance. Saturn was planned to be run mainly with local management, supported by a few expatriates to transfer know-how and management skills. Substantial retraining of the workforce was considered necessary.

Mighty Multinational was thorough in devising reasons that might reduce the effective share purchase price. Among the conditions, it was specified that the SPA had to guarantee the transfer of the local municipalities' stock to Mighty Multinational. Obsolete stocks, stocks sold at less than inventory price, and uncollected debts were to be further deducted from the price. No major decision concerning Saturn's business was to be taken without the prior consent of Mighty Multinational as from the date of the non-binding offer. All guarantees given by Saturn to third parties were required to be withdrawn, or undertaken by the SPA. Payments to non-working employees covered by a legal obligation (e.g. for maternity leave), bonuses to be paid to employees of Saturn in relation to the achievement of the privatisation of the company, as well as bonuses related to the achievement of the planned profit target, and costs and investments arising from an environmental audit were to be covered by the SPA. It was also required to guarantee that no penalties and/or increase of levies would be charged to Saturn for environmental matters within the following five years. Because its foreign ownership exceeded the limit of 30 per cent specified by the law, Saturn was also to be granted a full tax holiday for a period of five years, and a partial tax holiday for the following five years. Mighty Multinational also laid claim to export subsidies at a rate of 25 per cent of export revenues for a period of at least five years. Finally, a part of the purchase price would be retained as further security for the performance of the obligations of the SPA. Although some at the SPA objected to several of the conditions, there was a firm intent to negotiate and, eventually, sell Saturn to Mighty Multinational.

In the next few months, negotiations resulted in 'final offers' and their revision a couple of times. In the first version of its 'final' offer, Mighty Multinational increased the value placed on Saturn as well as the amount of debts to be deducted. It also specified some of its claims, naming especially Saturn's guarantee for an International Bank as an example of liabilities to be withdrawn or undertaken by the SPA. The part of the purchase price to be retained until the SPA fulfilled its guarantees was given as 10 per cent of the price, and the maximum length of the review period was shortened from two years to six months.

It was now the SPA's turn, first, to evaluate the offer and, second, to lay claims for the buyer's guarantees for the investment, an increase in exports, the maintenance of current levels of employment and the provision of necessary retraining, and that Saturn would not revoke its contracts with its current suppliers for at least a year. Certain conditions required by the acquirer were rejected, partly because the SPA had no authority to grant them and partly because they were considered exaggerated. So that the SPA could better argue, the General Director was asked to provide information on Saturn's current status. He updated the SPA on the amount of the firm's debts and specified the amount of Saturn's guarantee for a loan that had been taken by a Foreign Trade Company from an International Bank. Saturn inherited this liability from the times when it had been part of an industry-wide trust. The General Director could, by now, also inform the SPA that the munici-pality seemed willing to sell its shares at the purchase price as negotiated with Mighty Multinational.

Towards the end of the summer, Mighty Multinational acknowledged some of the SPA's proposals, mostly those that arose from the SPA's lack of authority to decide, such as subsidies and tax holidays. These were granted by law in any case. It also confirmed that it would stick to the prescriptions of the laws prevailing in Hungary with respect to employee ownership. This would not mean any support for an ESOP scheme, of course, but only the acceptance of issuing new employee shares from the sale proceeds. The SPA also wished to sell some shares to producers in return for compensation notes, but the acquirer was not in favour of the idea. On the basis of negotiations, Mighty Multinational prepared a draft share purchase agreement.

The SPA officials working on the Saturn case were aware of Mighty Multinational's strong position. They pointed out that the bidder had excellent information, and had formulated its terms and conditions after the failure of two tenders. The SPA considered two options: either accept the offer but with conditions more favourable to the SPA (for example, requiring the buyer to pay at least 80 per cent of the nominal value of the shares; 25 per cent + 1 vote to be sold to producers in exchange for compensation notes), or reject it (and offer the shares to small investors and producers). A draft proposal to the decision-makers elaborated the first alternative; in its final form, it was suggested that after concluding a contract with Mighty Multinational a press release should be made in which the SPA would state how much it was in the national interest to attract a major multinational company to the industry.

The Ministry objected to the sale to Mighty Multinational and wanted to see a more lucrative deal. Considering all the claims that could lead to a reduction of the purchase price, it concluded that 'then it may happen that the SPA will have to make a financial sacrifice in order to strike a deal'. It insisted that, as required by the provisions of the Property Policy Guidelines, shares representing 25 per cent + 1 vote be warranted to producers, and some shares be sold at a discount to employees – both in line with the government privatisation policy that, since 1992, had put emphasis on these forms of indigenous ownership. The Ministry also made the criticism that the draft agreement as drawn up by Mighty Multinational 'requested guarantees for everything but provided no guarantee for the buyer's undertaking'. In sum, whatever advantage it might bring in the future to have Mighty Multinational in this Hungarian industry, the 'one-sidedly dictated' terms and conditions attached to the offer were regarded as unacceptable, even from the internationally respected Mighty Multinational, particularly when good long-term market prospects for Saturn's products were envisaged. Finally, the Ministry suggested that in case negotiations with Mighty Multinational failed, a new call for tender should be announced. According to the General Director, the reason behind the Ministry's objection was two-fold: it was probably afraid of a monopoly situation, and it wanted to protect the producers. However, this position had to change later, under pressure from the exchequer.

In this situation the SPA made a decision which, while accepting the offer in principle, required further negotiations. It wanted to achieve about 70 per cent of the registered capital being sold for at least 80 per cent of the nominal value, employee shares with discount being issued, capital investment being carried out within two years, and a stock of 25 per cent + 1 vote being sold to producers in exchange for compensation notes (with Mighty Multinational's option on the shares not subscribed to). It was also decided that these target conditions could only be modified by the SPA's Board. As proposed, the Board's resolution prescribed that a press release should be issued after the conclusion of the contract, which was to emphasise that 'it is in the national interest' to draw a multinational into this industry.

The SPA made its decision in the absence of the Ministry's representative, although he had personally requested that the case not be discussed when scheduled because he would not be able to attend. His request was disregarded and a decision was made which he saw as being contrary to the Ministry's position. In a new tender he wished to see that only 50 per cent + 1 vote should be offered for sale, and the SPA's earlier decision on the possible extent of employee ownership should be enforced. He insisted that the Ministry's expressed objection should be entered in the minutes, which was duly done afterwards. The SPA management was then instructed to conduct negotiations with Mighty Multinational in accordance to the Ministry's position and bring back the issue before the decision-makers in the event that the negotiations failed to result in an agreement. At the company the Ministry's efforts were regarded as futile: 'If Mighty Multinational says it wants 100 per cent, it is in vain that the Ministry' held different ideas. 'It wasn't serious', commented the General Director.

The ongoing negotiations had resulted in Mighty Multinational's revised, 'final and definitive' offer in September 1993 for more than 80 per cent of the shares (instead of some 70 per cent as prescribed by the SPA resolution), so that it could have full control with at least 75 per cent + 1 vote after sales of shares to employees and producers. It also required right of first refusal on all shares not purchased by them, and on shares sold by any other shareholders (municipality, employees) at any time. The offered price represented 60 per cent of par. Accepting the SPA's request, it undertook to issue new shares to be subscribed by employees, but also wanted to be compensated by the SPA for any price discount on these shares given to the employees.

Clearly, this was not exactly what the SPA had hoped for. The offered price was only two-thirds of the claimed one. Yet, it was proposed that the offer should be accepted since the SPA official evaluating the offer believed that it was 'in our interest to attract them into the industry'. He also noted that in the case of two other firms in the same industry the SPA could only achieve price levels of 50 per cent and 85 per cent of the nominal value of the shares, which made Mighty Multinational's offer of 60 per cent in cash look acceptable.

According to a marginal note, there was a view within the SPA that the Ministry was just 'thwarting it [dragging its feet]'. Assuring its 'fellow state agent' that the SPA did not wish, nor was it in its interest, to take a position against the Ministry, the SPA asked the Ministry for its opinion on the revised offer. Anticipating that it would want to reject the offer, and in an attempt to try and involve the Ministry in devising a mutually acceptable solution, the SPA also wanted to hear the Ministry's view on 'how then should Saturn's privatisation happen' while keeping it viable and safeguarding the value of the state's shareholding.

The Ministry was still unhappy with the likely outcome of this privatisation, and kept fighting for more influential stakes for producers. It also spotted that Mighty Multinational had now indicated larger employee ownership than originally prescribed by an SPA resolution. This would also mean higher compensation from the SPA to the acquirer, resulting in an effective share purchase price of less than 50 per cent. If a price of 60 per cent was regarded as too low by the Ministry, this new figure was seen as simply 'beyond reality'. In fact, because of further price adjustments, even this amount might decrease. The offer was unacceptable: at such a price 'we do not recommend the sale', concluded the Ministry.

An SPA official reviewed the situation by comparing the offer to the SPA's expectations, particularly those that had formally appeared in earlier SPA resolutions. The latest offer was made for more shares than the SPA wanted to sell, reducing the size of the stock that could be offered to producers below the limit prescribed earlier. Striking a deal on these terms would yield less-than-hoped-for proceeds to the SPA, although somewhat more than offered formerly. It was also considered that the investor had made it clear: this was the last and definitive offer – no more major changes, please.

Apparently, the main obstacle to striking a deal was that the SPA, as it was also required to by law, had once acknowledged the right of producers to have an opportunity to acquire stock. This would prevent Mighty Multinational from acquiring absolute majority once the employee shares were issued. The negotiations had now been going on for about six months in the context of the potential acquirer's apparently superior bargaining position, and it was important to conclude a deal before the end of the year so that Saturn could be eligible for an automatic tax holiday. The SPA reviewed the situation and decided that the shares originally intended for sale to producers could now be offered to Mighty Multinational. It argued later that the producers could have submitted bids in the first two tenders but they had failed to do so. On the other hand, if this stock were sold to Mighty Multinational, the producers could count on a solvent owner of Saturn, and buyer of their products. The wording of the resolution makes it possible to speculate that the SPA's reasoning actually meant the following: since Mighty Multinational's offer left only about half of the stock originally intended to be offered to farmers (who would pay with compensation notes), we might as well sell this stock to Mighty Multinational (who would pay in cash). The investor was asked to revise its offer accordingly.

Mighty Multinational submitted its once again revised offer for all the SPA shares in Saturn. It also exerted pressure at high level for the deal to be struck quickly. It urged the conclusion of the agreement at a meeting with, and in a letter to, a Responsible Politician. Its intent was conveyed clearly: 'We want to acquire Saturn.' That such an acquisition would be very beneficial to the firm and the national economy was also elaborately presented. Timing was critical: the deal had to be struck before the end of the year. To that end, the Responsible Politician was asked to help in concluding an agreement.

The SPA accepted the offer, again with conditions. Further negotiations followed. Now all the SPA shareholding could be sold to Mighty Multinational at 60 per cent of par, and employee ownership was to be ensured to the extent of 10 per cent of the enlarged registered capital. The SPA wanted a guarantee that a substantial capital investment would be carried out within two years. The Ministry apparently agreed, but it was noted that 'Mighty Multinational took unfair advantage of its favourable bargaining [position].' According to standard SPA procedures, the final agreement was to be concluded within thirty days of the decision.

Upon the SPA's request, Mighty Multinational submitted its draft of the agreement. It specified some previous conditions, but also included new elements. Indemnification was to be limited to 25 per cent of the purchase price, instead of to a smaller extent as the SPA had wanted. Capital investment was to be undertaken by Saturn itself and not Mighty Multinational, allowing it to finance new machinery and fixed assets partly from Saturn's profits instead of new finance as the SPA had hoped. The acquirer wanted Saturn's release from a guarantee given to International Bank for Foreign Trade Company, and the guarantee to be assumed by the SPA – a claim which Mighty Multinational had already made but which seemed to be a new demand to some SPA officials, as we shall see later. Finally, it wanted English to be the language of the contract.

Closing with debate

Only a few weeks from the end of the year, an all-day-long meeting, supposedly the last before the signing ceremony, was held to finalise the agreement. Some issues were still being debated. An SPA report prepared at about this time noted that the buyer had the benefit of knowing that there was no bidder in the tendering, and it would 'get Saturn in one way or another in any case'. It was feared that the acquirer would oblige the SPA in various ways to pay indemnification to a considerable extent. In addition, the SPA believed that the employee shares – subsidised by the SPA up to 90 per cent of the nominal value – would be bought up by Mighty Multinational eventually. As an SPA staff member calculated, the worst possible scenario (if Mighty Multinational claimed all guarantees, price adjustments, and indemnification) would provide an income to the SPA which would be only slightly more than 10 per cent of the nominal value.

Mighty Multinational requested one more meeting, but with a higher-ranking SPA executive, while urging the SPA administrator assigned to the Saturn case to settle the issue of the Bank guarantee as soon as possible. Tension and possible misunderstanding of previous communication between the parties were indicated by a marginal note, which viewed this request as 'once again a provocation'. In his reply, the SPA administrator expressed his surprise at a request which seemed new to him, believed that the acquirer was hindering the conclusion of the contract, and shifted 'responsibility for your unusual action and all its detrimental consequences onto you personally'. He immediately prepared a report to his superiors on this matter. In a few hours the misunderstanding was cleared up, when Mighty Multinational's counsel, assuming a 'fatal misunderstanding', explained that Mighty Multinational had only tried to ask for the administrator's assistance in solving the problem of the guarantee, but had no intention of delaying the conclusion of the contract.

Had the administrator waited only a few hours before sending Mighty Multinational his excited reaction and preparing a brief for his superiors on the problems, as perceived by him, jeopardising the scheduled closing date, he could have saved himself some work. Now he had to prepare an addendum on the most recent developments, since Saturn was released just in time from the much debated Bank guarantee (assumed by the SPA).

On the eve of the signing ceremony some further objections were raised by legal counsel of the SPA. He criticised the buyer's one-sidedly favourable position and the lack of some formalities that he regarded as indispensable for the SPA to sign the contract responsibly. These minor problems disregarded, the parties signed the contract, although on somewhat different terms than had been formerly approved by the SPA Board. Mighty Multinational as the Purchaser thus acquired all the SPA shares, the price being subject to adjustments. It was to be compensated for discounted employee shares in such a way that the allowance given to employees when acquiring these newly issued shares would be repaid by the SPA to the Purchaser within 60 days of the issue. The Purchaser withheld 10 per cent of the purchase price to cover subsequent adjustments. A ceiling of 20 per cent of the purchase price was applied to indemnification. Regarding investments, Mighty Multinational guaranteed that within two years capital investment 'will be made' at Saturn 'up to' a specified amount. The transfer of know-how and the use of trade marks were subject to a separate agreement. Before the end of the year, the acquirer paid for the stock, and the shares were endorsed.

Saturn's new boards were elected in early 1994 at an extraordinary shareholders' meeting, which also increased the company's registered capital by issuing employee shares against capital reserve. About two months later Mighty Multinational informed the SPA that employee shares had been issued as contracted, and this had been recorded with the Registration Court. Therefore it claimed its money from the SPA, namely 90 per cent of the nominal value of the employee shares. In its reply the SPA could 'not construe this request', and asked for evidence that the Purchaser had met its contractual obligations. When Mighty Multinational again urged the SPA for compensation, it was rejected again and was told that employee shares could be issued only after an increase of the capital had been registered with the Court; thus, in order to lay claims to compensation, the acquirer should first provide evidence of that act. In fact, Mighty Multinational had already done so, but the SPA did not repay the employee allowance for months.

As this issue was kept in suspense until the middle of the summer, the acquirer found one more reason to submit a claim to the SPA. An International Auditor prepared a report on Saturn's balance sheet at 31 December 1993 and the company's asset value was considerably less than a year earlier, giving rise to a possible price adjustment of the same amount. Along with its claim, Mighty Multinational informed the SPA that the employee shares scheme had already been finalised 'to the full satisfaction of the employees'. Other developments included quality improvement programmes in co-operation with the producers, the relationship with whom was said to be excellent. Investments had already started, and the company was preparing to launch a new high quality product.

After the SPA paid the acquirer compensation for the employees' allowance, a report on Saturn's privatisation believed that the employees' shares had been bought up by Mighty Multinational, 'contrary to the spirit of the agreement'. This was confirmed by the General Director; in fact, these shares 'were not actually issued [i.e. printed]'. The employees received cash amounts equal to net wages of six months. He also added that the acquirer bought up the municipality's shares, too, resulting in the accomplishment of its original plan, the ownership of the whole stock. Although the said report also raised concerns with respect to Mighty Multinational's obligation to carry out a capital expenditure programme, the General Director spoke about an investment programme far exceeding the acquirer's contractual obligations, although with some delay. Benefiting from this, Saturn could then decrease its dependence on the commissioned business and concentrate on its core business.

At the time of closing this case history, some outstanding issues were still being debated. The case is ended here with a review of these issues, and the General Director's reflections on this privatisation.

Following the 1994 elections and changes in the SPA's management, the SPA attempted to close all outstanding issues with Mighty Multinational in early autumn. After paying tribute to the Auditor's well-attested competence and impartiality, it pointed out some errors and missing formalities in the report, and asked Mighty Multinational to specify its claims and reveal its position on whether, in its understanding, the 20 per cent ceiling upon indemnification included both price adjustment and various guarantees, since the recently submitted claim alone exceeded this ceiling.

The General Director regarded Saturn's privatisation a success, something that 'we can be proud of'. At the national level, Mighty Multinational's investment in Hungary was said to be 'barometric, an acknowledgement', that is, it indicates that the country is a safe place in which to invest. Its investment also provides market opportunities for Hungarian producers. The acquirer developed a good relationship with them, including financial support. Its business culture and long-term commitment have also been noted. The price it paid for the acquisition was subject to negotiation, but for Saturn, this was a matter of indifference. Employment was important, and it decreased somewhat, but the General Director viewed it as a necessary short-term sacrifice for better long-term prospects. He believed Saturn would soon advertise vacancies again and 'will be doing very well' as market opportunities improve and the business, on a healthier foundation, starts expanding. In reply to a specific question about the politics surrounding privatisation, he remarked: 'No, there was no politics. There are charismatic party leaders in [the region where Saturn is located] but regional politics could be kept out.' Reflecting upon his personal involvement, he pondered, 'I acted upon conviction; my colleagues sometimes said I was too virtuous; I think I facilitated a good privatisation.'

Less than two years after the agreement between Mighty Multinational and the SPA, the General Director left Saturn, apparently because he saw no future career opportunities in running a unit which was under tight control and 'needed only a shopfloor manager'.

5.4   Mars and Deimos: Brown and rough(-and-tumble)

'Deimos' had been a unit of an industry-wide trust which we shall call 'Mars'. It was turned into a 'subsidiary with legal personality' from mid-1991 and named Deimos Subsidiary accordingly. With more than 1,000 employees, a net book value of its assets in the range HUF 1.5–2.0 billion (US$ 20–27 million), sales of less than HUF 4 billion (US$ 53 million), and profit before tax of about HUF 0.5 billion (US$ 7 million), Deimos Subsidiary (or Deimos, for short) was a relatively large unit within the Mars group. Its main business included products for personal use, sold mainly in Hungary. The firm had a high market share, ranging from 30 per cent to 80 per cent in the main product lines, even if the products were somewhat 'brown and rough'. Imports had already been fully liberalised by the nineties, and this industry, contrary to the position in neighbouring countries, was not protected by tariffs and duties. Recession and low capacity utilisation in North America and Western Europe in the early 1990s resulted in increasing interest in Eastern European opportunities. Deimos thus faced growing import competition from 'white and soft' products of better quality.

Prelude: towards breaking up Mars

In the early 1990s, Mars was already operating as a group of several companies. Some were subsidiaries (legally independent units), while others had been established by contributing plants in kind to joint ventures with foreign firms. Since more than 50 per cent of the firm's assets had already been represented in company form, Mars was required by law to transform by the end of 1992. Following discussions with and instructions from the SPA, the first draft of Mars' Transformation Plan was submitted in the first half of 1992. Based on the sector's capital and R&D intensity and 'international experience', Mars' management proposed that the group should not be broken up. It planned a holding structure with the headquarters carrying out the asset management function for all the companies. Note that Mars was heavily indebted. The planned date of transformation was July 1992.

The Vice-President of Deimos' local Workers' Council complained to Mars' General Director and the SPA in June 1992 that he had been informed only from the papers of the fact that Mars had submitted its Transformation Plan, and asked for information. A week later he requested in another letter that the SPA find a solution that would protect employment. An ESOP Organising Committee was also established whose Leader promptly requested the SPA to 'deprive Mars of the assets of Deimos Subsidiary ... so that on the basis of these assets a company can be established and in this company an ESOP programme can be launched'. He argued that 'it has been for years a determined demand of Deimos' employees to be separated and to operate as an independent company. This effort has so far been made hopeless by the rigid opposition of Mars' management.' At a Workers' Open Forum held a week later with the participation of the responsible Ministry, the National Association of Workers' Councils, the Taking Part Foundation (a pro-ESOP organisation led by one of the SPA Board's members), Mars' General Director, and Deimos' Director 'promised to support the work of the ESOP Organising Committee'. At about this time, 'Phobos' (another subsidiary of Mars) made a similar move, in order to achieve independence from Mars and to implement an ESOP.

In the second half of summer 1992, a rival ESOP Organising Committee was launched (ESOP II; ESOP mentioned above now becomes ESOP I). From a joint memorandum from the two ESOPs to Mars' Enterprise Council it appears that they aimed at obtaining at least 45 per cent of the registered capital in the form of employee shares with a 90 per cent allowance to be granted by the SPA. For the 10 per cent to be paid for, the ESOP Organising Committees planned to take an Existence Loan. However, they held different views on how to achieve employee ownership. In the first way, preferred by ESOP I Organising Committee, the SPA would deprive Mars of Deimos' assets at the time of Mars' transformation (resulting in the SPA becoming the sole owner and Mars losing its control over Deimos), convert Deimos into a company, and grant the employees an opportunity to acquire ownership in it. In the second alternative, preferred by ESOP II Organising Committee, Mars would transform Deimos into a company before its own transformation, and Deimos would then be sold in part to employees. This meant that Mars would still be the majority owner of Deimos.

Because the Enterprise Council members received the memorandum only one day before their sitting, a resolution was passed that employee ownership was 'supported, to the extent that it is legally possible, in every unit of the Mars group'. To deal with the situation, Mars established a Central ESOP Preparatory Committee at headquarters level, led by one of the deputies to Mars' General Director. Discussions with the ESOP Organising Committees started. The Preparatory Committee's position was that employee ownership was acceptable to the extent that was financially feasible (less than claimed by the ESOPs); Mars 'would reinvest [in Deimos] dividends ... in every year, subject to evaluation of the company's [subsidiary's] capital requirements', which evaluation would certainly be made by headquarters. The Committee objected to the demand that the transformation of the parent company could only happen after Deimos was already privatised, but promised to provide the ESOP Organising Committees with a detailed business plan in a few weeks so that they could use it in preparing a feasibility study. The Committee's position was accepted only by the ESOP II Organising Committee which enjoyed the support of 45 per cent of the employees. This alternative was also supported by the subsidiary's management. ESOP I Leader, backed by 25 per cent of the employees, refused to acknowledge the authority of the Committee in a matter that had been addressed to Mars' Enterprise Council, and insisted on becoming independent of the parent company before transformation and privatisation took place.

It took some time for the SPA to evaluate the situation and to formulate a privatisation strategy for Mars and its subsidiaries. The SPA now faced two problems. The first problem was whether first to transform Mars and then turn the renegade subsidiaries into independent companies, or first to establish independent companies from the subsidiaries, causing considerable delay in the transformation and privatisation of the rest of the group. In the beginning the position of the SPA (or at least the administrator dealing with the industry) was that there should be no delay: only when Mars was transformed could employees obtain ownership.

The second problem was how to handle the rivalry between the two ESOP Organising Committees. The SPA attempted in vain to reconcile the two ESOPs, whose rivalry 'even raised anger'. It was concluded that 'an interference [by the SPA] with a word of authority may have disadvantageous results'. Instead, feasibility studies should be prepared, and the SPA should decide by considering the professional opinion of external advisors. However, political judgement gave new direction to the flow of events.

The Leader of ESOP I had been seeking support for his case from an MP. In his letter he attacked Mars and its proposal for a holding structure. He pointed out Mars' interest in a holding structure which would be 'vital for its further existence', since if Mars were dismantled, there would be no subsidiaries to direct from the top. If the SPA accepted Mars' proposal, it would, in ESOP I Leader's view, provide headquarters with an opportunity 'to continue its operations, just as in the earlier, socialist, megalomaniac industry structure'. On the other hand, acceptance of their, i.e. the ESOP's, proposal would 'impede power retention' by managers appointed in the communist era.

The MP asked a Responsible Politician for urgent help in Deimos' case 'before things completely get muddled up'. Utilising arguments provided to him by ESOP I Leader, he stated that the efforts to achieve employee ownership 'have in every possible way been thwarted'. The Responsible Politician passed the letter on to the SPA with a hand written note: 'Let's create an opportunity for them!' Parallel to the developments at Deimos, a similar story was unfolding at Phobos.

In September, ESOP I Leader met the Responsible Politician and asked for help. In a subsequent letter he also complained that the management had not provided him with information and money for preparing an ESOP Feasibility Study. In the meantime, a pro-ESOP consultant's free preliminary study concluded that an ESOP would be feasible if there was a tax shield granted to Deimos (for example, due to partial foreign ownership), and if a 13–15 per cent return on sales could be achieved. Deimos' management regarded a higher profitability to be necessary for Deimos to be able to finance its operations while covering the ESOP's debts.

To put the events in historical context, note that about a year earlier the same argument had been presented in a public notice sent to the SPA on 'squandering' a subsidiary. Mars' headquarters was said to have attempted to sell it at any price 'only in order to keep their individual positions at the top of an asset management holding'. Mars indeed wanted to transform this subsidiary (a legally independent form) into a so-called 'self-accounting internal unit' (a legally non-independent form). This was to serve the purpose of freeing it from irrecoverable debts, obsolete stock, etc., and to keep them in Mars' books when, in the second phase of the planned transaction, the subsidiary would have been contributed in kind to a joint venture with a foreign investor who would have had a majority. That is, Mars' headquarters (still state-owned) attempted to accumulate all the losses and contribute the subsidiary's assets to a (private) joint-venture clean of all debts and liabilities. The deal fell through later; the subsidiary was eventually acquired by the same investor who bought Deimos. In another case, the ownership split was again planned with a slight foreign majority. This deal was eventually struck, but only a few months later production by the joint-venture was 'suspended' by the majority owner whose other companies were said to have been hit by recession. Yet another deal of a similar kind that Mars intended to strike with a foreign firm was characterised at the SPA at the time as a deal in which Mars would simply give away controlling rights and 100 per cent of the assets of the subsidiary concerned, with the foreign firm's commitment being minimal.

Previous experience, the SPA's ongoing dispute with the foreign co-owner of Mars' large joint-venture, and immediate pressure from Deimos and Phobos (and soon a third subsidiary) must all have played a role in the Responsible Politician's judgement. His marginal note on a letter he had received from Phobos and passed on to the SPA made it clear that 'decentralisation is to be discussed'. Another note on an attached slip was absolutely unambiguous: 'Mars has to be decentralised [dismantled]!! The daughters [i.e. subsidiaries] have to be allowed to go independent! They [must] receive a positive reply!' A few days later the Responsible Politician noted again in a marginal note: 'Mars [must] be drawn under direct state control, and let us break it up by appointing a commissioner!' Mars' management was requested to examine the possibility of decentralisation, and an expert was to be commissioned to prepare in two to three weeks a detailed plan for implementing 'the decentralisation concept'. SPA administrators sent a 'positive reply' (copy to the Responsible Politician) to the ESOP Leaders at Deimos and Phobos, assuring them that nothing had been decided yet and that their interest was being considered. The MP received a satisfactory reply which informed him that 'preliminary studies show that the best possible solution seems to be letting the subsidiaries ... go before the parent's transformation'. Whether it would be a feasible solution was subject to further studies.

Other agents of the state thought otherwise. The Ministry, prompted by Mars' management, wrote to the SPA and stated that the examination of the decentralisation alternative should not cause any delay in carrying out '*the firm's transformation programme that has been agreed with the Ministry*', arguing that Mars' credit agreements with banks were soon to be renewed and any uncertainty might jeopardise debt management. It was also pointed out that an ESOP could be implemented after Mars' transformation. According to the Ministry's letter, there had been successful discussions on this issue between the employees and managements of the subsidiaries and Mars' headquarters.

This view gained further weight when most of the subsidiary directors, including the director of Deimos but not that of Phobos, sent the SPA a declaration. They stated that they wanted to transform their subsidiaries in a few months into companies within Mars (i.e. under a holding company to be established from Mars' headquarters), and urged the SPA to proceed quickly with their case since the 'viability of the units is jeopardised by the transitional state dragging on'. Mars' management suggested that the Enterprise Council, too, should vote for this position.

But again, ESOP I Leader raised objections in his letter to the SPA, also correcting the Ministry's statement: 'there has been no successful discussion with our ESOP Organising Committee, although you have been informed so by [the Ministry] ... which was worded on the basis of information provided by Mars' management'. In his view, Mars wanted to divide employees and had yet not provided them with the data and documents necessary to prepare the ESOP Feasibility Study. At about this time Phobos' similar efforts were made public through the press. ESOP I Leader subsequently often referred to Phobos, thus indicating that he was not the only one who was rocking the boat.

The 'Director' of Deimos and the Leader of ESOP II felt it necessary to present their view to the SPA so that it could make a decision on the basis of 'complete information'. Emphasising that the management and ESOP II represented 45 per cent of the employees, they put forward the 'ESOP within Mars' plan again, with Mars keeping the majority stake while employees obtained a minority in the range of 25–45 per cent (ESOP and employee shares combined). This proposal was also signed by two functional directors and several middle managers.

But to no avail: it was the 'decentralisation concept' that the Responsible Politician instructed the SPA to execute. The Ministry had by now changed its position too. Admittedly because of several requests made by the ESOP I Organising Committee, the Ministry 'considered the firm's transformation once more and concluded that it is necessary to change the position we have had till now'. However, it was suggested that the subsidiaries should be independently transformed into companies parallel to (but not, as demanded by ESOP I Leader, prior to) Mars' transformation. A higher-level official also elaborated the Ministry's current position in a letter to the SPA. As if the ESOP I Leader had written it, he listed the possible arguments Mars' headquarters might raise against decentralisation, and immediately fended them off in four pages (plus an appendix).

Before the end of the year, Mars was drawn under direct state control. The General Director's work was duly acknowledged; nevertheless he was relieved of his position and soon retired. The SPA appointed a so-called State Commissioner who had been a deputy to the General Director. He was given the task of drawing up a 'crisis plan' and a transformation and privatisation plan for the Mars group in thirty days. He was also required to examine whether there had been abuse of state-owned property in the process of establishing joint-ventures on the basis of Mars' assets.

Transformation

Mars' State Commissioner was also responsible for preparing a Transformation Plan for the Deimos subsidiary. He submitted it to the SPA in early spring 1993. The plan combined capital injection and employee ownership by 'subscription to employee shares or perhaps some other privatisation technique', which elsewhere was specified as an ESOP with the maximum possible discount.

At the same time the SPA also approved the privatisation proposal for Mars, including that much of the sale proceeds should be used to service Mars' debts. The State Commissioner was authorised to manage the sale of the subsidiaries, while Mars itself was to be transformed too, and wound up when all its units had been sold.

Deimos was soon converted into a joint stock company, wholly owned by the still state-owned Mars. The Director was confirmed in his position until the following year's Annual General Meeting of shareholders.

Employee ownership was still a high-profile issue. A separate section in the transformation plan elaborated the possibilities. An 'Employment and Social Plan' was also attached which envisaged maintaining the job of every employee, a 25 per cent increase in wages plus a so-called 'thirteenth-month salary', and continuing operations of 'social assets'. Later the leaders of the local union and the Workers' Council recorded in writing that they agreed to the proposed forms of employee ownership 'on the condition that various forms of acquiring ownership by employees taken together should make it possible for the employees to acquire majority interest'. At about this time the Responsible Politician assured a governing party politician in a letter that he supported the concept of decentralised privatisation and employee ownership by any means possible under the law, and that he had 'reminded the SPA of this task'. On Deimos' specific case, the Responsible Politician stated, 'I consider it most important to carry out an ESOP programme.' The importance attached to this issue is also indicated by the fact that a high-level SPA officer attended the workers' assembly at Deimos.

United ESOPs playing politics

In early summer 1993 the SPA approved the privatisation plan for Mars' companies. It was ready to accommodate bids from ESOP organisations. A public call for tenders was to offer 51 per cent of shares in Deimos, allowing bidders to use E-loan and compensation notes.

Meanwhile, a managerial contest began to arise within Deimos. A few weeks after its transformation, the two ESOP Organising Committees merged under the leadership of ESOP I Leader (ESOP Leader hereinafter). He had once belonged to, but fallen from, the so-called 'managerial reserve' of Mars; now he had become a man of influence and seemed to rely on political connections. However, a local party politician's request to replace Deimos' current Director was firmly rejected by the SPA. It was pointed out that the SPA's statutory obligations of promoting conciliation did not include political parties or their regional organs, and that it was the SPA's policy that the leader of an ESOP Organising Committee could not hold a top managerial position.

The now-united ESOP leaders, teamed with one of the functional directors, then presented the conflict within the firm. They blamed Mars' management for the unsuccessful privatisation process to date; yet, again this management was given an opportunity to manage the sale of the subsidiaries. They also attacked Deimos' Director who was said to intimidate them 'by making references to the banks' (note that the ESOP Organisation could not take a loan if the Director refused to allow the bank to register a mortgage on the firm's property). Fearing that in an open call for tenders the Director and his circle might submit a proposal that would be contrary to the ESOP's interests, they noted that he could obtain an unfair advantage from knowing the employees' offer. In addition, he was said to have monopolised discussions with state agencies, consulting firms, and banks. In their judgement, the top managements of Mars and Deimos were only pretending to co-operate, but 'they were in every possible way delaying, bargaining, and impeding, and they deprived the ESOP Organising Committee and the management at Deimos of the possibility of not only getting but also providing information [i.e. they prevented us from having our voice heard]'. The SPA official assigned to the Deimos case was also blamed for hindering the work of the ESOP. They also outlined an 'ESOP–management buy-out–Foreigner' plan. The ownership split would be worked out by a consulting firm which they hoped would be paid by the SPA 'since the employees cannot bear the costs of this'.

In a memorandum to the Responsible Politician, a high-level SPA official (the same one who was criticised by the ESOP) fended off the proposal, regarding it as 'all too messy and unacceptable to the SPA'. He believed that the ESOP Organising Committee did not really have specific plans for privatisation, 'except for one thing, namely that the incumbent director has to be replaced, and a person suitable to them has to be appointed'. The Responsible Politician requested that a reply be drafted for him 'on the basis of which the conflict cannot be intensified'. The ESOP and its manager-supporters were thus called 'to reach a consensus' with the Director until the soon-to-be-completed privatisation could put an end to the internal power contest, otherwise the implementation of employee ownership in any form might have been jeopardised. They were also reminded that the ESOP Organisation should 'operate according to the legal conditions, and take a position only on issues to which it is entitled to under the law'. The costs of an ESOP feasibility study were to be covered, within reasonable limits, by Deimos and not the SPA.

The ESOP Leader immediately wrote back to the Responsible Politician, thanking him for his help, and assuring him that they certainly adhered to the law. He also explained that they had declared their intention to acquire a majority stake in the company only to 'achieve [the goal] that the foreign investor's possible capital increase should be large enough to carry out the inevitable and urgent developments'. That is, if the ESOP acquired the majority of the existing shares, the foreign investor could obtain a majority position only by putting in a considerable amount of new finance. He noted that they had already contacted a foreign investor.

The ESOP Organising Committee prepared for the tender by commissioning a Consultant whose assignment was 'to harmonise a management buy-out with an ESOP acquisition', and 'to harmonise the outside investor's acquisition intent with the ESOP'. They also teamed up with a Foreign Holding, a possible investor, while their Consultant prepared an ESOP feasibility study.

Sale of majority stock

Towards the end of summer 1993, all was set for a call for tender for what was called in a newspaper 'one of the SPA's few remaining diamonds in the rough' owing to its high market share. But it was ripe for a major upgrade. The SPA's Advisor expected relatively easy privatisation and at least ten bids; later, a bidder said, 'the whole factory really is not much, but the local market is a big attraction'. Unlike other state-owned monopolies or near monopolies that had rapidly lost market share to foreign competition, Deimos' market share was not expected to change, because of anticipated local production of higher quality products.

First round of tender

A call for bids for 51 per cent of the shares was advertised. The first round was to serve the purpose of pre-qualifying the bidders on the basis of their business plans. In the second round they were to make a price offer.

The ESOP's feasibility study had been prepared by this time. Mars' State Commissioner, who evaluated it at the SPA's request, accepted all the conditions that were normally parts of ESOP deals, but objected to 'over-capitalising' the ESOP organisation since Deimos was expected to transfer a large amount to the ESOP organisation for good prior to the actual takeover, and to give an additional sum from its pre-tax profits. Basically, this transfer would have been the ESOP members' 'own contribution', a requirement for taking an E-loan.

Meanwhile, lobbying for the ESOP continued. The SPA updated a high-level official of the nationwide trade union on the developments, while the Responsible Politician reminded the SPA that 'Deimos' privatisation must be given topmost attention'.

In the first round of the tender, bidders whose offers were accepted included a Foreign Industrialist alone, the same Foriegn Industrialist in a consortium with a Hungarian Bank, and a Large Atlantic Company. A Domestic Investment Group was not invited to the second round. It included five people who had never been active in this specific industry. In response to the SPA's request to provide references, they referred to three industry experts who wanted to remain anonymous until the second round. The SPA considered a hostile takeover possible.

The ESOP–Foreign Holding consortium was disqualified because the SPA regarded the Foreign Holding as disreputable. It was allegedly a Western European firm, but the registration abstract attached to the bid indicated incorporation in a tax haven. For business reference, a name of a tiny foreign firm was given, 'completely unknown in international business' in the SPA's view. A consortium agreement, setting out the mutual obligations of the partners, was also missing from the bidding documents, contrary to the tender requirements.

A Disqualified Domestic Consortium could not proceed either, because of late submission. According to the minutes of the tender opening, its bid was received seven minutes past the official deadline. It is understood that the consortium also included some of the members of the company's existing management. They later objected to having been disqualified, arguing that they had submitted the bid just in time but by the time the receipt confirmation slip was filled in, it was already three minutes past noon. On the request of the SPA, the Advisor asserted that the consortium's dispatcher arrived late, adding that it was the representative of the ESOP–Foreign Holding group who, having just submitted their bid, called the Advisor's attention to the clock.

On the recommendation of the bid evaluation committee, which consisted of representatives of the SPA, the Advisor and Mars, the SPA offered the ESOP 20 per cent of the shares, out of the 49 per cent not put to tender this time, at a price equal to what the winner of the present tender was to pay. This implied not only that the employees would not be excluded from the acquisition because of having teamed up with a partner of questionable background but also that they would not have to compete with any other bidder. The proposal of the evaluation committee noted that offering the ESOP 20 per cent would most likely satisfy them, although it was probably clear to everyone that the ESOP leaders had been seeking a larger interest. This recommendation, thus, not only provided a favourable opportunity but at the same time limited the interest that the ESOP could, at least in principle, acquire. The bidders later considered legal action but gave up the idea when the SPA hinted that such a move might endanger the acquisition of even the 20 per cent stake offered outside the tender.

Some episodes occurring between the two rounds of the tender deserve mentioning. At the time of these debates, the Responsible Politician received some documents from an anonymous sender by fax which may reasonably be assumed to have served the purpose of strengthening the position of the Foreign Holding while attempting to discredit the Large Atlantic Company before the SPA. Deimos' contract with a small service-provider was revoked on the SPA's instruction because of suspected misdeed. The SPA also requested Deimos' Director to revise the contract with the ESOP's Consultant because of unjustified elements of its fee structure.

The ESOP once more sought support from Responsible Politicians. ESOP Leader and, on behalf of the MBO group, one of Deimos' functional directors stated that 20 per cent of the shares was not enough to attain their objectives, and asked for personal support so that they could buy the remaining 29 per cent of the stock on top of the 20 per cent which had been offered for sale to them. Interestingly, they referred to their 49 per cent minority position as a temporary state only, although their stated objective was to obtain the largest possible stake only for the purpose of encouraging any outside investor to put in a large amount of new finance. In another letter they stated that they were 'fighting a phantom battle', that is a fight against an invisible enemy in order to achieve employee ownership. In an attempt to share responsibility, they referred to previous encouragement they had received, which 'played an important role in the establishment of our ESOP organisation'. In other words, they claimed that they acted upon the instructions of their external supporters. They added, 'we cannot see why, despite successive promises and encouragement, there should be a phantom who continuously resists and hinders the rational [as interpreted by them] process, often with means beyond words'. They hoped the SPA would make it possible for them to acquire a 49 per cent interest which 'could be maintained for at least 1–2 years'. Note that holding a 49 per cent interest probably also implies one to two years' delay in achieving their alleged eventual objective, that is the implementation of a capital increase to finance developments.

On behalf of the original recipients of these letters, the SPA official assigned to the case drafted replies. The ESOP was condemned for having teamed up with an unacceptable partner; their judgement on the privatisation of the industry to date as catastrophic was rejected, as well as the insinuation that some sort of a phantom within the SPA would obstruct the ESOP's proposals.

Second round of tender

Invitations to make price offers were sent to the pre-selected bidders. The SPA's Advisor estimated a justifiable price of Deimos' shares in the region of 160–170 per cent of par value; 51 per cent of the registered capital was offered for sale, while 20 per cent was reserved for sale to the ESOP and 29 per cent was intended to be used for fulfilling the SPA's other duties. All three invited bidders submitted valid offers.

The joint offer of the Foreign Industrialist and the Hungarian Bank was disqualified because of its failure to meet some formal requirements. Foreign Industrialist's individual bid included not only a relatively attractive cash consideration and plans for developments but also a letter from representatives of Deimos' ESOP which assured him that 'We ... as representatives of the personnel and potential shareholders and partners would like to express our wish to co-operate with you.' The Large Atlantic Company's offer was less attractive and, depending on the result of a possible due diligence, reserved the right of withdrawal. Although only a few days before the SPA's decision the ESOP made one more attempt for a 49 per cent interest, Foreign Industrialist was announced to be the winner. The remaining 49 per cent of shares were taken from Mars to the SPA's portfolio; 20 per cent were to go within forty-five days to the ESOP at the same price, while the decision on the rest of the shares was postponed. At about the same time the Foreign Industrialist also won the tender for another subsidiary of Mars.

On the day of the SPA's decision the ESOP and MBO leaders reiterated their position. Claiming that the SPA administrator and the State Commissioner of Mars supplied the decision-makers with false information on their true intentions, they complained about 'an irrational lack of understanding' of their efforts. According to this letter, they wanted now to have a 49 per cent interest for five years instead of two as indicated earlier.

The SPA official dealing with Deimos' case was asked to draft 'a polite reply', including the SPA Board's decision of that day. The reply was sent without delay. Claims of an 'irrational lack of understanding' were denied, and the assignment of blame to SPA and Mars officials was firmly rejected.

The time had come to implement the SPA's decision. The Advisor prepared a draft agreement between the SPA and the ESOP, but the ESOP Leader and his deputy (once leader of ESOP II) informed the SPA that the ESOP could not take an E-loan because the Director had not provided a declaration on the company's guarantee for ESOP's debts. In this debate the SPA official supported Deimos' Director.

The Advisor also prepared a draft agreement with the Foreign Industrialist who then requested some modifications; most were accepted, allowing the Share Purchase Agreement to be concluded before the end of the year. Thus, Deimos became entitled to a tax holiday because of foreign ownership. The agreement upheld the investor's right to submit claims, should the information he had been given prove to be false. The SPA was to vote together with Foreign Industrialist on issues related to modifications of the Articles of Association and the sale of assets.

Sale of minority stock

In January 1994 the ESOP guarantee was further debated. The SPA reminded the Foreign Industrialist that pursuant to the agreement between them he was obliged to acknowledge and support the ESOP's acquisition of 20 per cent of the shares, and asked him to undertake a guarantee for the repayment of the ESOP's Existence Loan. The Foreign Industrialist was reluctant to do so, but the SPA pressed on. Meanwhile, Deimos' Director submitted a report to the Foreign Industrialist, in which he stated that the company urgently needed a large cash investment, and criticised his management methods. The SPA official later commented in an internal memorandum, that 'unfortunately some of the managers did not co-operate with the new majority owner'.

When the takeover was officially effectuated at an Extraordinary General Meeting of the shareholders in February, the ESOP Leader was appointed to the Board of Directors on the SPA's proposal, reflecting the expectation that the ESOP was soon to be a co-owner. At the same shareholders' meeting the Foreign Industrialist ensured his control with new appointments to the Board, but had to face the SPA's rejection of some of his proposals on changes in the Articles of Association. He then reminded the SPA that it should vote in support of him under the terms of the Agreement, and asked for time to become better informed before undertaking a guarantee for the ESOP.

The ESOP leaders had not given up their plan to get as many shares as might seem possible, and continued lobbying for their case. On the eve of the 1994 election, they wrote to an MP, and also requested an official investigation of the Deimos privatisation. Reflecting on past developments, it was recalled that 'we thwarted Mars' plans' by establishing an ESOP Organising Committee and submitting a claim to shares. In their view, Deimos' Director had immediately started a counter-action, which had aimed at discrediting the ESOP for eighteen months, and was supposed to have thwarted employee acquisition. 'Contrary to its promises of support', they believed the SPA's decisions had been repeatedly against the interests of the ESOP organisation, while 'the counter-interested lobby managed to achieve' the outcome that their foreign partner in the bidding, 'and thus the ESOP too', were excluded from the second round. They complained that 'information from the ESOP never reached those with decision-making competence, whereas for those who were counter-interested there was an open channel to those who were preparing the decisions'. The MP was asked 'to use [his] influence to help the employees acquire the remaining 29 per cent currently owned by the SPA'. Votes were offered in return: 'We are asking this not only to have an opportunity to influence our future by having an employee interest of 49 per cent but also for the reason that the voting of several thousand constituents belonging to [Deimos' employees] should not be accidental'. This letter was passed on four times down the hierarchy, only to reach the SPA official assigned to the case. The reply that the MP received to his enquiry stated that he had been asked for help 'on the basis of imprecise information'. The process of Deimos' privatisation to date was summarised from the SPA official's viewpoint.

Since the Bank insisted on having a guarantee from the company before providing the ESOP with an Existence Loan, the SPA was again asked to help, while a local union leader sought information on the matter of the ESOP guarantee from Mars' Commissioner. The Commissioner was 'unable to answer the questions' because that would require disclosure of the terms of the Agreement, which would be possible only with the Foreign Industrialist's permission.

In April 1994 the Foreign Industrialist submitted his proposal on dividends distribution to the SPA. His comments shed light on why he had been reluctant to provide the guarantee for the ESOP's loan. He claimed that he had been misinformed about the exact amount of funds that could be distributed, since, for example, overdue payments should have been disclosed. He proposed instead an increase of share capital, and a distribution of dividends a year later. The SPA sought advice from Mars' State Commissioner who agreed that distribution of the previously specified sum was impossible, but who also pointed at the Foreign Industrialist's interest in reinvesting profits instead of distributing dividends. He believed that the SPA could take advantage of the situation and strengthen its position in the debate about the Foreign Industrialist's support for the ESOP acquisition. The SPA then indicated its agreement with the proposal on postponing the distribution of dividends.

The Foreign Industrialist was not yet prepared to provide a guarantee; instead, he submitted to the SPA a statement he had made to Deimos' personnel: his support could be counted on if the employee shares thus obtained from the SPA 'can be offered for sale only to the Foreign Industrialist or the Foreign Industrialist Majority Company'. His support was also conditional on general relations between the employees and the owners.

The ESOP made an official offer for all the SPA shares in Deimos; they wished to acquire 20 per cent at the price the Foreign Industrialist had paid, and 29 per cent at par value, with all the usual discounts applied in combination. The Responsible Politician made a last attempt before the election to support them, asking whether at least 25 per cent + 1 vote was possible for the ESOP. Another Responsible Politician, once apparently in favour of ESOP ownership, noted that he did not 'really like it'. However, the SPA official drafted a reply to the Responsible Politician that not only regarded 25 per cent + 1 vote 'a proposal [that] can be realised without any problem', but asked him whether the sale of all the remaining 29 per cent to the ESOP should be proposed to the decision-makers. In another memorandum he noted that 'Foreign Industrialist is having discussions with an International Bank on a very important development' which seemed to be hindered by uncertainty concerning the final ownership structure.

However, the contract between the SPA and the ESOP was not yet to be concluded. Instead of providing a guarantee, the Foreign Industrialist announced his intent to acquire the remaining 29 per cent.

The Annual General Meeting of the shareholders took place in May 1994. It was preceded by a small dispute about the postponed dividends, while the Foreign Industrialist gave notice to the SPA that 'we have claims ... since when we took over [the company] ... we found the following conditions VERY DIFFERENT from the tender documents', referring to the less-than-expected cash to distribute, and worse-than-expected state of the machinery. Other claims under several headings were also formulated. The Foreign Industrialist also noted that three top managers 'appointed by SPA to Deimos to transfer the company to the private foreign investor were never present' after the takeover. He thus requested 'indemnification, the extent of which will depend on many factors'.

The Annual General Meeting was to be continued in June, since in the absence of the Foreign Industrialist's proposal on members of the boards, the SPA's representative had not been authorised to vote on these issues. Note that the appointment of Deimos' Director terminated as of the date of this shareholders' meeting.

Deimos' Local Union made an appeal to the SPA, protesting that the sale of 20 per cent of the shares had not been executed yet, thus 'the foreign owner in possession of a stock of 51 per cent controls Deimos Co. 100 per cent'. The morale had worsened further. They complained that 'we have not received many social and wage-like allowances to date although they are granted in the Collective Agreement, and the owner delays the discussions', adding that they did not intend to reinforce their requests with a strike – in effect, they were making a mild threat. (A Collective Agreement is made between an employer and employees; it usually specifies more favourable conditions to the workers than the standard rules of the labour law; if there is no Collective Agreement, labour law automatically applies.) The SPA's new official (who had replaced his colleague on this case when he had left for another state institution) argued to his superiors that 'the ESOP ... has not been given a bank guarantee', owing to the lack of support of the Foreign Industrialist. This, in turn, he attributed to conflicts between Deimos' management and employee representation organisations and the foreign owner. At the time of the takeover, the Director and a few of his colleagues immediately went on long sick leave, while the employee representatives acted offensively. He also provided a plausible reason for this tension when he pointed out that 'the foreign owner terminated the JGMs'. A JGM was a legal organisational entity, established by employees of a state-owned enterprise to carry out work in their free time by using the assets of the firm; they were paid by the firm under a contract; the legal predecessor of the JGM form had been devised to bypass wage restrictions that had applied in the communist era. Productivity of the company did not deteriorate; on the contrary it improved, but those participating in the JGM lost considerable extra income. The new SPA official also held discussions with representatives of the ESOP and Deimos' union. They asserted that they had been misled, because they had been promised that they would acquire the company. They had asked for 25 per cent + 1 vote. The new SPA official had requested them to co-operate with the foreign owner in the interest of the company.

Early summer 1994 was coloured by a false alarm on tax accruals. To the great surprise of the Foreign Industrialist, the Tax Office issued a notification that Deimos should have paid a 'dividend on state property' between 1991 and 1993 under then prevailing law. With interest and a penalty, the amount was indeed substantial. This decision was based on an incorrect interpretation of the law. Eventually the Tax Office admitted its fault; until then, however, the issue caused debate between the SPA and the Foreign Industrialist.

The Foreign Industrialist formally submitted a cash offer at par value for all the minority shares, or at least 29 per cent of the stock if the SPA insisted on giving the ESOP 20 per cent. The SPA acknowledged the offer but regretfully had to reject it, 'because the SPA doesn't have the authorization to sell a state holding bypassing tendering procedures'. Whether this rule should also have been applied to the planned ESOP acquisition was left unnoticed.

When the adjourned Annual General Meeting resumed, some issues could still not be resolved between the SPA and the Foreign Industrialist, apparently not because of lack of mutual understanding but only because of the need to adhere to formal requirements. Yet, this gave the Foreign Industrialist a further opportunity to re-submit his claim for indemnification. On the SPA's request, Mars' State Commissioner prepared counter-arguments, rejecting all of the claims. In return, the Foreign Industrialist sent the SPA notice of 'material breach of our contract' ahead of the reconvened Annual General Meeting, calling the SPA to vote with him on the modification of the Articles of Association as stipulated in their agreement. The SPA refused since it was stuck in its own regulations – it could not act contrary to the law and its earlier decisions – and tried to secure the possibility of selling shares to the ESOP organisation. The Foreign Industrialist was asked to understand the SPA's position, 'considering our excellent relations in the past and present'. The adjourned Annual General Meeting continued, but was then adjourned again.

At this time the Foreign Industrialist held discussions with a foreign bank about a large loan to finance planned developments in both Deimos and his other Hungarian acquisition. The SPA was afraid that if it forced the Foreign Industrialist to agree to ESOP ownership, the capital investment programme might suffer delay. They requested the ESOP to confirm interest in acquiring 20 per cent of the stock. The conflict between the Foreign Industrialist and the employees continued with a debate on the Collective Agreement; the atmosphere among Deimos' employees was described at the time as 'extremely bad ... [and] cannot go on like this for long!', while the ESOP confirmed its interest not only in this but also in acquiring as many shares as possible from the remaining 29 per cent of the stock.

By this time the ESOP acquisition enjoyed only half-hearted support. The Ministry, for example, agreed to it only if it was achieved in a way that 'Foreign Industrialist's interests are served'. They argued that 'considering the foreign majority-owner's plans to carry out major capital investment, special attention must be given to the issue of a possible sale of shares from the remaining 29 per cent to the ESOP, because the ESOP organisation might thus thwart the capital increase'. The SPA believed that the Foreign Industrialist was not against the ESOP acquisition *per se*, but he wanted to find a way of financing it which did not need the company to be involved in it as a guarantor.

The Foreign Industrialist was called to make a statement of his support for the ESOP. In case of failure to reach an agreement with him, the SPA approved that the ESOP could acquire 20 per cent of the shares by paying in instalments on conditions not worse than those of an E-loan. It was decided to offer the remaining 29 per cent for sale in an open tender for a 'cash only' price representing at least 135 per cent of the nominal value. With this decision the SPA in fact called Foreign Industrialist and the ESOP to submit competitive bids.

Towards the end of summer 1994, the new government's privatisation policy started to take shape, including the preference for cash over 'soft forms' of payment (those normally available to ESOP organisations), thereby indirectly strengthening the Foreign Industrialist's bargaining position. Apparently, he had been negotiating with the ESOP on how he could purchase shares from the employees after they obtained them from the SPA at a discount. By now, the ESOP was willing to co-operate.

The adjourned Annual General Meeting reconvened again and the SPA representative announced that a cash-only tender invitation would be advertised for 29 per cent of the stock at a set price; this practically meant the exclusion of the ESOP from the bidding. The conflicts between the Foreign Industrialist and the workers were also brought to the table, prompting the Foreign Industrialist to remark, '[this] issue is not on the agenda but we can listen to it'. He informed the SPA that workers received an amount 'as a bonus for presence and efficiency' but when he visited some of the units at 1.30 p.m. the day before, 'nothing was working'.

The once again adjourned Annual General Meeting reconvened in September, when an agreement with the ESOP had already been reached. The Foreign Industrialist expressed his appreciation to the ESOP for the co-operation, while the SPA representative noted that he did not expect any other bidder to the tender for the remaining 29 per cent, but if there were any, the Foreign Industrialist would have the right to match the offer. A few weeks later a Ministry official also reckoned that the only bidder would be the Foreign Industrialist, and commented with some irony that it would be quicker to 'simply give it to him'. This was certainly not possible under the law, which required the sale of state-owned shares to be sold through a tender procedure.

As soon as the SPA specified in writing what allowances were available to the ESOP for buying 20 per cent of the stock, the ESOP (now enjoying financial support from the Foreign Industrialist) specified the way they intended to finance the purchase of the shares. Combined with employees' discounts, they used compensation notes which were trading at the time far below face value but accepted by the SPA in privatisation deals at 'nominal value' (face value plus accumulated fixed-rate interest from the date of issuance). The SPA–ESOP share purchase agreement was soon concluded.

In October, the SPA prepared the call for tender, determined the asking price as 135 per cent of par, cash only. In fact, the SPA did exactly what the Ministry official remarked should be done, but in a legally acceptable way: the amount of the bid bond was set high enough to deter any bidder potentially interested in a minority stock. Not surprisingly, the Foreign Industrialist 'won' the tender. In the first few months of 1995, the ESOP's 20 per cent of the stock also changed hands, as had probably been agreed well in advance.

From December 1994, there was a new improvement every month at Deimos. An old production line, stopped years earlier, was put back in use again; new equipment was installed; new products were introduced; new plant and storage facilities were under construction; a workers' hostel was planned to be converted to a hotel. In total, investments amounted to several billion forints. All financial indicators showed improvements from 1993 through 1994 to the planned results for 1995; employment was slowly decreasing while production was increasing. The ISO 9001 quality standard was introduced and audited. Similar developments, although to a lesser extent, occurred in the Foreign Industrialist's other Hungarian acquisition. The two acquisitions were merged later in 1995.

5.5 Neptune: Delayed refashioning

'Neptune' was one of the largest firms in a certain branch of the apparel industry, operating across several plants, with headquarters in Budapest. Its sales to the Soviet Union had completely ended owing to the buyers' insolvency, and domestic sales had also decreased, partly because new firms had entered the market. By the early 1990s most of Neptune's production was exported to Western Europe and the USA, exclusively under long-term production contracts with Western firms (to the extent of almost 80 per cent of its total production capacity). Neptune did not sell own brands on Western markets, mainly because of the poor quality of materials from domestic sources. The industry had two seasons, autumn–winter and spring–summer. After a steady decrease in labour force, the number of employees totalled a couple of thousands in 1989 and continued decreasing. On assets of more than HUF 0.6 billion (US$ 10 million), the firm made moderate profits in 1989, but only just broke even in 1990. The management reasoned that this was partly due to a shift in market orientation, and partly due to a wage increase that had been effected following an agreement between the management and representatives of the workers in order to maintain the labour force.

The initiative

Preliminary talks on joint-venture opportunities with potential investors, mainly business partners, started in 1989, and an asset valuation was carried out. At the same time, 'Continental Investors' (two people, one a financial specialist and the other a renowned apparel industry expert) discussed business opportunities in the Western world and decided to seek an opportunity in Eastern Europe, with the focus on Hungary because of 'economic considerations, how safe [they felt], how skilled [the workers] were, [and] accessibility to the Western world'. They contacted various firms via a banker friend, and chose Neptune as a potential target. They were backed by a 'Financier' who was to provide most of the capital to invest when the opportunity arose.

In 1990, the incumbent top management established a limited liability company with a foreign buyer, and built a new plant in the town where one of Neptune's better performing plants was located. The new establishment lured half of the employees from Neptune's plant, and Neptune lost large orders. What remained was a plant without skilled workers, and without a buyer.

The next year witnessed the appointment of a new General Director (previously director in charge of economic matters). The management commissioned the 'Consultant', who was later to become advisor to the Continental Investors. Towards the end of the year, Neptune's Enterprise Council approved a transformation plan. Some members of the management wished to implement a management buy-out. Others believed that the firm needed a resourceful owner. This view came out as the winner, and a closed tender was planned. They hoped to attract investors who could put in new finance but would not buy existing shares. These, instead, could be acquired by the management and employees. One of the directors, and the vice-chairman of the Enterprise Council (who was to become the ESOP Chairman) were in favour of a management buy-out. The General Director and some others were against it: 'We were able to convince them that there is no other way. We just did not have the money.'

In late 1991 and early 1992 the management sent an information memorandum to business partners and others possibly interested in privatisation. After all this preparation, Neptune announced its transformation intent to the SPA and discussions began.

By this time, the Continental Investors had thoroughly investigated Neptune, and were ready to structure a deal. As one of them explained, 'We made an offer for Neptune because we thought we could reorganise the company, turn it into a profitable company and make money ... pure businessman approach.' The transaction they devised did not include any purchase of existing shares, but, rather, a capital increase and asset management of Neptune for three years, to be followed by flotation. In return for the investment and management services, they required a stock option, a share of profits, and 70 per cent of the capital gain upon eventual sale of shares. The business plan reflected the Continental Investors' declared turnaround strategy for Neptune. It included substantial capital investment to be spent on machinery, volume expansion, technological developments, and a new incentive system for workers. This proposal was conveyed to Neptune through the Consultant. The Continental Investors urged him to proceed with the negotiations as quickly as possible. They reasoned, 'We are aware of a number of similar privatisations in the apparel industry in other countries in the old Eastern Bloc which will increase the current overcapacity.' They also pointed out that Neptune was currently loss-making, which was further draining its reserves and affecting its cash flow. They wanted to be in management control of Neptune by the end of the summer at the latest.

The Enterprise Council reviewed the Continental Investors' offer and specified that employee ownership with the investors' financial support, and 'organisational integrity' were at the top of their priority list. Complying with the SPA's request, the Enterprise Council also approved an open (instead of the previously planned closed) call for tenders.

Investment tender

As a preparation for transformation and, eventually, privatisation, the valuation of Neptune's assets was updated in June 1992. The (new) Auditor believed that the assets had been overvalued earlier. With the

SPA's approval, Neptune's management advertised a call for tender, while they also sent an information memorandum directly to potential investors. Bidders who would inject fresh capital and undertake to 'support employee ownership from their own resources' were favoured.

They received two bids. One of them, which bid for only one plant, was disqualified, while the Continental Investors undertook to maintain employment, develop exports, double the value of the SPA's shareholdings, and implement sale or flotation within three years.

The amount they placed on Neptune was subject to adjustments. The Continental Investors would have complete control under a management agreement until flotation or sale. No dividends would be paid until then. They would provide new machinery in three years, for which they would be allocated newly issued shares at par equal to the value of the equipment. In return for management services they would receive each year an allotment of existing shares at par. Upon sale or flotation, they would receive a further 50 per cent of the SPA's capital gain on the sale of existing shares. An employee trust would acquire 5 per cent of the SPA's shares, and the investors would provide half of the necessary funds to facilitate this acquisition. The trust would also have an option to acquire a further 10 per cent of SPA's shares. Conditions included that the deal be concluded in a couple of months, an audit be carried out by an internationally recognised firm, and the value placed on Neptune be reduced by any undisclosed liabilities, and by losses incurred since the end of 1991. The crux of the Continental Investors' business plan was 'to double production with the same labour force' and to achieve considerable pre-tax profits.

All the relevant parties seemed to welcome the Continental Investors' offer. When the Enterprise Council approved Neptune's transformation plan, it already included parts of the Continental Investors' offer and business plan, although higher employee ownership was envisaged. The Ministry agreed to transforming Neptune into a joint stock company, and agreed with the Auditor that the assets had earlier been overvalued, compared to the firm's actual market value. Neptune reported a loss for the first half of 1992. The SPA Administrator assigned to the Neptune case was in favour of the offer, too. As he argued, the firm was in the red for the first time since it had been established, and its financial position was rapidly deteriorating. 'Without a quick implementation of privatisation, the threat of bankruptcy will arise.'

The SPA thus accepted the bid and approved Neptune's transformation. This turned out to be the beginning of a lengthy negotiation that was 'ludicrous' and took 'longer than it should have', according to a Continental Investor. As he reflected,

The company was losing money. When a company goes through this process [of privatisation], it's in a sort of abeyance ... They needed ... rapid surgery ... It was the privatisation process [which took] time; this time was extended because we didn't get the contract. Basically, the company was 15–16 months in the course of being privatised. And it drifted because of that, because of lack of investment in many previous years, ... because the company didn't think it could make changes.

Negotiations

Neptune's General Director reported to SPA in October that 'the value of the company's own capital has decreased' by a considerable amount. He argued that owing to the lack of financial resources there had been no significant development in the previous three to four years, thus they could not increase the production volume, and for this reason they had run into the red in the first eight months of 1992. Because of problems with product quality, they had to concentrate all their efforts on trying to keep their existing markets and avoiding necessary lay-offs. The logic was that once privatisation occurred, increasing output would require the same staff, which therefore had to be kept even at high cost. The General Director also emphasised that the firm was in a very difficult situation, particularly with respect to its cash flow and indebtedness, and added that the investors had indicated their willingness to put in new finance. He asked the SPA to decide fast. Later an Enterprise Council member also urged the SPA to make a quick decision, using almost the same words and arguments as the General Director.

The asset valuation was again updated, and approved by the SPA, while negotiations with the Continental Investors continued. As an SPA official explained, 'The negotiations have been successfully concluded, but in the meantime the firm's economic conditions have been further deteriorating. [Thus], the investors ... wished to modify their offer.' The subsequent negotiations resulted in a compromise. The revised offer included lower registered capital of the company to be established by way of transforming Neptune, lower investment, lower capital reserve, some dividends from 1994, and a higher management fee. The SPA official supported this claim of the investors. After allowing for his very bureaucratic style, what he may have been trying to say in a progress report was something like this: Neptune is in deep trouble. We tried to get a better deal but couldn't. Either we give it to the Continental Investors who, in all probability, can turn it around, or Neptune will go bankrupt.

In early 1993, an SPA official took the view that the SPA's earlier decision on the acceptance of the offer was based on incomplete and incorrect information. More precisely, he claimed that his colleague had not presented correctly and thoroughly the Continental Investors' offer to the decision-makers. According to the Consultant, this claim was not true: the representation of the offer was correct, partly because he himself had actively been involved in its writing, thus helping a newcomer to the SPA who really 'did not understand' the way the offer was structured. The Consultant believed that the SPA official had probably just wanted to improve the SPA's position, but he could not say that the decision-makers 'had been stupid, that's why he took on' his colleague. However, he could not improve the SPA's position because 'Neptune was indeed on the verge, there was indeed no other buyer, and the Continental Investors insisted.' The Consultant's experience was that 'the more complicated you make it, the slower it will get through ... but the cheaper it will be'. Later the case was placed under the authority of another SPA official, who 'negotiated hard, too, and hesitated ... but ... did not want to thwart the planned deal altogether [as the previous SPA official seemed to]'. A Continental Investor's view corresponds:

we made a firm, clear, distinct offer. This was accepted. The SPA then tried on three occasions to change the rules, to change the terms ... [T]hey didn't understand the deal very well ... [because of] lack of expertise, [and because of] inexperience ... and they were losing their option because the company was going into a decline. [To sum it up,] They [the SPA] paid quite dearly for the delay [because] the company continued to lose money ... basically at the expense of the SPA.

Make deal or no deal

In the first few months of 1993, letters from the Consultant, the investors and their lawyer, the General Director, Neptune's ESOP Leader and the local union leader urged the SPA to make a decision. They argued that 'The process has been proceeding so slowly ... that it now risks not only the privatisation but also the very existence of the firm', owing to continued losses, a deteriorating financial position, and because 'The firm's most important partner ... has announced that unless the firm is privatised within a reasonable time, it will terminate its co-operation with the firm, since it cannot see that ... quality problems will be [solved otherwise].' The investors gave emphasis to their words: 'UNLESS THE CONTRACT IS FINALISED ... OUR OFFER WILL BE IRREVOCABLY WITHDRAWN', and if Neptune lost its contract with the partner, 'we would not take over the business EVEN IF YOU GAVE IT TO US FOR NOTHING'. All the other letters referred to Neptune's business partner who was considering terminating business. This was a concerted effort to push the deal through as one of the investors explained later: 'The pressure [on the SPA] was orchestrated because it was in everybody's interest that this deal was done.' The investors believed that, viewing the situation at the national level, the price was much less important than other sides of the issue: jobs, exports, a huge contribution to the social security budget. Although the business partner was indeed asked to put its complaint in writing so that it could be shown to the SPA, the problems existed regardless. However, according to the General Director, it was unlikely that it would actually terminate business with Neptune.

Regarding other forms of pressure, a leader of the national union was also enlisted to lobby for the deal. A National Bank executive, once colleague of the Consultant, also argued for the deal at the SPA. However, both the General Director and the Consultant noted that 'there was no political influence'.

While discussions dragged on, the Continental Investors declared they had no objection to employee ownership, while a Bank was willing to consider providing an Existence Loan for employee acquisition. An ESOP Feasibility Study was prepared, and attuned to the Continental Investors' offer; it aimed at the acquisition of the whole SPA stock from E-loan. When the SPA again attempted to improve its position by limiting the Continental Investors' interest obtainable under the management agreement, the investors were willing to make concessions, but only in favour of the employees. They suggested that the ESOP should be allowed 'to acquire the SPA's holding in Neptune. If, and only if, this happens would we then be prepared to renegotiate' some elements of the deal. In a letter to the Consultant, one of the Continental Investors explained,

If he agrees then, given the circumstances, [the SPA official in charge] will have won big concessions for the SPA and I cannot see how anyone could criticise him. If he doesn't then, it won't help us ['and the firm's employees', added the Consultant in the Hungarian translation which he forwarded to the SPA] but I understand that there will be a big political storm.

The agreement and the adjustment

Although there was a view within the SPA that the offer should be rejected, it was overruled by the decision-makers. According to one SPA official, who apparently based his evaluation on a direct comparison of the firm's asset value and the amount of new finance provided by the investors, 'they would acquire a major firm with a relatively small investment'. Others reached a different conclusion.

Meanwhile, a joint ESOP–Continental Investors offer was being prepared, combining Continental Investors' original offer and an ESOP acquisition of existing shares, and including some concessions to the SPA. An addendum to the investors' original business plan revised the timetable within which certain objectives were to be achieved, since they had expected a faster completion of the privatisation process and had not taken into account the substantial losses in 1992. 'The basic plan has been set back at least eight months' with the result that 'it will not be possible to influence marketing and sales or to introduce our own product range in 1993 as we have missed the spring selling season for autumn deliveries. Furthermore, the whole capital expenditure pro- gramme and the reorganisation of the company has inevitably been delayed.'

The time to sign the share subscription and syndicate agreement (the Agreement hereinafter) between the SPA and the consortium of the investors and the ESOP came in April 1993. Neptune transformed, retrospectively, into a joint stock company, and the investors acquired about a 30 per cent interest in the firm, which was to increase because of the stock option under the management agreement. The SPA's holdings were to be reduced by the amount of the audited losses in 1992 (the Adjustment hereinafter), and eventually sold to the ESOP.

The official closing day of the contract was not until June. According to an interviewee, this privatisation process consisted of two phases: when the SPA was delaying it, and when the firm and the investors were delaying it. The SPA did so by raising objections against the structure of the deal, and the company did so by insisting on an audit to be carried out according to international accounting standards. Because of the delay caused by the SPA, the company and the investors missed one of the new seasons; for them, it was an objective to start business under new management at the beginning of a season.

During the summer, the investors subscribed to new stock and took control of management. They introduced changes quickly: the first new piece of equipment was installed within a few weeks. Except for the General Director, who kept his title but became subordinated to an active Chairman and a President, managers were dismissed before the end of the year. According to the Consultant, 'The main problem of Neptune has always been that the top management was bad. It is not good even now', after the takeover, as the Continental Investors were acting as top managers. Before we outline changes that the new owners brought about in Neptune's operations and management, it is timely here to discuss some developments related to the Adjustment that were to modify the ownership split of Neptune.

As stipulated in the Agreement, an auditor completed a report on the amount of the Adjustment by which the SPA's interest in Neptune was to be reduced. The Auditor calculated the firm's net asset value (according to international accounting rules) as of 31 December 1992, after taking account of the loss for the year then ended, and compared it to the net asset value (Hungarian accounting) a year before. The difference was considered to be the amount of losses in 1992, that is the Adjustment. The SPA's interest was further to be reduced by the stock to be transferred to municipalities. What was left could now be offered by tender to the ESOP organisation.

The SPA accepted the Auditor's report. A resolution of the extraordinary shareholders' meeting of September 1993, and an agreement between the SPA and Neptune then prescribed that the firm's registered capital was to be decreased, against the SPA's stake, by the amount of the Adjustment. Technically, the SPA would transfer shares free of charge, which the company would take into its treasury; these shares would then be cancelled. To comply with the Hungarian law, which limited the stock that could be held in treasury, the transaction was divided into two parts.

It appears that the consequences were not all clear to everyone. While a hand written marginal note asked, 'The SPA will remain 50 per cent owner, won't it?', in fact, the SPA was to hold about 30 per cent after the Adjustment, and even less following an increase of the registered capital to be approved a few months later.

Three-party conflicts

Events in the next period revolved around conflicts between the SPA, the ESOP Chairman, and the company (including the investors). The question was how much was the ESOP stake, and in how much registered capital?

At about this time, the Consultant was acting as Neptune's director in charge of economic matters. Rereading the Accounting Act he noted that redemption of the shares concerned would give rise to tax liability which they wanted to avoid. However, the agreement they had already made with the SPA required this share redemption, with all its consequences. The investors and the management then thought they would just wait until they could sort out this problem with the ESOP as co-owner, instead of the SPA. They did not anticipate that it would drag on for long.

However, the call for the 'ESOP tender' was postponed several times, making it necessary to deal with the SPA in the matter of share redemption. According to an SPA staff member, the investors attempted to have the resolution of the previous shareholders' meeting cancelled, but there were no certified minutes on this issue. The General Director asserted, however, that 'The SPA voted for the proposal [to cancel the resolution], too.'

After several postponements the SPA called a tender for its shares. Only Neptune's ESOP made a bid, but the tender was declared unsuccessful because a bid bond had not been deposited. Whether it should have been provided prior to, or could have been deposited subsequent to, the submission of the bid, was a question viewed differently within the SPA. Nevertheless, the bid included only a note that the company would deposit the bid bond if necessary.

Other factors also hindered the ESOP acquisition. The Bank provided a promissory note, but required considerable guarantees from the company in return for an Existence Loan for the ESOP. Providing such guarantees, however, 'would have jeopardised the company's own chances to take a loan which it wanted to do for modernisation purposes', as an executive reflected. They did not want to take this risk at a time when they had been holding discussions with an International Bank to finance a large loan for further developments, and when the results of the investment and new management had already started to manifest themselves.

Although Neptune made some losses over the whole year 1993, these were partly inherited from the pre-privatisation period, and were partly due to restructuring costs which could not yet be compensated by the increase in sales. From the time of the investors' taking it over in the middle of the year, Neptune's weekly output increased, considerable sums were spent on new machinery, the production process was restructured, quality improved, the labour force reduced, productivity and wages rose, and the firm opened a large new apparel products retail outlet. Also, one of Neptune's plants was sold as it was considered nonviable by the management. (The plant sold now was the same one that went into decline in 1990 after the previous management had established a limited liability company with a foreign partner.) The General Director praised the achievements: 'Survival was at stake. Without them ... we would be bankrupt by now. Apart from a car for [the chief executive], all the money was spent on machinery [and equipment which] were new ones.' Changes started to infiltrate the organisation. As one of the investors observed, '[modernisation] needed discipline, ... we invested ... quite a lot, it needed a big cultural change, ... [my partner] started [work at] six o'clock, suddenly [the workers] saw the chief executive on the factory floor, at six o'clock!' This cultural change was said not to have been without difficulties. According to the General

Director, 'Workers complain that [the chief executive] shouts. Of course, but first he asks, and shows personally how to do it. He then leaves, turns around, and they just don't do it that way.'

A second 'ESOP tender' was advertised in early 1994 for the SPA stock, which represented about 30 per cent of the registered capital, a smaller proportion than had been offered for sale earlier, owing to the Adjustment. The ESOP, as the only bidder, indeed made an offer, based on its agreement with the investors and the company on how to finance the acquisition of the SPA shares. They were offering 120 per cent of par value according to their calculation, but the SPA later pointed out that the net present value of the offer represented less than 110 per cent. Payment was to be made in compensation notes and could be effected in instalments with an interest rate of 7 per cent (that of an Existence Loan), thus combining the advantages of various forms of preferential payment. This combination was later considered to be legally acceptable. The idea of taking an Existence Loan from the Bank had been dropped because it would have placed too much liability on the company's assets. Instead, the Continental Investors undertook that Neptune would provide the ESOP with the necessary money at a fixed interest rate, subject to reductions if the Board of Directors was satisfied with the performance of the ESOP members. Until the ESOP repaid its debt to Neptune, the company would have a charge over the ESOP shares.

Before the announcement of the tender results, an extraordinary share-holders' meeting took place. The SPA vetoed the investors' proposal to increase the registered capital, since it would reduce the relative size of the SPA stock now being offered for tender. According to an SPA report, this was 'to the great astonishment' of the investors who reminded the SPA of the obligation it had undertaken in the syndicate agreement that it should vote along with them. The SPA's lawyers insisted: the SPA could not approve the capital increase until the tender was closed. In addition, as it was later emphasised, the Agreement clearly stated that the SPA indeed agreed to vote along, but the exceptions included the matter of raising or reducing the registered capital of the company. The management, however, believed that the true reason for the objection was not legal subtleties but something else. 'Actually, they did not dare to take responsibility for the fact that they had agreed to an increase of the registered capital to be subscribed by the Continental Investors which was decreasing the ESOP chunk.' Apparently, the SPA took a cautious approach but the reason why it did so became apparent only later.

The extraordinary shareholders' meeting was reconvened with the same agenda. The issue of increasing the registered capital remained a sensitive one, prompting the SPA to seek the ESOP's reaction to such a move in advance. The ESOP declared that if they won the tender, they would agree to the increase in the registered capital. The only objection came from the ESOP Chairman who was overruled by the six other trustees. The SPA thus probably felt safe voting for the proposal. Some thought the ESOP was under considerable management influence.

After the ESOP Chairman had submitted a proposal, offering 80 per cent of par for the shares, payable in compensation notes at the time of concluding an agreement, the SPA declared the tender unsuccessful on the same day. However, it also decided to offer the stock to the ESOP 'outside the tender process on the basis of the terms and conditions' proposed by the ESOP Chairman, who then confirmed that the ESOP wanted to take the opportunity. Apparently, both the ESOP Chairman's offer and SPA's decision to declare the tender unsuccessful but to offer the stock to ESOP were the results of a preceding agreement between the parties. The stock offered for sale now represented less of the registered capital, some 20–25 per cent. The percentage that the SPA stock represented of Neptune's registered capital at this time differed in two distinct documents. Keeping an up-to-date account of its shareholding had apparently proved a difficult task for the SPA throughout the process. Bookkeeping was not a strength of Neptune either, as the Auditor's report indicated later.

Preparing for the forthcoming Annual General Meeting, the management made a new proposal on the issue of decreasing the registered capital because of the Adjustment. As one of the Continental Investors recalled, they had taken only legal advice, but had not been 'advised by [the] Auditor [that] if we cancel the shares we will incur tax liability ... So when we realised this, we said 'we don't cancel them, we distribute them in specie' [according to the current ownership split, leaving it practically unchanged; yet the] SPA got so excited about this.' The Auditor, the Hungarian arm of a foreign firm, was later replaced by one of the largest international accounting firms. The SPA's excitement was also due to its realisation that the company had not yet registered the resolution of the September 1993 shareholders' meeting to decrease the registered capital. Soon it had another problem to deal with.

When the investors and the General Director declared that the company would provide the ESOP with the necessary funds by not later than 31 October 1994 to purchase compensation notes to be used in paying for the SPA shares, the ESOP Chairman was able to submit a draft agreement to the SPA accordingly. The SPA revised the draft so that it would be entitled to half of the profits made on any possible resale of ESOP shares. When all seemed set for a quick conclusion of an agreement, the ESOP Chairman suddenly requested an explanation from the SPA as to why the proportion of stock offered to the ESOP had decreased. He was a mechanical engineer by profession, and had once acted as vice-president of the Enterprise Council. In 1993 he had run for a directorship, but had not been supported by the General Director, who considered him a great mechanic but less likely to be a great manager. The ESOP Chairman now insisted on obtaining the original proportion of the voting rights, as offered in the tender, and required a detailed presentation of Neptune's ownership split 'because it is unclear, cannot be legally followed, and financially is almost incomprehensible to us'. This was what the SPA had been afraid of when it did not agree to an increase in Neptune's registered capital earlier. With a hint at possible 'invisible privatisation transactions behind the open tender', the ESOP Chairman demanded a copy of the syndicate agreement with all its appendices and amendments.

According to the Consultant's explanation, the ESOP Chairman may have been playing a defence strategy. The company's Chairman, himself an expert and actively involved in running day-to-day operations, decided to close a unit in the capital for pure efficiency reasons and wanted to move this line of operations to another plant where labour was abundant. What he did not know was that the ESOP Chairman worked in the unit to be shut down. Neither did he discuss his relocation plan with other executives who could perhaps have warned him. Recognising the threat, the ESOP Chairman devised his defence. If he was dismissed, he would take the company to the labour court (arbitrating disputes between employers and employees). He would make the affair appear as if his dismissal was not due to a simple decision to increase efficiency, but because he was the ESOP Chairman who did not want to lay down for the Continental Investors.

We did not know why he had gone mad. He did not know that we did not know [the reason for his behaviour]. He threatened the SPA ... The SPA got worried, but they didn't tell us that they were scratching [slang: meaning approximately, 'making a fuss'] because of the ESOP Chairman. Nobody knew why the other was [making a fuss]. In the end, it was all ulcerated [meaning, approximately, 'a big mess'].

The company had good reason to try and settle the problem, since a public action could have disclosed that it had not redeemed the shares and that the amount of the Adjustment might also become subject to reconsideration. The ESOP Chairman's mistake was that 'he prepared a report for the SPA which [a company executive] received in writing'.

The Annual General Meeting of shareholders was adjourned because the SPA had not received sufficient information on some issues. Owing to 'extremely chaotic conditions' that were attributed to the lack of accounting personnel, the Auditor could not approve the company's balance sheet and profit and loss statement, which were then submitted to the Registration Court with amendments and a suspending clause. The clause pertained to the registered capital of the company since Neptune had not entered the free transfer of the stock from the SPA in its books. The Auditor also pointed out that the losses of 1992 had already been written off and thus could not justify a free transfer of shares from the SPA to the company. The choice for the SPA at this point was between accepting that Neptune would not decrease its registered capital, despite the Agreement and the resolution made in September 1993, and keeping to its previous decisions and forcing Neptune to execute what had been decided.

During the summer a limited liability company appeared as a co-owner of Neptune; its shareholding was equal to the second part of the amount of the Adjustment, and lower than the amount requiring the approval of the shareholders' meeting. It is understood to have been a technical manoeuvre, made necessary by legal provisions prohibiting a company having more than 30 per cent of shares in treasury. It was planned, and in due course implemented, that the shares thus 'deposited' in this vehicle would be bought back at a nominal price and distributed among the shareholders in specie as soon as the ESOP deal was finished, without having to negotiate with the SPA.

When the ESOP Chairman pressed on, an SPA executive urged his colleagues to 'try and close' the matter. The ESOP Chairman soon received a letter that requested him to do his best to conclude the transaction, or the whole issue of the ESOP acquisition would have to be reconsidered by the SPA.

While this tug-of-war continued, the SPA spotted in the Board's report on 1993 that the company had sold one of its units and believed that its approval should have been sought for this because of the amount involved. For this reason it was suggested that the SPA should not accept the Board's report. The investors argued that payment for the unit was made in instalments, each instalment within the authority of the Board, and not that of the shareholders' meeting (including the SPA). However, the SPA based its opinion on the standardised Deed of Foundation because it had not received Neptune's actual one. 'We knew our rules better than they did', said a company executive. The discretionary limit of the Board was higher than the SPA had assumed, since it was specified not as a percentage of Neptune's registered capital (as it usually was in the standard SPA version) but as a percentage of its 'own capital' (registered capital plus capital reserve). There were objections to voting for Neptune's board's proposals within the Ministry, too, with the

Ministry suspecting 'manipulation of the company's capital' which adversely affected minority interests. Contrary to the SPA's objections, the reconvened general meeting approved the Board's proposals.

The SPA considered the possibility of legal action in order to have the resolution of the general meeting declared null and void, since it believed that the balance sheet, with a suspending clause, could not have been lawfully approved. It did file a suit, but more than a year later the legal process was still suspended.

Clearing up

In an attempt to try and obtain a clear picture of the changes in the registered capital, the SPA requested the company's Supervisory Board to prepare a report. Meanwhile, the ESOP Chairman complained that the company was not willing to cover the ESOP's legal expenses. The investors and the General Director explained that it was only a misunderstanding, 'since the company has done all in its capacity so that the employees can be owners'. To that end, they were also 'willing to pay an acceptable fee to any legal firm that is competent and experienced, and thus able to properly inform the ESOP'. An ESOP lawyer who could not speak foreign languages, did not have experience in company law, and wanted to charge a certain percentage regardless of the results was not acceptable to them. Next time a renowned international law firm was commissioned to assist the ESOP.

The Supervisory Board's Chairperson comforted the SPA. He had consulted with the General Director, and obtained a written statement from Neptune's lawyer. According to the information thus received, Neptune did submit the minutes of the general meeting of September 1993 within the legally required period to the Registration Court. This certainly does not mean that the resolution was executed and the shares cancelled.

The investors made an effort in September 1994 to solve all outstanding issues with the SPA in a letter that reviewed past developments and current difficulties. They regarded the Neptune case as 'probably one of the most successful privatisations in Hungary' on the basis that a well-established Hungarian company and its trained labour force had been combined with the capital and the marketing and management skills of foreign investors. Reviewing the progress the company had made since the takeover, they referred to the installation of new machinery, increasing production volume, quality improvement to an extent that 'not only do we no longer have complaints from customers, but we have managed to increase our prices significantly', a wage increase, the opening of new retail outlets, export achievements, etc. However, 'besides the successes the company also has to face serious problems'. Owing to the accumulated losses and the cost of the reorganisation and the expansion of the business, there were short-term liquidity problems which they solved by advancing a loan to the company. Similarly, they were funding further investments in machinery and equipment without changing the shareholding structure of the company.

Turning to their relations with the SPA, they remarked that 'unfortunately there have been misunderstandings ... due to the lack of communication between the parties'. Particularly, these misunderstandings included the issue of the reduction of share capital. The fact that the company did not cancel the shares was said to be purely a technical breach of the agreement with the SPA, made in the best interest of the shareholders and the company, which resulted in damage to no-one. The SPA's veto on the increase of share capital, on the other hand, did cause damage to the company.

However, the most important problem was that the privatisation had not been completed. The Continental Investors pointed out that despite the SPA's contractual obligation to sell its shares to the ESOP, the ESOP's two tender offers had been rejected. Employees were thus held in uncertainty about their ownership, and the company could not benefit from the incentive effects of employee ownership.

In reply, the SPA urged the ESOP Chairman to send their version of the contract. While the ESOP Chairman had been attributing the delay to the company's reluctance to provide finance for the share purchase, the SPA believed otherwise. The investors had already made it clear, when the SPA made its decision, that they would not have the money to lend to the ESOP available until the autumn. The SPA decided not to withdraw but to hold out until the ESOP could execute the acquisition. Before the actual ESOP acquisition, however, several developments took place that are worth reporting.

Towards the end of 1994 a new position of Chief Executive Officer (CEO) was created, reporting to the Board. The General Director now reported to the CEO, which position was filled from outside. According to the General Director, the CEO became 'the real boss'. The Financier was said to have lost his patience and wanted to see gains on his investment. To some extent, delays in producing expected results may have been due not only to the protracted privatisation process but also to the managerial incompetence of the Continental Investors. They were said to have been 'in effect fired already' as executives of the company, although they formally stayed with the firm because any dismissal would cast a shadow on the planned flotation. 'The [new] CEO runs it, because they [the Continental Investors] could not achieve what they were expected to' is how the General Director described the situation. The Consultant saw several reasons for the investors' managerial failure. He believed that 'the firm is too big for them, it is Hungarian, and it is spread all over [in several plants]. They could not oversee it.' There was an element of human relations with the mostly female workforce, too: 'They [workers] dislike them [foreign executives]. The new CEO doesn't make such mistakes, although he doesn't go down to the shopfloor either ... but he is not so bad at human relations.'

Problems were also witnessed at the second level of management. Between 1993 and 1995, Neptune had several directors in charge of economic matters. The one who held the position at the time of the Agreement was dismissed because of apparent incompetence. The Consultant took over for a short period at the end of 1993 and found that 'almost nothing was true in the books', simply because of lack of expertise. Then the General Director did the job, moonlighting: 'he worked 24 hours a day and could straighten things out more or less'. However, the Consultant believed that the investors 'did not accept [the General Director] because he doesn't speak the language, but they knew they needed him to console the people's spirit. He doesn't have many places to go at his age; he labours through.' Two others followed, one senior and one freshly graduated. According to the Consultant, neither of them knew the profession well. 'Continental Investors appreciated the fact that they could speak the language. But they are not willing to pay for a proper man. And they will not get a proper financial manager for this money.' Later the job was again given for some time to the General Director, whose latest position was Personnel Director.

Neptune closed the year 1994 with profits of a size that could also have been represented as losses; according to the Consultant, it was purely creative accounting. In early 1995, the contract between the ESOP and the SPA was eventually signed. The company immediately lent the ESOP the necessary money, the shares were bought, and they were put in the company's safe as a guarantee for the loan. Reflecting on the ESOP, the General Director 'very much regretted it'. At the time they thought 'ESOP was important as an incentive to the workers, but it took longer than the privatisation itself'.

Soon afterwards the ESOP Chairman left Neptune for another firm, but officially still held his title and thus could attend the Annual General Meeting in May 1995. It did not go without a hitch. The ESOP Chairman was said to have stated 'in front of everyone that the balance sheet is incorrect, the ESOP will go to court', and to have managed to take the whole general meeting in such a direction that his agenda would be discussed seriously. The General Director described him as 'a bell-wether' of the flock and compared his position to that of a local party or union leader.

It is only he who counts, the others only give him power by legitimacy. Workers view the ESOP as a representative of their interest [like a union] and choose the loudest [person]. He probably thought that the ESOP Chairmanship meant power that he could not obtain elsewhere.

The issue of distributing the treasury shares in specie among the share-holders instead of cancelling them was once again brought before the Annual General Meeting, which confirmed the cancellation of the September 1993 resolution and now approved the distribution. The SPA, having already sold its shares to ESOP, was no longer a shareholder,and apparently just 'forgot about it', as the General Director commented.

The conflict with the ESOP Chairman was about to end in late summer 1995, when the ESOP members officially elected a new leader. Although a company executive was sure that they would win the case should the ESOP Chairman decide to enter an action, it would have been 'expensive and bad PR'. In the end, he was said to have been given compensation.

Reflecting on the whole process, a Continental Investor believed it was a 'model privatisation'. 'The company would have gone bust by now'; instead, in 1995, Neptune was making profits; wages were up by 26 per cent in the first half of the year; exports were rising; its largest foreign buyer – once said to want to terminate the relationship – accepted an 18 per cent price increase 'because we are indeed better'; flotation was postponed in the spirit of 'taking the long-term view'. However, if they were 'starting again two years ago, we would have made much firmer and quicker moves to get it [the company]' so as to implement changes earlier. The General Director also regarded this privatisation as a success. Although the proceeds to the SPA were modest, 'the budget should eventually benefit from corporate tax'. However, 'with the benefit of hindsight, I would be firmer, and lay off people even before the Continental Investors came in ... And I would think of myself more – I don't mean money, just to get the same result with less personal effort.' Finally, the Consultant believed, 'With a good top management, the results would be even 30–40 per cent higher.'

5.6   Venus: Fading beauty

'Venus' was created as an industry-wide concern with headquarters in Budapest during a centralisation campaign in the early 1960s. It had once been the only domestic producer of a wide range of consumer products, and its market position was protected from import competition. Venus had several plants, all but one in the capital, and a separate R&D establishment. Venus also produced licensed products, and had a joint-venture with a Western firm. Its labour force amounted to more than 1,500 in 1990. Exports were less than 10 per cent of total sales of several billion forints, on which the firm made pre-tax profits of a few hundred million. Short-term loans exceeded half a billion, but the firm's financial position was still stable.

By the beginning of the 1990s, the firm's market share had decreased dramatically, to a (still remarkable) 40–50 per cent from an earlier 80–90 per cent (for the average of its main product groups), most importantly because of import liberalisation and subsequent market penetration by Western companies with enormous expenditures on advertising. Some domestic competitors' new brands had also overcome Venus' positions, mainly in the upper segments of the market.

Venus was run by the General Director from 1990, when his predecessor retired. In September 1990 the Enterprise Council confirmed him in the position. During this year other members of the top management were also replaced owing to retirements.

The management's initiative

Authorised by the Enterprise Council, the management announced their transformation intent to the SPA in October 1990. Asset valuation was already under way, and they had already had preliminary talks with potential investors. The management believed that Venus needed additional resources in order to stop further decline, to modernise machinery, to develop quality and packaging, and to keep up with increasing competition. Following investment, environmental problems could also be alleviated, particularly in Venus' Least Advanced Plant whose production was ordered by the municipality to be halted by the end of the year because of pollution. Venus had no resources to move to another site; the deadline was later extended and the plant remained operational for several years. What the management hoped to achieve by transformation and subsequent privatisation was to draw on resources with which it could implement its business plans. On the SPA's request the management additionally submitted a report on their previous talks. Among those interested in an investment were foreign firms and Expander (known already from the Mercury case). Discussions with an American Institutional Investor were soon terminated because the management reckoned it placed too low a value on Venus. A Diversified Global Leader (DGL), one of whose brands Venus produced, intended to establish a joint-venture based on only one product line. The management proposed acquisition of shares after transformation instead. A Major German Company was more interested in contractual production, while setting up its own trading arm in Hungary, but later expressed its interest in acquiring Venus' Most Advanced Plant. A Continental Licenser, whose licensed products represented about 20 per cent of Venus's sales, wanted to maintain, or possibly extend the licensed product range. A few months later an employee at Venus' Most Advanced Plant, on behalf of employees and unspecified foreign investors, also expressed an acquisition intent for that particular plant, but the SPA disregarded his announcement. Of all these potential partners, Diversified Global Leader's interest developed into a letter of intent in which it offered technology transfer and emphasised strategic fit between the acquirer and the target.

The formal Transformation Plan, with asset valuation attached, was approved by the Enterprise Council, and was subsequently submitted to the SPA in February 1991. The management believed that the firm's still remarkable market share, its stable financial position and some of its properties, particularly an unused building in the capital, were attractive for potential investors. It was also acknowledged that the current employment level was high. At the heart of the transformation would be the involvement of a 'serious, capital-strong professional firm' with a range of businesses matching that of Venus. The management wanted to avoid the option of 'privatisation in parts', i.e. breaking up the firm into pieces and selling them separately, because they thought this would lead to drastic downsizing and redundancy, and the elimination of the Venus brand from the market. However, one of Venus' operations, Basic Material, was planned to be sold in an 'asset protection procedure' with the proceeds to be spent on reducing indebtedness.

Venus' Consultant did not agree with the result of the asset valuation, and argued that the firm's real value was about 25 per cent less than appraised. When the SPA approved a privatisation strategy for Venus in March 1991, however, it set the minimum asking price for Venus at the appraised value. On the basis of previous interest in investment, transformation and 'genuine' privatisation were to be carried out in one step by way of a closed (invitational) tender. A stock was reserved for employees which they could purchase at a discount of no more than 50 per cent. In exchange for the shares thus secured for the employees, the company was to waive its entitlement to 20 per cent of the proceeds of the sale of shares. Separate sale of Basic Material was approved. The Enterprise Council then wished to have better conditions of employee ownership, and requested free employee shares up to 10 per cent of the equity, while it also remarked that it had no authorisation to waive the entitlement to

20 per cent of the proceeds; only the board of the company after transformation could make such a commitment. This triggered the SPA to increase its price expectation since, if the SPA repaid the company 20 per cent of the proceeds, the investor would obtain free the part of this amount that would be left after financing the issuing of employee shares.

Deal with Diversified Global Leader falls through

Following the SPA's decision, several firms were invited to submit a bid. Basic Material was offered for sale separately. A foreign company won that tender, offering more than the asset value of Basic Material and promising capital investment and to maintain employment. The deal, however, was not concluded, according to a later SPA source, 'because of the buyer's [unspecified] fault'. Talks on the sale of Basic Material were still being held a year later.

Regarding the tender for the whole company, a Focused Global Leader considered Venus too diversified, producing too many products with too complicated an internal structure. Streamlining the firm and integrating it into the network of Focused Global Leader would require much time and many resources. Besides, it was not their policy to produce other firms' licence products, but cutting them out of Venus' operations would mean an immediate 30 per cent decrease in sales. Therefore, Focused Global Leader declined to take an interest in Venus and chose other ways of entering the Hungarian market.

The Major German Company was unable to reach the minimum price for the SPA's shareholding in the whole firm, but offered 'proportionately much more' for Most Advanced Plant alone.

Diversified Global Leader, however, submitted a bid for the whole firm. Its vice-president was 'truly excited by the prospect of a DGL–Venus partnership', despite the long journey to this point. They had been in discussions with the management for more than a year by then. He found that the 'strategic fit is perfect, our people work well together, our bid fully reflects the future value of the Company', and emphasised that Diversified Global Leader wanted 'to be your partners'. Although the up-front cash consideration was less than half of the asking price, the bidder would assume debts, carry out a substantial capital investment programme, and offer 50 per cent profit-sharing to the SPA. Of the proceeds, 20 per cent was asked to be paid back to the company, with half of this sum to be spent on issuing employee shares. The bidder's detailed business plan envisaged increasing sales, arising mainly from its own brands. Venus would pay royalties for the use of trade marks and patents, and a management fee for the services provided by the acquirer's personnel. Diversified Global Leader planned to reduce Venus' product range considerably, but those products remaining in the portfolio were planned to receive significant advertising and marketing support. It considered Venus overmanned by about 25 per cent, but promised that 'we do not plan dramatic personnel reductions' and emphasised the weight they would give to the issue of employment.

The management estimated that the up-front cash price could be increased by several hundred millions without causing the bidder to lose its interest. They criticised the extent of royalties and the management fee, and also wanted the acquirer to cover the current level of debts, which had increased considerably during the year above the amount that the bidder had used in its calculations. The management emphasised that 'staying alone' was out of question; it would 'lead to Venus' falling to pieces', to frittering away of its real value that lay in the market share and qualified personnel, to liquidation of the R&D base that represented significant human capital, and to simple contractual manufacturing of licensed products in the units thus created. They warned that the situation of the firm had 'severely deteriorated since 1990', and concluded that the firm's relatively high market share and its qualified personnel had been acknowledged by the bidder as Venus' biggest source of value. If this value continued to decrease 'at an accelerating rate, then at a later date the privatisation process can only be started again with worse conditions'. No doubt the firm had, and would have in the future, no resources sufficient to strengthen its market position and financial stability, and the managers were aware of this. They believed that the sooner privatisation took place the better, since 'for the time being we still have a chance', Venus' remaining strengths could improve its bargaining position, but this would diminish as these strengths eroded. The Enterprise Council approved the management's evaluation at a meeting where the vice-president of the bidder personally presented the main points of the offer.

Diversified Global Leader (DGL) was then holding discussions with the management and the SPA, and was still willing to go ahead with the deal. Following brief visits to a plant and several stores, its Chairman, President, and CEO was satisfied about 'the appropriateness of a partnership between Venus and the DGL companies'.

Both the General Director and the firm's Consultant urged the SPA to make a deal. What the management was afraid of happened faster than expected. What remained of Venus' strong market position continued to erode. Sales revenues were less than planned in the first half of 1991, putting Venus' operations in the red. For the second half of the year, projected sales opportunities were expected to be even worse, which would further increase losses, despite plans for radical cost-cutting. Debts were now more than twice as great as at the end of the previous year. With no internal resources available, any improvement was possible only by getting in new finances through quick privatisation. The General Director also warned the SPA that in the event of a protracted decision, the bidder's offer could significantly diminish in the light of the firm's difficulties. He raised the question: 'Why don't we speed up the privatisation process, since as time passes by the market value of the firm is continuously decreasing?'

The Consultant went even further than the General Director, emphasising his disagreement with Venus' management as to the 'slack' in the bid of DGL. It pointed out Venus' worsening situation: 'sales revenues are stagnant, stocks are growing, the firm's debts have increased, market share is continuously diminishing, but the number of its competitors is very much increasing, ... [the firm] has no resources available for modernising [its operations]'. The Consultant emphasised that assuming, as the management did, a 'cash reserve [in DGL's bid] is not realistic', especially if Venus' poor financial results in the first six months of 1991 were considered.

Bright prospects began to dim. From various sources it was apparent that the bidder was unhappy with the length of time it was requiring to reach an agreement, and was considering an alternative of a greenfield investment. It had already set up a tiny subsidiary in Budapest to establish its presence.

Two months after the opening of tenders, the Venus case was taken over by a new administrator at the SPA. Meanwhile, Empire Builder sent a letter of intent over acquiring 51 per cent of the stock, but his interest was disregarded by the SPA owing to ongoing talks with Diversified Global Leader.

With its decision about the bid, the SPA effectively put Venus on the path of a long privatisation process, and was apparently not determined to strike an immediate deal. The privatisation tender was declared unsuccessful because no bid met the tender requirements, that is the SPA's price expectations. The SPA management was authorised to hold talks with DGL, and other investors if necessary, in order to improve the offer, and was asked to conclude a consulting service contract with an investment bank to obtain new offers. However, the minimum asking price could now be lower than previously. Venus was also to be transformed into a company form prior to the actual sale, which was explained by the SPA in its letter to the management by the need to accelerate the privatisation process.

Soon afterwards an SPA staff member publicly insinuated a misdemeanour by the management. The press, on the lookout for conflicts, asked him if the management 'could be condemned for their conduct'. The SPA official explained that the firm's management naturally urged privatisation 'since they wanted to have security for themselves as well as their company as soon as possible'. Judging personal responsibility, however, was said to be a very difficult issue, 'since bad faith cannot be presumed'. Interestingly, the management was later to be condemned for delaying privatisation. In the same interview it was also indicated that the SPA could 'not prolong the decision more than two months', but it might have to announce a new tender. Of course, this meant prolongation.

Prior to his meeting with the SPA, the vice-president of Diversified Global Leader indicated that they were still interested 'provided that negotiations can be concluded' in a matter of weeks. However, a review of both the current macro-economic situation in Hungary, and the financial results of Venus' operations during the first half of 1991 'will necessarily have an impact on our position', implying a definite reduction in the original offer. The bidder's position, as summarised by its lawyer, was that if the SPA wanted to increase the amount or improve the terms of the bid, as suggested in published press reports, it did not wish to engage in negotiations. In that event, discussions should be terminated immediately. On the contrary, DGL reduced its offer and claimed an increase in the amount to be transferred back to the company from the proceeds of the sale, since the financial results of Venus' operations indicated an accelerating downward trend, while several competitors had aggressively entered the Hungarian market. Referring to the declaration of there being no winner of the tender, it was noted, in passing, that the validity of DGL's bid would have expired at about this time in any event. The bidder seemed to have been prepared to abandon its interest in the privatisation.

Negotiations then followed with the involvement of a Foreign Investment Bank (FIB) that had been quickly appointed to advise the SPA. Offers, revised offers and counter-offers were exchanged in a few days. The deal was given the green light by the Competition Office, but the offered price and the conditions were unacceptable to the SPA. Its net proceeds from the sale would be about a third of its initial price expectation; some of Venus' assets, including the Least Advanced Plant, would be left in state ownership; the bidder expressed its intent – but it would not be obliged – to make substantial capital investments. A number of conditions applied. The SPA pressed for better conditions, until the potential acquirer announced its withdrawal from the deal.

As DGL's vice-president reasoned, they had 'undertaken a more comprehensive review' of the target's positions and prospects and found that the passage of time and the deterioration of the business had adversely affected the company's fundamental values. Witnessing the failure of privatisation of a major consumer goods firm, the Press kept the topic alive for weeks. Some of the newspapers were persistently seeking 'the true reason' for why DGL stepped back, and thought they had found it in the slow, clumsy, and complicated state procedures and, eventually, in DGL's lack of trust in the current government. It was also believed that DGL's withdrawal may have been motivated not only by Venus' gloomy results and prospects, but also by its own restructuring efforts at that time, including lay-offs of several thousand employees around the world. A foreign analyst later compared the SPA's bargaining power to that of a stall-owner trying to get rid of a load of rotting fruit, since Western multinationals had been busy eroding Venus' market share and, referring to events yet to happen, 'poaching its best executives'. Venus' marketing head was to leave the company for Diversified Global Leader. The analyst concluded that Western multinationals had by now built up local sales and distribution organisations to the extent that 'they do not really need Venus' whose market share was, though large, perishable.

According to its advisor, the SPA could now either seek revised terms with DGL, or approach Major German Company to see whether it was still willing to pursue its earlier proposal for the Most Advanced Plant. A third option, to make fresh approaches to a limited number of alternative purchasers, was also possible in principle but considered as 'not a simple undertaking', given the deteriorating financial condition of Venus. In response to the SPA's request for more options, the advisor listed other, less likely or less satisfying alternatives, including public flotation, more licence agreements, and 'an orderly liquidation of Venus' assets'. It also gave the SPA some general advice, concluding that 'had [we] been involved in the Venus privatisation from its inception, or even from the date of the bid deadlines, we believe the outcome would have been different'. Foreign Investment Bank stated it could achieve results despite its late involvement, and remained committed to the privatisation process in Hungary.

Having been lectured, the SPA indicated that it was not satisfied with the advisor's recommendations. It also signalled that there would be no need for further services, particularly as an 'old-new' bidder, Expander, had reappeared on the scene. Following some argument between the SPA and Foreign Investment Bank, the bank's contract was revoked, and the advisor's last invoice was settled. In its letter to the SPA, FIB assured it that 'FIB has enjoyed our harmonious day-to-day relationship' and was keen to continue to work with the SPA on any occasion, although it was 'surprised and disappointed' by the abrupt termination of its engagement.

Privatisation postponed

The services of the advisor may have seemed unnecessary because Expander, when news that the deal with DGL had fallen through appeared, confirmed its interest in acquiring 51 per cent of the shares. It placed a value on Venus similar to DGL's valuation, but wanted to acquire only 10 per cent of the stock with an option on the remaining 41 per cent until the end of the following year. For the option period it requested total management control over the company's operations. The SPA was given a couple of weeks, and then some additional time, to think about this offer.

Reviewing the situation, the SPA excluded all of the alternatives that Foreign Investment Bank had listed. The view that Venus' financial collapse was not an immediate threat was becoming adopted, particularly because Venus' partner in a joint-venture intended to buy out the company's share, and this possibility promised financial relief. A new strategy for Venus was formulated, in the spirit of 'transformation first, then privatisation'. It was hoped that a transformed Venus would implement streamlining measures and sell some of its assets (an unused building, Basic Material, the interest in the joint venture) in 'asset protection procedures' for the purpose of decreasing its indebtedness. The privatisation of the whole company was thus postponed to the following year.

The SPA was holding discussions with Expander in the meantime. A staff member suggested that Expander's offer should be considered as an invited bid competing with DGL's offer, although that tender had already been closed. Legal counsels insisted on obtaining at least one more offer; thus the SPA requested a competitive offer from a Little Mediating Firm that was said to act on behalf of an unspecified foreign investor. This firm then offered no more than (unspecified) consulting service in tandem with an (unspecified) investment bank.

On the SPA's request to submit a detailed offer, Expander put forward a proposal that was even less favourable than its original one. Several items were deductible from the cash payment, contrary to the requirements there was no business plan and employment policy, and the option period with total management control would now span three years. At the same time an employee of the Most Advanced Plant, on behalf of unspecified 'individual investors', repeated their interest in acquiring this plant. The SPA decided to refuse both. The SPA management was required to contract with a new advisor, and Venus was to be sold in a new open tender.

Meanwhile, transformation preparations continued. The SPA and Venus signed an agreement according to which Venus, once re-established as a joint stock company, would waive its right to retain 20 per cent of the proceeds from share sale if it received free employee shares equal to 10 per cent of the equity. When Venus was actually transformed, its registered capital was established in the range between the asset value (as appraised formerly) and the value that offers the SPA had received to date placed on the firm. The SPA owned more than 90 per cent of the registered capital, the rest being spread among local municipalities.

At the end of this phase of Venus' privatisation process, there were two further developments worth mentioning. First, Venus' union informed the SPA that it 'could only accept' privatisation with a 'capital-strong' partner who would guarantee Venus' further development, develop production with capital investment, maintain the present level of employment, and create new jobs. This only indicated the employees' attitude towards privatisation; despite the wording that might suggest a strong bargaining position, it had no relevant effect on what was to come. Second, although its relevance will be apparent only later in the process of privatisation, it is recorded here in appropriate chronological order that a Tiny Private Company with the least legally possible capitalisation was established by a handful of individuals in 'MAP town', where Venus' Most Advanced Plant was located.

Half-hearted privatisation

Efforts to sell selected individual assets continued, with some misunderstanding and only partial results. A foreign investor made an offer for Venus' unused building. The management's counter-offer was considered informal and unprofessional by the investor, who noted in a letter to its representatives in Hungary that it wanted to receive answers to all its proposals in the form of its original offer, with the appropriate marking or addendum signed by the Venus management, because 'this is the businesslike manner' to develop a contract. The representatives were also instructed to convey a copy of this letter, properly translated, to the Venus management, 'so that they will know we are serious business people'. The building was to remain in Venus' ownership for long afterwards. The sale of Basic Material had not been implemented either. Only Venus' interest in the joint-venture was sold, for which the foreign partner had offered a very attractive price.

A new potential acquirer laid eyes on Venus in early 1992: 'Focused

Atlantic Corporation' (FAC), owner of a few brands of worldwide reputation. Its 'Assistants' (a small Hungarian firm with a mostly technical role, mediating between FAC and the SPA) were making preparations for the visit of FAC's President throughout the spring. Their approaches to the SPA were left unanswered, causing the cancellation of the planned visit; instead, the President of FAC Europe was to visit the SPA. Meanwhile, 'Emerging Investment Group' (EIG; also known from the Mercury case) exhibited interest in an acquisition, but it was not willing to enter an open bidding process. For some time EIG was treated by the SPA as an independent potential bidder. EIG was actually acting on behalf of FAC throughout this phase. Its leader had good relationships with both FAC and Expander; these two firms were business partners in the Hungarian market. Soon it turned out that EIG was mediating only, when it informed the SPA that an Atlantic company (then unspecified, but apparently identifiable as FAC) was contemplating investment in Eastern Europe. Following his discussions with the SPA, the President of FAC Europe confirmed in writing an interest in acquiring all the shares in Venus and agreed to submit a bid in a tender, but emphasising that the transaction should be completed in a speedy process. The letter was left unanswered. Meanwhile the SPA was advertising a tender for advisors, and in due course selected a foreign Advisor.

When the SPA was urged to send a reply to FAC Europe, a draft was prepared. This apologised for the delay in replying and asked for a concrete offer, in the knowledge of which the SPA would announce the terms and conditions of the sale of Venus in a closed tender. The draft, however, was never finalised and sent. When FAC's Assistants again urged a reply to the letter that they knew had been given to a staff member to draft a reply, they were informed that a draft had indeed been prepared and was to be forwarded for signature by an SPA executive. On further inquiry, they were told that the official assigned to the case was with the SPA no longer. Later, in June 1992, the Venus case was completely taken over by another directorate of the SPA.

Coinciding with these events the Annual General Meeting of the shareholders took place. This increased the value limit up to which the management could take decisions without prior approval of the shareholders' meeting, that is the SPA. The General Director, who was confirmed by the SPA in his position earlier that year, once again urged the company's main shareholder, the SPA, to conclude privatisation quickly: 'time is passing by ... how long shall we wait?'

In the middle of the summer 1992 there seemed to be an intent to sell Venus. The SPA decided that the company could be acquired by Focused

Atlantic Company without it having to enter into competitive bidding, if it offered conditions as good as Diversified Global Leader had once offered – and which had then been rejected. The SPA specified these conditions to FAC at a meeting and subsequently in writing, requesting a detailed offer within a month. Expecting a deal to be struck without major hurdles, the SPA informed the selected Advisor that its services were not needed, but it would be contacted again in the event the FAC deal fell through.

The leader of EIG, on behalf of FAC, asked the SPA for some clarification of the expectations, and requested that negotiations on the possible sale of Basic Material be terminated. His request was accepted.

While FAC's offer was in preparation, representatives of the SPA, the company's General Director, its Chairman and the Union Leader held a meeting. Apparently, company representatives were anxious to learn about FAC's business plan for Venus, and insisted on being involved in the discussions with FAC before the sale of Venus was concluded. The meeting also discussed a previous agreement between the SPA and Venus in which the company waived its claim to 20 per cent of the proceeds from privatisation in return for free employee shares. Those present confirmed that the agreement was still valid. However, 'the legislation and circumstances have changed' so that the SPA could not issue new, free employee shares. (Despite the fact that the unlawfulness of the said contract was recognised at this point, it was not declared null and void until the end of the year.) Instead, the SPA now undertook to give the employees ordinary shares representing 5 per cent of the registered shares. Interestingly, they specified a condition to be applied to these shares such that 'in the event of dismissal the owner is obliged to buy them back for twice their nominal value'. In other words, if FAC acquired Venus and made redundant an employee who was a holder of such registered shares, it would have to buy the employee's shares at 200 per cent of par.

This subsection is ended, again in chronological order, with an event the relevance of which was to become apparent only later. Some owners of Tiny Private Company in MAP town sold their interest to other owners; it was also entered in the minutes of the owners' meeting that its managing director had made a contract with Venus. According to this contract, Tiny Private Company obtained exclusive rights to wholesale Venus' New Product Family.

Enter insiders, bidder deterred

Around the middle of the year, when the priorities of the government's privatisation policy shifted in favour of domestic and employee ownership, the management (including all plant managers) announced their intent to buy out the firm, complete with its employees if there was an interest on their part. They argued that 'the country needs an enterprise in [this industry] the greater part of which is in Hungarian ownership'. By Hungarian ownership they believed it could be ensured that there would be products offered in the domestic market at prices affordable to everyone. The firm's 'human capital' could thus be preserved, too, and profits would be reinvested in Hungary.

However, some interviewees indicated that the buy-out attempt had also been triggered by fears of Focused Atlantic Company. Management saw it not as a potential partner but as a firm 'negotiating on the basis of a three-minute run around the factory'. They felt raided. One may infer other reasons from later events.

Venus' interim financial report showed profit, although only to a very modest extent. The sale of the interest in the joint-venture and some streamlining measures seemed to have borne fruit. The stock of Venus' own products and its short- and long-term debts had dropped by half. This may have contributed to how the SPA started to change its view of Venus' positions and the prospects of its privatisation. An internal analysis, prepared for SPA executives, concluded that the privatisation strategy for the company should be modified. Apparently based on information from the management, it argued that the problem was neither poor product quality nor managerial incompetence. (According to laboratory tests, the quality of Venus' products was in some cases better than the quality of products produced by Diversified Global Leader and Focused Global Leader.) What the real problem was believed to be was the lack of interest-free resources of an amount which would allow the company to finance production and sales, and to buy new machinery. By the end of the year considerable profits were expected. Therefore, it was proposed that instead of professional investors, that is Western firms in the same industry, the SPA had better look for financial, that is institutional, investors, and after a two- to three-year period of recovery it should sell the existing shares via public flotation, which would give the SPA proceeds close to the original target it had hoped for in 1991. In another report the same SPA staff member repeated these arguments and noted, after analysing Venus' balance sheet, that 'it would not be advisable to do Venus' privatisation in too great a hurry'. As if echoing the management's view, he added that this would also be advantageous since there would be no threat that the new owner would liquidate the existing businesses and 'fill up the market, dominated by Venus so far, with its own products' produced outside the country. This, as a threat, was considered possible if FAC acquired the company.

When Focused Atlantic Company sent the SPA a draft agreement, it indicated an acceptance of all the SPA's conditions with only minor modifications. By this time, however, the SPA's determination to privatise Venus seemed to have evaporated. In the light of the new privatisation law which was to come into force within a few weeks, the SPA anticipated that its stringent requirements for tender processes would also be applied to ongoing matters. Therefore, it seemed unlikely that FAC could acquire Venus outside a tender process, as had been decided earlier, without attracting severe criticism of the SPA. The management-employee buy-out offer was also considered a fact that made it 'almost obligatory' to make a new call for tenders, indicating that it was a matter of opinion what exactly was obligatory for the SPA. In addition, the company's improving performance gave rise to a need to reconsider the speed and manner of privatisation. It was therefore proposed that in the discussions with Focused Atlantic Company, the SPA should 'take a position which would result in no agreement'.

For a long period during summer 1992 a high-level executive of the SPA was on holiday. At the time it was speculated that he was wanting to wait until he could see if his position was secure enough. In the meantime, the Venus case was handled by another executive. When the next meeting between the SPA and FAC took place it was, for a short period, also attended by the Chairman and principal owner of the potential acquirer. Subsequently, the decision-makers deferred the discussion of the FAC–Venus deal. In the meantime, FAC's reaction to several questions was sought. The questions included whether FAC would accept the SPA retaining a 'golden share' in Venus, whether it would be willing to submit a bid jointly with the employees who would have at least 25 per cent of the shares in addition to the 10 per cent already designated as employee shares, and whether it would accept a future flotation of Venus shares. Other questions were listed on a further one and a half pages. Finally, it was hinted that the SPA did not plan to sell Venus immediately but that a new tender might be called.

In the meantime, an internal poll showed overwhelming employee support for a buy-out attempt. They established an ESOP Organising Committee, comprising three plant managers. Within the SPA, a new tender was suggested in which FAC and the employees would be competing bidders. The Ministry favoured this solution, questioning the need to sell Venus rapidly to FAC. Others recommended combining foreign investment and employee ownership. A Responsible Politician did not support the tender or the sale of a significant proportion of stock to employees because that would not provide much needed capital;

instead, he proposed to try and improve the conditions with FAC. The decision-makers accepted this view and decided that negotiations with FAC should continue while 15 per cent employee ownership would be permitted.

This was certainly not what the potential investor had expected. Soon after FAC was informed of this decision and invited to further meetings, it let the SPA know that it was withdrawing from further proceedings. Its Assistants explained that the SPA had come up with entirely new demands as if the preceding discussions had not occurred. This was said to have made the principal owner and the executives of FAC very angry, particularly as FAC had offered what the SPA had earlier required for its shares. The Assistants hoped that FAC's withdrawal would 'teach the SPA that business cannot be done in this way'. Not that it wanted to.

After the high-level executive returned from his holiday, however, FAC's withdrawal became a subject of intense correspondence. FAC's Assistants furnished the refreshed SPA executive with copies of the correspondence between his colleague and FAC, although several weeks later an inter-office memorandum still showed some staff members' unawareness of the withdrawal and all the events leading to it. 'Did FAC indeed step back from the transaction?', asked those who were supposed to furnish information. Some weeks later the SPA executive attempted to renew contact with FAC but it was reluctant to engage in talks and blamed his temporary replacement.

Venus' Board was also unaware of the withdrawal. One of the Board's outside members, 'Dissenter', argued in a fax to the SPA against the FAC deal, weeks after the withdrawal. He believed that FAC's owner, 'Raider' was 'a real estate agent by his original profession and one of his major businesses is buying and selling firms'. For that matter, the Chairman and principal owner of FAC was indeed an active boat-rocker, initiating many organisational and ownership changes in the industry, as it was reported in a Western professional journal. He was also known as an orchestrator of leveraged buy-outs in the USA during the 1980s. Dissenter also hinted at Raider's good relationship with a foreign company that was known to be an ally of Expander in Hungary, implying that FAC's acquisition attempt may have been an attempt to pass Venus onto Expander. Expander already had an interest in the related retail sector, and had also exhibited an interest in acquiring Venus but had apparently been reluctant to engage in any formal tender procedures. This was all shooting at an imaginary enemy, since by now FAC had already withdrawn.

Sinister or scapegoat

The SPA solicited a Feasibility Study and a detailed buy-out proposal from the ESOP Organising Committee in autumn 1992. The submitted Feasibility Study aimed at the acquisition of all or, alternatively, 51 per cent of the registered shares. The management was reported to welcome a foreign partner, but they opposed a sale of the whole firm to a foreigner. The General Director argued that it would involve simply a takeover of Venus' market share and the termination of Hungarian production and research and development. The Ministry strongly supported this view which the SPA, presumed to prefer foreign investors' cash to employees' payments, was said to be unable to disregard any longer.

The SPA took the position that the ESOP Feasibility Study should be accepted if no more than 30 per cent of the SPA shares were sold in this scheme because Venus' survival would be at risk in a majority employee ownership. (A staff member assumed even now that Focused Atlantic Company was still interested, and suggested that its 'actual offer' should be treated as one bid in the new tendering process.) Before any decision was made, however, other issues captured the interest of some of the players.

Dissenter insinuated to the SPA that many of the company's top executives, including some fellow members of the Board, had been receiving unjustified income from the company. This prompted the SPA to commission an 'Investigator' to look into the matter. The Investigator's assignment also included an examination of the financial interest that Venus' management presumably had in Tiny Private Company. The SPA believed that these interests of the management existed to 'such an extent that they are impeding the Company's privatisation'. At about the same time the SPA instructed the General Director to convene an extraordinary shareholders' meeting where the ESOP Feasibility Study would be scheduled for approval.

Venus' Board supported the ESOP, despite Dissenter's dissent. The Chairman, once a colleague of a Venus executive, and the Board in general were already considered incompetent at the SPA when the bids submitted by consultants had to be evaluated earlier that year. Dissenter pressed the General Director to provide information on numerous issues so that he could better evaluate the Feasibility Study. Although in principle he was in favour of employee ownership, he did not agree to the extent and way it was planned to be implemented at the company. When he criticised specific details of the Feasibility Study and asked for further information at a Board meeting, others reminded him that 'checking the details and numerical errors is not the task of the Board'. In the voting, Dissenter was overruled on this, as well as on other issues including the increase of the General Director's salary and the extent of those payments which he assumed provided unjustified income for the management. Some days later Dissenter sent the SPA a detailed evaluation of the ESOP Feasibility Study, noting that 'it is financially impossible'. He also pointed out that the ESOP plan must have been calculated backwards, starting from the Existence Loan necessary for the acquisition, matching it with an amount of profit from which the loan could be serviced, and 'adjusting all other figures to this'. An SPA staff member shared this view when, doing some arithmetic in the margin, he noted: 'Dream! Full of contradictions!' Thus he proposed that the Feasibility Study should be accepted with only a 10 per cent ESOP interest. He also hinted at the management's misdeeds, now under examination. In another brief, the management's attitude as presumably impeding privatisation was again mentioned.

The SPA instructed the General Director to change the date of the extraordinary shareholders' meeting from November to December, and also informed him of the Investigator's assignment. He stated that the law required the SPA to have the value of shares appraised by a registered expert, and for this job the SPA had commissioned Investigator, to whom General Director was required to grant access to information.

Dissenter kept fighting the management in the meantime. In a fax he sent to the SPA he objected that the management was acting without involving the Board, criticised the lack of recovery measures that should have been taken, and believed that the ESOP 'would only serve to strengthen the position of the present management, as it manoeuvres for freedom from the control of the SPA'. He reckoned that the employee buy-out attempt was doomed to fail because of lack of resources, and this would drive the whole company into bankruptcy in a year or two.

The Investigator's report for the SPA seemed to confirm previous assumptions. It pointed out possible misdeeds arising from personal association between executives and Board members, and providing an opportunity to reap unjustified benefits covered from company resources. The report concluded that the management had a vested interest in the business relationship between Venus and Tiny Private Company. Venus allowed Tiny Private Company as commissioned merchant to wholesale its New Product Family and pay in the thirty days after goods were sold. Tiny Private Company, with the legally minimum possible capital, had no stocks, warehouses, or previous experience in trade. Its owners included relatives of some members of the incumbent top management team, including the manager of the Most Advanced Plant and the General Director, who had been the manager of the same plant. However, sales through Tiny Private Company were not flourishing, and the total amount involved was negligible. While some sources indicate that those implicated had already devolved their interest in Tiny Private Company when, and perhaps because, it contracted with Venus, the Investigator's report, and later the SPA, referred to them as current owners. This gives rise to some speculation that those involved were perhaps scapegoats just as much as being ethically challenged, particularly in the light of the General Director's defence given sometime later.

On the basis of this report, high-level decision-makers were informed that the management's unethical behaviour had been proved. The SPA also jumped to the conclusion that the management had been impeding privatisation. The leader of Venus' local union attempted to support the General Director in letters to the SPA, a Responsible Politician and the chief of the national union, but to no avail. Allegedly at his own request, submitted in a one-sentence letter which is understood to have been backdated, the General Director took early retirement, later to be attributed to 'health reasons'. A new Managing Director was appointed at the extraordinary shareholders' meeting. The Board of Directors was also subject to changes. Dissenter remained a member. The SPA also decided that the ESOP Feasibility Study needed major revision.

The new Managing Director's tasks for securing a bonus included the development of a new business strategy, executing a cost-cutting programme, and 'getting things straight' with some activities of Venus which seemed to be the source of unjustifiable managerial income. The most important and most highly rewarded of his tasks, however, was to facilitate privatisation in the year just about to begin.

Overdue condemnation and defence

Three months had already passed when high-level SPA officials came to discuss the privatisation strategy for some large companies, including Venus. An SPA executive acknowledged that relations with Focused Atlantic Company had not been managed well. It was falsely reported that, in demanding that stealing state property should be stopped, he was referring to Venus, when he actually meant another firm. However, the ethical issue at Venus was also brought up. Interestingly, events of the past such as the Investigator's report and the top management's interest in Tiny Private Company were treated as facts of the present, and the management (without regard to the recent changes in top managerial ranks) was reportedly condemned for unethical behaviour and for impeding privatisation months after the General Director left the firm.

Prompted by this news, the previous General Director protested to (another) Responsible Politician who simply fended off his arguments. The General Director stated that he had clearly proved his ethical conduct. His relative had terminated interest in Tiny Private Company even before it had entered a business relationship with Venus. Yet, he was told only a day before the extraordinary shareholders' meeting that he was going to be dismissed and that the new Managing Director had already been designated. He agreed to submit a request for early retirement, backdated, since he had no other choice. The retired General Director also claimed that as the records clearly showed, it was a false accusation to attribute the failures of Venus' privatisation to the management and himself. On the contrary, he blamed the SPA for delaying the process at several points and for setting the price higher than the management had suggested. He noted that some apparently wanted to shift responsibility to others even by insinuation. In sum, he asked the Responsible Politician to have an investigation conducted which would judge his role, otherwise he would turn to legal action and publicity. His letter went down through all the levels of the hierarchy to an SPA staff member. The reply, written on behalf of and signed by the Responsible Politician, simply fended off the arguments by stating that it was the General Director who had requested early retirement, and asking why, in any case, his relative had had a share in Tiny Private Company. The matter was considered closed, although the General Director kept fighting, with partial success, for his severance pay at least, which had earlier been rejected by Venus' Board.

Preparing for sale

The company started 1993 still in state ownership, and with new management. The new Managing Director soon set to work on strategic and organisational renewal, and introduced tighter control over purchasing, limits for maintenance work and wages, etc. 'These are things we do not make jokes about', said an executive in an interview at about this time. However, work on organisational issues and on a strategic plan had already started under the previous General Director.

A new privatisation strategy for Venus was emerging. However, it took several months to advertise a call for tenders. As the privatisation strategy was debated, the Ministry objected to an open, unrestricted tender. Echoing the management's view, known from the announcement of their buy-out intent, the Ministry wished to maintain Hungarian majority ownership in Venus in the belief that this was the only way to ensure the availability of products in everyday use at a price affordable by low-income strata of the population; this would also discipline import price levels, and the pricing policies of foreign firms operating in Hungary. It was proposed in the study that Hungarian majority ownership should preferably be achieved through the use of an ESOP and management buy-out with an Existence Loan. When this view was presented at a meeting of the company's Board, it declared support for the proposal and suggested that profits should be retained instead of distributed.

The SPA seemed to try and limit the stock to be offered to employees to around 20 per cent, while it was also considering reserving some shares for other purposes, such as free stock transfer to the Social Security Fund. It was discussing the matter with the Managing Director and the ESOP, requesting the former to convince the latter not to aspire to a larger percentage of the stock.

The SPA also had discussions with the Advisor, a Western consulting firm, which had already been selected in a tender about a year earlier but had been put in reserve at the time. Although its capabilities were questioned by some within the SPA, and the required fee was also the subject of debate, the SPA contracted with the Advisor. One of its first tasks was to estimate Venus' market value which it then calculated as somewhat more than 50 per cent of its registered capital (less than a third of the expected proceeds the SPA had once hoped for). A few weeks later the Advisor recommended a minimum asking price of more than twice as much as the estimated value of the company.

Potential investors were expecting Venus to be offered for sale again soon and made approaches to the SPA and the Advisor. Most importantly, the foreign firm that had been attempting to acquire Basic Material for a long time, now pressed the SPA to sell it at last. At the end it offered a handsome amount which an SPA executive considered was worth thinking about. He argued by experience: 'if there is a good offer, there is rarely a better [one]'. Others objected because they thought this would make the sale of the whole of Venus very difficult. The SPA eventually kept Basic Material as part of the company, now to be offered for sale again.

The last tender

The Advisor directly invited fifty-one potential investors, and advertised a call for a two-round tender. About 80 per cent of the registered capital was offered for sale, requiring the bidders to deposit a large bid bond.

Cash, Existence Loans, and instalments were all acceptable forms of payment. By this time the ESOP had revised its Feasibility Study and produced two alternatives, aiming at acquiring 15 per cent or 25 per cent of the shares. The Annual General Meeting of the shareholders – effectively the SPA – accepted the Feasibility Study. It also approved the company's business plan, noting that the profit target for 1993 was unrealistically low, and insisted that all profits after 1992 were to be distributed, that is to be paid in mainly to the SPA.

As the date of opening the tenders was approaching, the Managing Director informed the company's Board that Domestic Investor and Co., including himself, was going to submit a bid. At the request of the SPA the Advisor issued a declaration, stating that the company's management had ensured each potential bidder equal and sufficient access to information, thus the fact that the Managing Director was a member of a bidding group would not constitute a case of insiders' asymmetric information. This potential problem aside, however, the Managing Director now had to face a Board that wished to exercise greater control. A resolution was made, with three members for and two against, that contracts above a relatively small amount were to be approved by the Board. The Managing Director was also required to submit monthly written reports to the Board.

By the deadline, three bids had been submitted. Others expressed only a possible interest; these included a small Hungarian bank, said to be representing a Hungarian financial investor who in turn had good relationships with international strategic investors. It stated that it would only be interested in an acquisition if conditions were better. Circumstantial evidence suggests that this bank actually represented Expander. Those who did submit a bid comprised a Large Overseas Corporation, Domestic Investor and Co. (DIC), and the ESOP Organising Committee.

Large Overseas Corporation's offer, attractive as it might be in terms of cash considerations and further investments, was only tentative. It also failed to meet the tender requirements by not putting up the bid bond.

DIC and ESOP referred to each other in their bids. The ESOP Organising Committee bid for 15 per cent of stock at par, to be financed mainly from an Existence Loan. They stated that they would be pleased to co-operate with Domestic Investor and Company. DIC's offer included the condition that about ten members of the management team would receive shares (an unqualified minority holding in total, with the Managing Director receiving three times more than the others). It claimed to have an agreement with a foreign firm that would subscribe to new shares, thereby acquiring 31 per cent. Flotation was planned to occur by the end of 1995, and there would be a parallel increase of registered capital by a minimum of 20 per cent by public offer. DIC supported the ESOP's bid, and its offer was presented with two alternatives, corresponding to whether the SPA accepted or rejected the ESOP. In DIC's business plan for the company, the profit forecast was higher than in the plans prepared by the management, whose achievements in Venus' financial consolidation were acknowledged. 'Developments', presumably purchase of new machinery and equipment, would be undertaken to a considerable extent within a three-year period, financed from the sale of some property and from capital increase. The offered price represented 110 per cent of par, financed mainly from an Existence Loan, but partly in compensation notes and cash. A middle-sized bank's promissory note on providing the Existence Loan, in consortium with other banks, was attached in case DIC won the tender. The bid bond was deposited for DIC by another bank.

Domestic Investor was a successful entrepreneur whose experience in private enterprise and the management of state-owned firms went back for decades. He was said to 'sit down with every manager', including the ESOP leaders, who were inclined to co-operate since an independent ESOP acquisition had been ruled out by the SPA. One interviewee, apparently having unpleasant memories of a former possible takeover by Raider, believed that DIC 'seemed to be the last resort'. In a prior agreement the ESOP had received the necessary guarantees from DIC Leader; thus it became possible that 'considering the circumstances the employees would not be excluded from this new asset distribution [or appropriation]', as ESOP Leader put it. He added, 'with this minority, ESOP had to undertake a flexible, co-operative approach'.

Evaluating the bids, the Advisor concluded that the Large Overseas Corporation had to be excluded because of not meeting the tender requirements. The other two bids actually meant only one. The Advisor considered it 'unlikely to meet the SPA's expectations' because only a small part of the price was to be paid in cash. It noted that although the offered price seemed favourable in relation to the company's expected profitability, the SPA would probably not accept to such a large extent a state-subsidised loan. The Advisor finally recommended modifying the tender and allowing for individual acquisitions of certain assets only. Contemplating the possible reasons for receiving far fewer bids than expected, it remarked that several potential investors seemed to have been deterred by the unusually high bid bond requirement and insufficient information on the target.

The SPA had other ideas. Although this was only the first round of the tender when non-binding offers were being invited, it was recorded as a black mark that the Large Overseas Corporation's offer did not constitute a binding agreement between the bidder and the SPA. Of the alternative options of following the Advisor's recommendation, or accepting DIC's offer combined with the ESOP's and asking them to modify their offer in the hope of a higher price, the second was proposed to the decision-makers, it being pointed out that this would also satisfy the Ministry. Some marginal notes indicate that others did not really believe it was possible to achieve a higher price. It was at this time that the SPA thought of the need to obtain a declaration from the Advisor on lack of insiders' information advantage, which indicates the possibility that the declaration was backdated.

Amid some problems regarding authority and operating procedures, it was decided at the SPA that a second round should be announced, inviting DIC and the ESOP to submit their final and binding offer. It then rejected the Large Overseas Corporation's request for more information on Venus, and received the Advisor's invoice regarding the success fee due after the first round.

Before the second round of the tender was closed, an extraordinary shareholders' meeting took place, which modified the Managing Director's bonus tasks. A bonus for bringing Venus' privatisation to a conclusion by the end of the year was still offered, but only if he was not one of the acquirers; the profit-related part of his bonus now required profits double those specified earlier. The Managing Director did not welcome the SPA's decision on curtailing his likely income and requested an explanation from the SPA's representative. In two different versions of the minutes of the meeting two slightly different explanations were recorded, both referring circumspectly to 'new factors to be considered'. One Board member agreed with the SPA, while Dissenter recalled that the first ESOP study had not long before expected a four-times-higher profit level than was now set as a target for the Managing Director.

In the second round of the tendering process, the Large Overseas Corporation confirmed its preliminary, still not binding and somewhat revised, offer, and needed 30–60 days to submit a final offer. It was not considered as a valid bid. Domestic Investor and Co. lowered its bid, referring to further analysis revealing that Venus' prospects were worse than thought. The bidder was willing to pay par if 20 per cent of the price was repaid to the company. It claimed all dividends after 1993. The proportion of the Existence Loan compared to other forms of payment further increased, while the proportion of cash decreased, practically to the amount of the already deposited bid bond. Promissory notes from a small and a large bank on providing the smaller and larger parts of the Existence Loan were attached. The ESOP's final offer was for 15 per cent of the shares at 80 per cent of par, financed largely from the Existence

Loan or, alternatively, at par if 20 per cent was repaid by the SPA to the company.

Following some deliberation on which alternative it should accept, the SPA believed that – considering the Property Policy Guidelines, the prospects of the industry, the company's loss of markets, and dynamic developments made by its competitors – 'it seems expedient' to sell Venus at par value to DIC and the ESOP. The SPA management was authorised to negotiate on the 20 per cent and settle this issue in the contract. The SPA's negotiations with DIC and the ESOP did not immediately result in an agreement, but in a few weeks the Share Sale Contracts were concluded with both of them. Eventually, DIC acquired 51 per cent of the shares at par, with the sale price being reduced by 20 per cent (and with no transfer to the company) against which employee shares were to be issued; the remaining SPA stock was to be converted to non-voting shares bearing fixed interest; at least 25 per cent of profits in 1993 were to be distributed; the acquirer was to be penalised if it failed to 'initiate' an increase of registered capital of a specified amount, and also if failed 'to attempt' flotation before the end of 1995. The ESOP acquired 15 per cent at par. In late summer and early autumn 1993 the company was thus eventually sold – or it seemed to have been.

Deal concluded in conflicts

The SPA considered the deal exemplary which justified the efforts 'all the long way on this bumpy road', although later an executive viewed it as the 'the least bad way' of privatising Venus. The Managing Director reported on cost reductions, improving profitability, and a narrower, but more profitable product mix. All seemed happy until Dissenter raised his voice again.

Dissenter prepared a long report for the SPA on the company's operations and performance in the first half of 1993. It was not so much a report as an attack on the management and the deal that had just been struck. He evaluated the management's work as 'practically zero', noting that they were not going to become 'stallions [i.e. superb managers] just by becoming owners themselves'. In his view, this only meant that the management could 'continue stealing without any control'. He expected that the firm might go bankrupt in no time if Domestic Investor 'does not hit the table [i.e. introduce tight control]' and remove his partners from managerial positions. Elsewhere Dissenter proposed to reprimand the Managing Director and eventually to dismiss him because he had not achieved any of the objectives set at his appointment. The SPA calmed Dissenter and, with due respect for his worries, called him to 'co-operate' in the interest of the company, pointing out that DIC and the ESOP had won the tender and the contract was then being finalised.

Dissenter had also submitted a similar evaluation to the Board of the company, but withdrew it from discussion at the Board meeting because 'it has lost its relevance'. By now, the mood had changed. A few months earlier the Board had introduced tighter control over the management by passing a proposal from Dissenter by a three to two vote. Now proposals aimed at relaxing this control were put forward by the Chairman (a young outsider) and the Managing Director. Thanks to the vote by one of the Managing Director's deputies, a Board member himself, these proposals were passed against recorded 'firm objections' of Dissenter and another Board member.

A few weeks later the whole acquisition seems to have been at risk. Domestic Investor and Co. sent the SPA an additional clause to the contract which indicated its difficulties in securing the Existence Loan. Soon afterwards these difficulties were confirmed, when DIC requested the SPA to approve a modification of the agreed terms of payment. It argued that it had been forced to look for a new co-financing bank, in addition to the small bank involved, and to work out a new structure for the deal owing to the large bank's delay in evaluating the loan. The proposed new structure of financing the acquisition involved a lower cash amount, a much higher proportion of compensation notes and a smaller Existence Loan. The proposed structure was more favourable for the buyer because of the higher proportion of cheap compensation notes. On the other hand, it meant a larger immediate financial burden.

The problem with the bank must have taken the acquirer by surprise, since an extraordinary shareholders' meeting had already been convened to effectuate the takeover. It then turned into an information session and was adjourned. Interviews suggest a more detailed explanation of why Domestic Investor had to propose a change in the structure of the deal despite the fact that he had obtained a promissory note from the large bank and, upon request, he had financed a study that showed enough guarantees for repaying the loan. Expander may have attempted to acquire Venus without entering into the bidding process. The bank's unwillingness to grant the Existence Loan was suspected of having been motivated by the assumption that in the event the winning bidder, because of the loss of its bank support, was rejected by the SPA, Venus could be acquired by Expander outside of a tendering process. The large bank 'wanted to play it into the hands of others', as an interviewee put it. That it did not happen was due to the support of another bank and particularly the SPA's willingness to change the terms. The other bank's support was won partly because of personal relationships. Domestic

Investor was later reported to be 'disillusioned about Hungarian banks', emphasised the importance of domestic ownership, and urged mutually favourable business co-operation with foreign investors.

Meanwhile, Dissenter made one more attempt to block the deal and announced his retirement from the Board would take place if and when DIC took over the company. Note that another Board member had already quit, allegedly because of the Board's being captured by the management. Dissenter argued that the Board, because of its personal composition, was unable to reprimand the management for lack of economic results, for 'creative accounting', and for successively not observing the company bylaws and Board resolutions. He accused the Chairman of delaying the discussion of his analysis of the company's situation, and then making it impossible to discuss it at the Board meeting, whose minutes, he claimed, provided a false account of what had actually been said. Noting that he did not want to represent the SPA's interest more strongly than the SPA itself wanted to, Dissenter asked for instructions. Dissenter misspelled the name of the SPA official who then misspelled Dissenter's name in his reply and encouraged him not to worry.

Venus' executives believed that Dissenter's critical attitude may have been loaded with personal ambition as well. According to the Managing Director, the reason behind the 'everyone steals, cheats, and tells lies' kind of memorandum that Dissenter prepared was his intention of becoming managing director himself. The Managing Director admittedly did a 'couple of things that were not absolutely in the spirit of the company bylaws', but blamed Dissenter for not understanding that the company could have easily been paralysed by tight rules. The Managing Director was focusing on keeping the firm operational and ensuring stability (e.g. by tightening budgets) rather than on major changes. He did not want to take the risk of introducing major changes before closing the privatisation process: 'I did not do a lot of things; decisions were made in a "just not to cause any problem" way.' Not only replacements in the top management but also the planned strategic and organisational changes (technological developments, renewal of the marketing unit) failed to be implemented. In the stability versus rocking the boat dilemma, he opted for the first approach. Some improvements were indeed achieved. In addition, 'inventories were replenished, since it had an influence on our start in 1994'. Another executive, also a Board member, stated, 'then we felt that somehow our latitude was limited', not only because of uncertainties that surrounded privatisation but also because of 'the incompetence and obstruction of [some members of] the Board that tied up the hands of the management' leaving no room for independent decisions at all. As he explained, Dissenter did not have a partner in the first year (under the previous General Director); Board meetings at that time ended with four-to-one votes. From 1993, Dissenter could team up with new members of the Board. After a few months, however, he had only one ally left, since first the Managing Director, then the Chairman of the Board changed position. In a consultant's view, the Managing Director, in his 'somewhat masculine rivalry with Dissenter', formed an alliance with the existing management against one whom he thought to be a challenger. Dissenter's behaviour may have been motivated by politically loaded instructions from outside. According to the consultant, Dissenter, as well as the Managing Director himself, were supposed to 'politically clean' the firm. After some time, the Managing Director did not want to comply with this expectation since he realised that a total confrontation with the existing management would do more harm than good to the company which was said to be driven by 'fossilised bureaucratic routines that are not easy to change in long discussions' that the Managing Director had with the existing management. The Managing Director drew the following lesson:

One should not be put [obviously by the SPA] into a situation where the execution of impossible tasks is expected when privatisation is in progress. For a thorough rationalisation, three years would have been necessary, but in the meantime we had to consider privatisation, when you cannot make a move. By handing over an operational firm, I fulfilled what was expected from me.

A Responsible Politician, in support of the request, blamed the bank for thwarting the sale of state property. The SPA, emphasising that it did not want to set a precedent, accepted Domestic Investor's request. Payments were then made and the shares were endorsed. At an extraordinary shareholders' meeting the takeover was effectuated by re-electing the Boards. From the previous members, the Managing Director and the Chairman remained on the Board of Directors, although in modified positions. The ESOP was represented on the Supervisory Board. A political appointee involved in privatisation decisions, who attended the extraordinary shareholders' meeting as a guest, was elected to Chairman of the Supervisory Board several months later, no longer holding responsibility for privatisation. The company bylaws were also modified, depriving the general meeting of shareholders of fundamental strategic decisions. The SPA's remaining shares were converted to non-voting shares with fixed dividends, which had earlier been opposed by some within the SPA because of the loss of 'the opportunity to have an influence'. The company undertook a guarantee for all the debts of the ESOP and Domestic Investor and Co., the latter with the SPA's objection but without its voting, in the belief that its shares, just converted, were already non-voting. The process of Venus' privatisation concluded when the SPA transferred a success fee to the Advisor.

Before the Annual General Meeting in 1994, the private owners announced their intent to acquire most of the remaining SPA shares that had been reserved for fulfilling other duties of the SPA. When a new staff member took over the Venus case at the SPA, he intended, in a proposal to the decision-makers, to deal not only with this issue, but also with some problems he found when learning about past events regarding, for example, the voting rights of the SPA shares and earlier decisions apparently taken without authority. He believed that his colleague, working on the case formerly, had made mistakes, then moved with his boss to another position, and that now they were trying to cover up the problems. Apparently, his diligence was not welcomed. As he explained, 'I am getting the reprimands now and am looking for a job', and he was not foreseeing a career at the SPA after having rocked the boat. However, an investigation conducted later uncovered no well-founded reason which would justify action.

Is the fun just starting?

At the time of the bidding in summer 1993 some industry analysts believed that Venus was bound to fail under pressure from 'multinational bullies'. A foreign executive reckoned that the market would be really tough after Venus had fallen out. That is when 'the fun will start'. A journalist speculated that Venus' fall would be slow if the Socialists won the next election. Following the acquisition of Venus by Domestic Investor, it was again envisioned that without significant capital investment and know-how from a multinational company, Venus was likely to continue losing market share to the foreign competition and would either go bankrupt or again be put up for sale.

Venus started 1994 in mostly private ownership, and, with renewed management, prepared to try and prove the contrary. New executive positions were created, outsiders were brought in, and the existing top management was reshuffled. During the spring, Venus' advertising activity was apparently intensifying, although it was still behind foreign brands that were reported to be gaining market share. Within the company, the management launched rationalisation programmes in several fields, and introduced a computerised management information system.

Contrary to earlier plans, no shares had yet been sold to foreign investors. Since Venus thus did not enjoy a tax holiday due to foreign ownership, the new owners encouraged managers to prepare proposals for projects with could secure tax concessions and preferential loans. Venus was indeed granted tax relief later, owing to its undertaking a capital expenditure programme that satisfied some legally specified requirements such as the protection of the environment and maintenance of the current employment level. Some other preferential sources of finance were also secured.

A few months after the takeover, and some time before the 1994 general election that was to bring victory to the Socialist Party, Domestic Investor passed over the position of CEO to an outsider, while remaining President. The newly appointed CEO had previously worked for the ESOP and Domestic Investor as a consultant, and had been a Board member since takeover. Even earlier, he had pursued a political career, and was allegedly involved in transforming Communist Party owned property into private property. He had abandoned this political career in 1990 in order to start business consulting as founder and leader of his own firm.

Later in 1994 Venus attempted to enlarge its scope of business by making an acquisition in retail sector, apparently teaming up with foreign investors, but competing with another bidding group of domestic and foreign investors. Neither managed to conclude the deal. Already in 1995 the company was reported to be launching a capital investment programme for the next five years of a considerable size – comparable to what Diversified Global Leader had intended to invest in the firm within five years, starting from 1991–92. Flotation did not seem on the immediate agenda.

Company executives considered this privatisation a success. They clearly saw the necessity of teaming up with a foreign company, and acknowledged that 'they could just wash us down [i.e. drive the company out of business]'. However, Domestic Investor said: 'I'm not a loser type.'

6   Corporate governance and politicking

In this chapter, we discuss the main concepts in the political bargaining framework through an analysis of the cases. The main findings are then summarised, and subsequently compared with expected post-privatisation performance.

6.1   Politics, strategy, and performance

In this section we consider two aspects of politics: organisational politicking, and politicisation of the context of privatisation processes. We take the cases one by one and evaluate them by these concepts. Similarly, we analyse two aspects of strategy: the process of strategy-making, and its outcome, the behaviour patterns of firms. This is followed by an examination of firm performance during the privatisation process.

Politicking
Throughout the privatisation processes in these cases politicking was rife, in some cases to a greater extent than in others. A notable exception is Saturn's privatisation. In contrast to Pluto, this firm avoided raging conflicts. The management and the boards of the company were apparently working in tandem, in the interest of financial stability and a successful privatisation. Saturn did not become the subject of oversized ambitions. We saw no example of any party attempting to have its own way by political means. Indeed, there was no need to use political tactics; sheer economic bargaining power and its use to the full appear to have determined the course of this privatisation.

We can group the *tactics of organisational politicking* that appear to have been used by players in other cases under a number of headings:
- building a coalition
- manipulating information
- manipulating time

- shifting up responsibility
- exerting pressure by going public.

Building a coalition.   Although coalitions are usually of a hidden, sometimes even illicit nature (Stevenson, Pearce, and Porter, 1985), the cases provide ample examples of coalition-building. In privatisations, one usually has to take sides. In Pluto's case, which provides most of the illustrations of politicking tactics, some actors were understood to be close associates of the General Director. Others took the other side. Initially, only two people were on this side, but soon it was three, and then four when a middle manager who later became Independent Union Leader was asked to join. By the time this group entered the arena publicly, its size had increased to about ten. It consequently continued growing, which indicates how people gradually join the side apparently on the path to become the winner. It was about this time that this group received support from important sources. The first of these was a deputy general director who had been a professional mentor of the two who started to organise the opposition. He did not take either side openly for a long time and completely withdrew to his strictly defined professional area. Yet, by providing his middle managers with access to information, he enabled the opposition to make a calculated case. Second, the middle managers established an independent union which dozens, and soon hundreds, of workers joined, which meant signatures were attached to every protesting letter in numbers no one could ignore. Third, and partly consequent to the growing social support, the middle managers could successfully seek alliances with politicians and the local community. This also indicates that coalitions in privatisation processes often cut across organisational boundaries, whereas a supposedly unified group of actors – for example, the management, which is often viewed as a group with a common interest – may be divided in the extreme.

The General Director's similar efforts to build a coalition were less effective. Regarding outside supporters, he attempted, with very modest results, to line up customers and technical experts. Because of his political background, there was limited opportunity to enlist political supporters. As to internal allies, the middle manager who got a seat on the Supervisory Board upon General Director's proposal did not desert. The General Director's other efforts – sending a middle manager on a business trip to a Western country, and promises of promotions – again proved mistaken.

Examples of attempts to build coalitions in other cases, with more or less success, are also abundant. Deimos' case shows a prominent example of turning points in the flow of events caused by politicking. Some subsidiaries' lobbying activity caused the Ministry to turn its earlier position upside down. They achieved, even if not exactly in the way they wished, the dismantling of Mars, despite considerable resistance. Venus' case seems the opposite: the plants whose managers became ESOP Trustees and the headquarters apparently struck a compromise, without exhibiting any serious conflict.

Another point to be noted in Deimos' case is that to raise a 'voice of discontent' effectively, to achieve the objectives of lobbying, and to develop a coalition with external powerful supporters, it is necessary to find *direct communication channels* to the decision-makers, so as to overcome the bureaucratic routine of passing the issue down the hierarchy until the complaint that is originally directed to the highest level is handled by the very same person whom the complaint is about. This requirement, however, seems to drive those dissatisfied with the current path of events into playing politics. This is what the middle managers of Pluto were good at. By using various means of politicking they ensured that they were listened to. The ESOP leaders of Deimos also attempted to communicate directly with top-level decision-makers, but less and less effectively as time passed by.

What makes politicking special in Deimos' case is, first, the conflicts between the parent company and the subsidiary and, second, the rivalry between the two ESOP organising committees, which later turned into a conflict between the united ESOP supported by some managers on one side, and the Director and his allies on the other. An implication of this is that tracing alliances becomes more difficult for the outside observer since there are more possible partners to team up with and more possible links between them. However, when the Foreign Industrialist took over the firm, he was confronted with a situation that seems to resemble the Bedouin proverb on quarrels:

> I against my brother,
> I and my brother against our cousin,
> I, my brother and our cousin against the neighbors,
> All of us against the foreigner.

Quoted by Bruce Chatwin in *The Songlines*, ch. 30, 'From the Notebooks' (1987). *Source:* The Columbia Dictionary of Quotations. Copyright © 1993 by Columbia University Press.

Neptune's privatisation presents a clear example of alliance-building. In addition to lobbying by a banker and a national union leader, the investors, their consultant, the management and the firm's suppliers acted in concert to put pressure on the SPA. This case also gives a brief example of internal organisational politicking within the SPA.

Coalitions may be temporary; sometimes they shift and rearrange as Venus' case illustrates. After a relatively short period, some members of the Board of Directors deserted Dissenter, resulting in a change in the balance of power. However, while it appeared intense in some personal relationships, politicking remained localised in that conflicts usually involved a small number of people, unlike Pluto and Deimos. This case also provides an example of coalitions across organisational boundaries in a latent conflict between the top management and Focused Atlantic Company, in that the former apparently attempted to prevent the latter from implementing the acquisition, and to that end the management sought to ally with the Ministry and SPA officials. These, in turn, could represent the management's views before decision-making fora. Other coalitions with powerful players seem to have been formed to influence the outcome of the somewhat concealed rivalry between two different groups of possible domestic acquirers, the first led by DIC Leader, the second (allegedly) led by Empire Builder (first introduced in the Mercury case), each supported by different banks. Finally, as in some other cases, external investors and insiders, in Venus' case both the management and the ESOP, allied to achieve their shared objective. The lack of strife between the management and ESOP on the one hand, and the outside investors on the other made the transitional period relatively smooth.

A contrast to Pluto and Deimos, and similar to Venus, is the case of Mercury. Even when politicking was present in its privatisation process, it typically did not involve long and hostile periods of strife. It took some lobbying to convince decision-makers not to auction the whole firm shop by shop. Then the external investor's and the ESOP's tactics to increase their odds by trying to ally with the decision-makers are worth noting. The primarily business-like conflict between the ESOP and the Bank was devoid of politicking, except for the ESOP's efforts to win the SPA over to its case, and the Bank's attempt to back the General Director. Although the change in the top management involved some politicking in the form of alliance-building, it took place quickly.

Manipulating information. Variations of this politicking tactic were frequently used by many in the Pluto case. The General Director and his associates *withheld information* from the opposition, and used the tactic of setting the agenda, for example at the Enterprise Council meeting that was to choose between the offers.

An alternative way of manipulating information can be labelled as *swaying opinion.* This was used, for example, by the General Director when he commented in favour of one proposal and made a declaration of being committed only to the Enterprise Council and the employees.

A similar technique is *hinting*. The group of middle managers, for example, hinted in a protesting letter that the sale they were against would solve the problem of 'some missing stock'. The innuendo certainly implied a misdeed done by the General Director.

Another variant of this tactic is *giving false assurance*, used by the General Director when he stated he could take measures against a possible unfavourable decision taken far above his level of authority. Similarly, the new Managing Director and his deputy (probably somewhat deceiving themselves, too) assured their colleagues and the employees' assembly that they were on the way to finding the best possible investor for Pluto. SPA officials sometimes gave false assurance whenever they calmed protesting employees by saying that their interests were being taken into account.

Probably the most direct way of manipulating information is *providing false information*; for example, Pluto's General Director and his deputy giving false information on the poor prospects of the firm, thus promoting Expatriate Investor's proposal by implying that he came to the rescue. Another example is the General Director's presentation of the advantages of the purchase of used equipment through Expatriate Investor. Providing false information was also used repeatedly by state bureaucrats, when they described Expatriate Investor's offer as the best and concluded that the offer was advantageous both to the firm and the country.

A more sophisticated way of manipulating information is to *conceal* it, that is to make it public in a way that will attract the least possible attention. This tactic may be necessary when due observation of legitimate procedures is unavoidable and does not permit more blatant ways of making information available only to those pre-selected. In April 1990, for example, new bidders were invited, in principle, to submit bids but the short public announcement placed amongst information irrelevant to potential investors certainly did not reach the widest possible audience.

Finally, the opposition may simply be *excluded from access to information*. Leaders of protesting middle managers, for example, were not members of the Enterprise Council. However, when one of them was proposed by the General Director to sit on the Supervisory Board in a mistaken effort to gain his support, the challenged let the challengers get close to the information.

Manipulating time. This tactic also appears in variants. In the *braking variant*, players attempt to delay a process. Typically, efforts are made to postpone a decision until more favourable circumstances obtain, such as when new opportunities provide the players with a better chance to see their interests met. Venus' insiders' acquisition proposal for all the shares without appropriate finance may not have been solid enough to consider it seriously; but it had to be dealt with in any case.

Alternatively, in the *accelerating variant* of this tactic, efforts are focused on pushing through an issue towards an *a priori* defined and favoured outcome. Note the hurry with which Pluto's Enterprise Council meetings were convened, and the state bureaucrats' successful move to rapidly put the issue on the decision-makers' agenda.

The accelerating variant often results in *cementing biases*, by putting the unfolding events on a path that severely limits the range of subsequent choices. A prominent example may be the letter of intent, which was followed by the option granted to Expatriate Investor just before the new government took control of privatisation. These were commitments which any newly elected democratic government would be inclined to honour.

Another way of manipulating time is *setting deadlines with a hidden agenda*. It may be important that a deadline should precede a certain event, or the time span for a certain activity should be restricted, or both. This was the case with the tender announcement in 1990 that allowed fourteen days to submit bids for Pluto on the eve of the general election.

Finally, to conclude the examples of this type of politicking tactic, note the use of time at Deimos. Mars' management, for example, submitted the memorandum of Deimos' ESOPs to the Enterprise Council, knowing that it would not discuss it owing to its late receipt. By the time of the next Enterprise Council meeting, the whole issue was dealt with by a newly created committee (itself a tactic of politicking) led by a deputy of Mars' General Director.

Shifting up responsibility. Pluto's Independent Union Leader and middle managers, and Deimos' ESOP and management buy-out leaders occasionally employed a tactic that we label *shifting up responsibility*. It closely resembles the tactic used by state-owned enterprise managers under the communist regime, who shared responsibility with their party-state superiors for the results of mistaken decisions. Targets of this tactic are again politicians and state officials. Thus, Pluto's Independent Union Leader put the blame on the SPA, and Deimos' ESOP and management buy-out leaders referred to encouragement they received from politicians.

Exerting pressure by going public.   This was perhaps the most efficiently used group of tactics of the discontented middle managers of Pluto. Press campaigns, public demonstrations, court litigation, and floods of protesting letters are examples, where going public may only mean letting one more person know what the opposition would rather like to keep secret. In some cases, an additional element of these tactics is that the target of the protest can be made aware of similar efforts with other targets, producing mutually reinforcing results. This seems to be the case in Pluto when, for example, those who were discontented not only protested but also let the target know that they had already protested (or, as a warning, would protest) in other fora, probably expecting that the recipient of their letters would want to avoid being questioned by other outside influencers. If the targets are in hierarchical relationship, this tactic is in fact a hidden threat. One would be inclined to label this the playground bully tactic: 'give me the ball or I will tell your father'.

The playground bully tactic appears in Neptune's privatisation, with the ESOP Leader threatening the management and the SPA. What is most characteristic in this case is the intense politicking after the majority interest had been obtained by private owners, and thus privatisation, strictly speaking, had already occurred. Because of the hostile conflicts between the ESOP Leader and the management, and because the ESOP Leader did have some bargaining power, turnaround efforts noticeably suffered delays.

Politicisation

As with politicking, some privatisation processes were more politicised than others. Pluto's privatisation process again scores high on this factor. The authorities' expeditious commitment to the Expatriate Investor's offer occurred at a time when the government was in effect an interim one, yet was facing the responsibility for divesting power in an organised way. In this situation, the bureaucrats' remarkably swift action in committing themselves to one of the possible alternatives may have been driven either by a self-interested attempt to reap benefits from a situation still under their control, or by a desire to show an example of their compliance with preferences (including the encouragement of foreign investment) that the new government was likely to exhibit. In any case, it was probably the political changes that induced swiftness which, by setting the process on a certain path, resulted in far-reaching consequences. The political climate in 1990 was clearly encouraging the organisational-level revolution of middle managers. Only a couple of months before, and particularly after the general election, Pluto's middle managers could rightfully assume that the time had come for them to do local justice. Their discontent appeared politically legitimate. Similarly, the growing nationwide movement of independent unions provided the background for local opposition. This could be used by the discontented middle managers to build up support from below and, in yet another way, politically legitimise their action. The argument over issues of authority that developed in March–April 1990 between the newly founded SPA and the Ministry that had earlier exercised nominal governance over Pluto is an example of the institutional instability due to political changes that enabled middle managers to seek justice from one representative of the state when they perceived unjust treatment on the part of the other. At a time when earlier spontaneous privatisation received much publicity and attention, the transparency of privatisation became an important political priority. This required the authorities to announce an open tender, contrary to the Ministry's argument for a closed one. While there was growing concern both at the SPA and the Ministry that they should probably withdraw from the planned deal, it was still decided to go ahead because a decision to withdraw could have appeared as an example of unfair treatment of foreign investors in Hungary. This decision, however, also meant that by the time this route eventually proved to be a dead end, considerable damage had been done and valuable time had been lost. Later political developments encouraged management and employees to enter the bidding and to use politically loaded arguments. Indeed, throughout the privatisation process, players who were active in organisational politicking were seeking support from politicians, sometimes at the highest level. This suggests that politicisation of the context in which the privatisation process evolves provides fertile ground for playing internal politics.

Mercury's privatisation, on the other hand, exhibits a low level of politicisation. One of the few major decisions that appears to have been based at least in part on political considerations was that the SPA Board prescribed selling further shops in the pre-privatisation scheme. While this decision created problems for those (SPA administrators and the firm alike) who were expected to execute it, no dramatic turning point in the flow of events resulted from this decision. Second, the appointment of a politically well-connected person to Mercury's Board of Directors as an act of political patronage did not have any apparent effect on this privatisation. Third, the general political climate was favourable for an ESOP acquisition, again without major influence since the ESOP–Bank bid did not need to be supported politically to win against the rival bidder's low-value offer.

Saturn's privatisation process exhibited some political influence, but apparently with only limited effect on the final outcome. It was said to have been devoid of party politics. Cross-ownership and management-employee majority (the latter never seriously considered by the management) were ruled out relatively early, mostly because of economic considerations. The

Ministry's attempts to secure a larger stake for the employees and the farmers were probably driven in part by political objectives, but these attempts eventually failed. The Ministry's objection may have made the negotiation process a little longer than it would have been otherwise, but it did not initiate a turning point in the flow of events. The process still remained based in economic bargaining between a resourceful and determined acquirer and a seller with low bargaining power. Similarly, although a Responsible Politician was involved in the process towards its end, his involvement served to bring about a quick conclusion of the agreement and not any discernible political objective (other than an *economically* successful privatisation, that is). The SPA's decision to emphasise, in a press release, the national interest in drawing a multinational into this industry reflects a political consideration, but only one relating to the perception of the deal *a posteriori*, not the deal itself *a priori*.

Like Pluto, Deimos scores high not only on politicking but also on politicisation. The involvement of a Responsible Politician and party politicians clearly initiated a turning point in the flow of events in 1992, but was less successful towards the end of the government's term. The reasoning of various parties often included political justifications. For example, breaking up Mars was considered necessary not only because of the economic rationale, but also because in that way retention of power by the old *nomenklatura* would be impeded. An interesting element in this regard is the SPA's rejecting, yet informative, reply to a local party politician who wanted to have a bigger say in the process, and particularly in determining Deimos' top management.

While Neptune's privatisation does not show signs of decisive political influence, Venus' privatisation process seems to have been moderately politicised. From summer 1992, the insiders' buy-out attempt and the subsequent change in the SPA's strategy for the firm's privatisation were probably encouraged by the politically motivated changes in the overall privatisation policy. However, it may have only been a tactical move to force the SPA to consider their offer as a competing bid to Focused Atlantic Company's, and thus to prolong the privatisation process in the hope that FAC would withdraw in the meantime. A Responsible Politician's and the Ministry's reasoning for Hungarian majority indicated political motives at work. Dissenter's dissent may have been backed by political supporters, just as was the appointment of the new Managing Director.

Strategy and performance

Pluto's strategy-making was vague, and the content of its strategy was aimless. The firm was deep in organisational politicking; strategy-making was suppressed by tactical moves with motives related to privatisation rather than business strategy. In fact, some business decisions seem to fit a personal strategy for privatisation rather than a corporate strategy for business conduct. Pluto's market share was continually decreasing in an increasingly competitive market. Financially, it made substantial losses, indebtedness was rising sharply, liquidity problems became frequent. At a time when competition was getting more and more intense, drift in practice meant sinking rapidly; no wonder that Pluto dropped back from third to fifth in the league table, and that its financial position deteriorated seriously, placing the firm at the mercy of the Bank.

Neptune was also losing money and accumulating losses, bringing the threat of bankruptcy – but not because of escalating conflicts. It was simply not capable of doing better, of devising a sound strategy for renewal (because of managerial incompetence) and implementing it (also because of lack of resources). The firm was 'in abeyance', in the investor's words, 'and it drifted'.

The third company whose strategy-making was vague and strategy content a drift was Deimos. Strategy-making, as in Pluto, was subordinated to privatisation. It focused on achieving independence from Mars and preserving workers' benefits but remained vague in terms of setting priorities for business policy. In contrast to other firms, however, Deimos faced a more benign environment. Vague strategy-making and drift produced less dramatic consequences in terms of performance, since the firm was less pressed by competitive forces. Although its high initial market share was not seriously challenged by competition, after the takeover the new owner seems to have found a few skeletons in the cupboard, including less than expected profit for distribution, substantial overdue payments, and a call for urgent capital investment, not to mention managers who had deserted and low morale amongst workers.

Similarly to the features of its privatisation process, Venus is also between the extremes in terms of strategy-making and strategy content. Strategy-making appears to have been focused enough in terms of priorities set by the management to cope with environmental challenges. The content of the management's intended strategy even reflected an attempt to implement recovery. However, in Venus' case it seems particularly important to distinguish between intended and realised strategy. While the management may have had firm intentions for what they should do, for a while realised strategy still resembled drift rather than recovery. It was only when the new Managing Director took his position that the firm indeed implemented some measures aimed at stabilising Venus' position. However, even in this period action seems to have been impeded by inertial forces in this large organisation, and by uncertainty surrounding privatisation. Similarly, Venus' performance was between the extremes. Its initially dominant market share had decreased by the time the privatisation process began, and it continued being eaten up by the competition. However, from a rapid financial decline it could achieve (albeit modest) financial stability.

Strategy-making during the privatisation process became increasingly focused at Mercury. From about 1992, when competition was already in full swing, measures aimed at recovery were taken, and these gained impetus after the conclusion of the privatisation in 1993. Its market share declined, but the firm later started to regain some of it, while a period with a deteriorating financial position was followed by gradual stabilisation, although a year after the end of the privatisation process, the situation was said to be 'still tight'.

Saturn is the only example of focused strategy-making and – at least attempted – recovery. Facing growing competition and decreasing domestic demand, and being hit particularly by the shrinking commissioned business, Saturn was rapidly losing profitability. The management considered it a top priority to keep the firm viable not only because of the bank's judgement but also because of the forthcoming privatisation. Once the main objectives had been defined, various measures were introduced to achieve them. 'Tough cost-cutting measures' that were 'unusual, different from previous practice' were taken. Efforts were also made to increase revenue. The management introduced organisational changes that aimed at improving the firm's relationship with the market. They also placed greater emphasis on co-operation between marketing and production. While maintenance work had to be delayed, quality remained a priority. Following a brief flirt with the idea of a higher management and employee ownership, the management and the Boards acted in concert. Regardless of all the efforts, the firm's position certainly deteriorated. Yet, by the end of the privatisation process it was still in business with a relatively healthy financial position and moderate profits despite severe shocks, and was ready to reap the benefits of resource replenishment by the acquirer.

6.2   Scenarios, outcomes, and turnaround

We begin this section with a summary of the case evidence presented so far, so as to facilitate an understanding of the relationships between concepts. This will be followed by three general scenarios of the privatisation process. We then match these scenarios with the outcome of privatisation in terms of corporate governance and resource replenishment. To complete the analysis, we examine how both the process of

Table 12. *How do firms score?*

Case	Politicking	Politicisa-tion	Strategy-making	Strategy content	Performance
Pluto	High	High	Vague	Drift	Decline
Mercury	Moderate	Low	Increasingly focused	Drift/Recovery	Decline, then stabilisation
Saturn	Low	Low	Focused	Recovery	Maintained stability
Deimos	High	High	Vague	Drift	Modest decline
Neptune	Moderate then High	Low	Vague	Drift	Decline
Venus	Moderate	Moderate	Moderately vague	Drift/'Hesitant' recovery	Decline, then stabilisation

privatisation and its outcome are likely to determine the post-privatisation performance of the firms.

Table 12 shows an evaluation of how firms score on various concepts of our framework. This evaluation is based on a careful analysis of available case evidence, making use of qualitative data analysis. Methodological references are provided in the appendix.

Politicking and *politicisation* seem to correlate in many cases. This relationship is apparent in cases with the same (high, moderate, or low) levels of both politicisation and politicking (Pluto, Saturn, Deimos, and Venus). Two other cases with low politicisation (Mercury and Neptune) show only moderate levels of politicking (which turned into intense but localised strife in the 'follow-up' phase of Neptune's privatisation). This suggests that macro-level politicisation may create favourable conditions for micro-level politicking. The fact that some level of politicking seems almost inevitable in privatisation processes may also be explained by the transitional nature not only of macro-level systems of society and economy but also of micro-structures of firms. In particular, legitimacy of the management or, in other words, the existing power structure may be subject to challenges. In cases like Pluto and Deimos, where the challengers succeed in involving outside, usually political, influencers and thus in increasing their bargaining power, the 'normal state' of politicking may be further heightened, resulting in a politically loaded organisational upheaval.

Firms also differ according to their *strategy-making* and *strategy content* during privatisation. It is important here to distinguish between intended and realised strategy, as well as between the processes from which they result (see figure 3). Venus is perhaps the most characteristic example of the formulation of intended strategy being focused, yet of

Privatisation process	Strategy-making – Strategy content	
	vague–drift	focused–recovery
Low politics		Saturn
Moderate politics	⇒ Mercury ⇒ Neptune ⇒ Venus ⇒	
High politics	Pluto Deimos	

Fig. 5. Mapping cases by privatisation process and strategy.
The arrows, where applicable, indicate change as the privatisation process proceeds.

strategy-making (the formation of realised strategy) remaining vague. In other words, the management may have rather well-defined priorities for what should be done but the pattern of behaviour of the whole organisation does not reflect those priorities. Similarly, Venus' intended strategy appears to aim at recovery, but its realised strategy has attributes of drift. The properties of the strategy concept also tend to correlate, vague strategy-making producing a drift strategy, and focused strategy-making producing a consistent pattern of behaviour aimed at recovery.

A third important relationship that our findings suggest is between different concepts, namely the *process of privatisation* and *strategy*. This relationship is illustrated in figure 5 which maps firms by privatisation process and strategy. We have combined properties of strategy-making and strategy content into 'factors' (vague–drift versus focused–recovery) since these properties were found to be interlinked. Similarly, 'low politics' and 'high politics' denote cases with either low or high scores on both politicisation and politicking, whereas 'moderate politics' encompasses the case with moderate scores on both concepts and two cases with moderate politicking and low politicisation. The pattern to be noted in figure 5 is the diagonal arrangement of the firms. It appears that the more intense the politics in the privatisation process, the more feeble the strategy. How does this affect performance?

The six cases show different *performance trends in the course of privatisation*. Saturn, the only firm with low politics and a focused–recovery strategy managed to maintain its stability in the face of severe shocks. Three firms were in decline throughout the privatisation process. Pluto is a clear case of high politics and a vague–drift type of strategy. With the same characteristics, Deimos' deterioration was only modest

	Scenarios		
Properties	Going through	Muddling through	Struggling through
Privatisation process			
• politicisation	low	both moderate, or	high
• politicking	low	opposing	high
Strategy			
• strategy-making	focused	in between, or	vague
• strategy content	recovery	progressing	drift
Performance during *privatisation*	maintained stability	delayed stabilisation	decline

Fig. 6. Overall scenarios of privatisation, strategy, and performance

owing to its relatively benign environment. Neptune, although scoring only moderate on politics, showed decline consistent with its vague–drift strategy stemming from resource deficiency and managerial incompetence. In two cases (Mercury and Venus), both with moderate politics and a trend towards more focused strategy-making and a recovery, initial decline turned into stabilisation towards the end of the privatisation process.

These findings suggest three overall scenarios that encompass properties of privatisation process, strategy, and performance during privatisation, and will be called *privatisation scenarios* for short. We label these scenarios as *going through, muddling through*, and *struggling through*, and summarise their properties in figure 6.

Going through.   In this privatisation scenario, a firm is going through the process in the sense that it is hit by environmental shocks and has to face challenges while equipped with inadequate resources, yet it endures the transition experience with the least possible losses. Its privatisation process is devoid of raging conflicts and jockeying for positions, which enables the dominant coalition to concentrate on keeping the business as healthy as possible while facilitating a privatisation that will bring resources for completing a turnaround. The example of this scenario in our sample is Saturn.

Muddling through.   Some firms are muddling through the transition period. Their privatisation exhibits moderate levels of politicisation and politicking, or a moderate/high extent of politicking with a lower level of politicisation. Internal conflicts may be generated by organisational members who see an opportunity to increase their power, but are unable to enlist enough support to overcome the existing dominant coalition, like Dissenter in the case of Venus. Alternatively, as at Mercury, the conflicts may be resolved by the removal of a key person. In any case, conflicts appear to be limited in scope and effect. Once the issue of legitimate power is resolved, privatisation is no longer hindered by unsettled power contests, and organisational efforts may be more effectively directed to pursuing recovery. Since these efforts have been delayed, the firm enters its post-privatisation era with a handicap.

Struggling through. Firms like Pluto and Deimos are struggling through several years of interregnum. Organisations are in a constant state of flux emanating from long-drawn-out strife between clashing interests. The bargaining power of the contenders may be raised by their taking advantage of high politicisation of the privatisation process. In the absence of outside restraint, self-control, and forbearance, politicking can drag on and on. Considerable energy is diverted from managing the business and is consumed in the political arena, leaving performance to be determined by the momentum of habitual routines rather than any deliberate and concerted effort to achieve recovery. Pluto's example suggests that the young Turks' game, if played out to the extreme, may result in a negative overall payoff. Figuratively, this privatisation story suggests that following a struggling-through scenario the winner only has the remnants left after destructive warfare. Players going for a bigger slice of the cake may deceive themselves, assuming that the size of the cake will not be affected by their action. Analogously to Pinkley, Griffith, and Northcraft (1995), we might label this the 'fixed pie expectation'. Alternatively, they may simply not care since the winning position is perceived as the size of the slice post-privatisation compared to the size of the slice before privatisation, regardless of the size of, and the damage to, the whole cake. 'Growing slice expectation' seems an appropriate label here. The firm struggles through if there is no corporate governance in place to manage effectively the fierce clash of interests. In short, the firm entangles itself in a downward spiral where unrestrained power contests and lack of resources exacerbate drifting. This leads to the firm's position deteriorating further which may intensify the strife over the slices of the shrinking cake.

From the process of privatisation we now turn to its outcome. In particular, we identified the *effectiveness of corporate governance* and the *levels of resource replenishment* resulting from privatisation as factors that are probable determinants of the post-privatisation performance of firms, in particular the success or failure of their turnaround.

Defective corporate governance and low resource replenishment characterised Pluto. It was acquired by management and employees, mostly from an Existence Loan. Not only were they unable to refill the company's resource base but they also drew on the company's resources in order to repay their debts. In addition, Pluto did not become entitled to a tax holiday. Effective corporate governance was absent for a long time. The same persons controlled the company's top management and its Board of Directors, and they also held a relative majority stake in the vehicle which nominally owned the firm. After a while Independent Union Leader, in his capacity as a director of the vehicle, made a hesitant attempt to introduce some outside control but his efforts did not represent a significant challenge for the top management, partly because he believed that another row among management would inevitably lead to the firm going under. It was not until about a year after the sale of the shares that the Bank introduced more effective control.

Effective corporate governance was coupled with high resource replenishment in three cases. In contrast to Pluto, Saturn was acquired by a resourceful foreign company. Both effective governance and a high level of resource replenishment were in place, as applied under the acquirer's corporate strategy. However, being subordinated to Mighty Multinational's global corporate strategy meant not only access to substantial resources, but also being downgraded to the status of a production unit. From early 1995, the Foreign Industrialist owned all the shares in Deimos, and later that year his two Hungarian acquisitions were merged, which suggested that effective corporate governance would be ensured. There were also signs of considerable levels of resource replenishment. We may assume, however, that a part of the additional resources had to be used on compensating for the 'skeletons in the cupboard', that is the assumed, but not found, profit for distribution, and other unexpected drawbacks. Neptune's privatisation resulted in both effective corporate governance, with two of the investors/owners being in top executive positions, and a high level of resource replenishment, with an apparently less-than-sufficient focus on managerial know-how.

The available evidence allows only assumptions about two others. In Mercury's case moderately effective corporate governance may have been ensured by the Bank which appeared to have a larger influence than its minority interest in the firm would suggest and which could also exercise control through its credit policy. Resource replenishment, however, seems to have been rather low. The amount of capital-raising was modest; Mercury's resources were being used to repay ESOP debts. Management was still gradually implementing a turnaround strategy, a relatively risky one since there were really no resources to finance the necessary developments. At Venus, corporate governance resulting from this privatisation appeared to be moderately effective on the basis of the ownership split, and because the majority owners may have had to give some concession in return for the support received from the management and the ESOP in the course of privatisation. Similarly, resource replenishment was only moderate. Although new financial resources seemed considerable, in comparison with the largest competitors, they only allowed for modest progress. In addition, some of the new resources were apparently obtained from the state which may have diverted the management's focus.

Note that there are two 'pure combinations' of both properties of privatisation outcome being either high (effective governance – high replenishment, three cases) or low (defective governance – low replenishment, one case). At the risk of oversimplifying, the other two cases (where moderately effective corporate governance is coupled with moderate or low levels of resource replenishment) will be collapsed into one 'in-between' case hereinafter.

In our sample there was no case with defective corporate governance and high resource replenishment – a situation that one might label as a manager's heaven. This finding should come as no surprise. Intuitively, such a situation occurring after privatisation would be difficult to explain, considering generally accepted theories of the objectives of economic actors in market economies based on private ownership. In fact, the transition of Central-Eastern Europe, at least in its economic dimension, may in essence be about the termination of the manager's heaven where poorly performing firms were continuously refilled with resources taken from better performing ones.

There was also no example of effective corporate governance coupled with distinctly low resource replenishment – the asset-draining scenario. Had Dissenter's fears and some analysts predictions happened to come true (see the last two subsections of section 5.6), the case of Venus would have fallen in this category.

In most of the cases, it seems too early to say if firms have *ended up* as examples of *turnaround success* or *turnaround failure*. Post-privatisation performance data for a sufficiently long period are not yet available. However, we do have one firm in the sample that has gone through two post-privatisation phases already! The other cases provide some evidence on the basis of which a plausible evaluation can be made of whether these firms are at least *moving towards* a successful turnaround or not.

Pluto is a clear-cut example of turnaround failure. It was only Domestic Investment Group that took firm measures to stem the losses and to put the company on the path of recovery, while the completion of the turnaround was left to the major international company which eventually acquired Pluto almost two years after the privatisation had been completed. The story this case tells is simple: the ownership arrangement of an organisation that is torn apart by a fierce privatisation process and left without the inevitable prerequisites of a sound strategy will likely be ephemeral.

For Saturn, on the other hand, turnaround success seems granted. With the resources provided by Mighty Multinational, the company can now prepare for better market opportunities.

Most importantly because of low resource replenishment, Mercury's turnaround seems to be handicapped and is being carried out at a slow pace. It is indicative that flotation, which at the time of bidding was planned to happen in 1995, has now been postponed to an unspecified date. From early 1995, impressive improvements at Deimos were reported. On the basis of limited public information the company is, eventually, on the way to a successful turnaround. However, similar improvements could have started earlier if Foreign Industrialist had taken full control earlier. There is no doubt that Neptune is on the way to a successful turnaround. However, despite the high level of resource replenishment, the firm has as yet not produced expected results. Managerial incompetence and cultural clash may provide a plausible explanation. In addition, it also appears that because of the delay in the privatisation process and the subsequent tug-of-war with the ESOP Chairman, Neptune started the implementation of a turnaround strategy with a handicap. Venus' turnaround can reasonably be regarded as handicapped by the privatisation process, in that the firm had lost valuable time while its competitors strengthened their positions. Venus is one of the cases that point to the relevance of procrastination for privatisation. It seems that the first tender could have resulted in a successful privatisation for both the state and the firm. DGL's offer, if accepted, would have yielded considerable proceeds to the state budget. It would have also ensured Venus' future development. Moreover, turn-around could have started as early as autumn 1991. In contrast, the privatisation process was put off for two more years, and ended with less cash for the state and fewer resources for the firm.

In sum, Pluto has clearly failed, while Saturn is most likely to succeed in terms of achieving a strategic turnaround. In all the other cases, turnaround seems to have been handicapped. Within this group, Deimos and Neptune appear to have a high probability of overcoming the

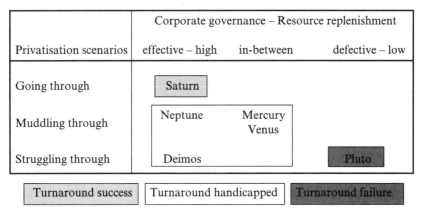

Fig. 7. Mapping cases by privatisation scenarios and outcomes.

handicap and eventually achieving turnaround success. Whether Mercury and Venus will follow suit remains to be seen.

To summarise, figure 7 maps the firms according to the *privatisation scenario* they were undergoing and *its outcome*, and indicates their *post-privatisation performance* as discussed above. There are two pure extreme cases in the sample: Pluto is characterised by the struggling-through scenario and an unfavourable outcome of privatisation on both of its properties, whereas Saturn is an example of the going-through scenario and a privatisation outcome that is favourable for future performance. The rest of the cases represent variants of mixed conditions. The pattern that this figure reveals largely corresponds to our propositions (summarised in figure 4).

There was no case in our sample that followed the going-through scenario and ended with a privatisation outcome unfavourable for turnaround attainment. This might be attributed to the small number of cases. One could also theorise, however, that the joint occurrence of the going-through scenario and owners who exercise defective governance and bring no resources may not happen, and conclude that such a case does not exist in the population of privatised firms. This might be the case. Let us assume that actors can, with a sufficient degree of confidence, predict whether a potential owner would bring about effective governance and high resource replenishment. In the case of two or more potential owners, the ability to distinguish them would be a sufficient assumption. Let us further assume that the objective of at least some of the actors who are able to influence the outcome of privatisation is to improve the firm's performance. These actors, themselves resource-deficient and therefore employing political tactics, will probably attempt to resist a takeover by weak and resource-deficient acquirers, who may just give up. Alternatively, they will have to rely upon politicking in order to increase their bargaining power against the resistance, forcing those resisting to engage even more deeply in politicking. Thus, the privatisation process will turn into one of the other two scenarios.

7 Conclusion

In this final chapter we summarise and evaluate the framework, now in the light of the case evidence, attempt to place this study in a broader context, formulate policy implications, and suggest some directions for further research.

In chapter 1 we asked under what conditions can privatisation facilitate the turnaround of privatised state-owned firms. We found that privatisation can not only facilitate the turnaround, as commonly assumed, but, under specific circumstances, it can also severely hinder a turnaround, depending on both process and outcome characteristics of privatisation.

The dominant economic approach to privatisation emphasises post-privatisation corporate governance – incentives and constraints – to produce efficiency (chapter 2). This provides a general understanding of privatisation as seen from the agency theory perspective. Although it may be sufficient to justify large-scale privatisation in the long run, when dealing with organisations in a transitional context, this perspective seems to have shortcomings (section 3.1) and yields only a partial understanding of the observed variety that is apparent from an overview of privatisation policy in a transitional economy (chapter 4) and lessons from a pilot study (subsumed in various sections).

The political bargaining framework that we developed on these foundations (section 3.2) explains post-privatisation performance with (1) the level of *politicisation* of the bargaining process in which the question of future ownership gets resolved, (2) the intensity of organisational *politicking*, (3) the effectiveness of *corporate governance*, and (4) the level of *resource replenishment* brought about by privatisation. Turnaround attainment is influenced by both privatisation process and outcome variables, whereas strategy-making and strategy content provide the mechanism through which privatisation plays out its effect.

Longitudinal case studies (chapters 5 and 6) provided substance for building the framework and revealed the following relationships:

(1) Low levels of both politicisation and politicking seem to facilitate focused strategy-making and recovery, whereas high politicisation and politicking produce vague strategy-making and make firms drift.

(2) Consequently, performance of firms during the privatisation process varies between the opposites of sustained stability and decline (which may be cushioned by the 'benevolence' of the firm's environment).

(3) Typical scenarios, as dynamic configurations of politics, strategy, and performance, are likely to occur in the transition period.

(4) These scenarios, coupled with different privatisation outcomes, are probable determinants of post-privatisation performance.

Essentially, it is suggested that the more drawn out and politicised the privatisation process, the more handicapped the turnaround, which will make it more costly to turn the firm around post-privatisation – since both the exercise of effective governance and the replenishment of resources require the new private owners to incur costs. These are extra costs of investment of which any investor needs to be aware before making a decision whether to stay put or 'Go East', and if the latter, whether a greenfield investment is a better option then engaging in local politics and incurring some extra costs. Similarly, for an investor who is late getting on the privatisation train, it may save time and effort to learn first about earlier events that may seriously restrict the range of possible choices for all the players.

The results of this study are in line with and extend previous literature. In privatisation studies of this kind, economics and organisation theory are really complementary theoretical approaches, but applicable at different levels of analysis and with different time horizons. The dominant agency perspective emphasises corporate governance resulting from privatisation as being superior to that under state ownership, and focuses on the final outcome in the long run. The political bargaining theory that has emerged from this study maintains the importance of corporate governance following privatisation. However, it also directs attention to corporate governance *during* the privatisation process, which avoids the attention of the agency perspective because of the latter's aggregate level, long-term view. Corporate governance resulting from and immediately following privatisation may also be defective. In addition, the role of *resource replenishment* is explicitly considered.

By establishing a process view of privatisation, the political bargaining framework sheds light on some previously unexplored issues that appear relevant both for theoretical advancement and policy evaluation. It suggests that *corporate governance in the course of privatisation is more often than not defective.* In the only case where the privatisation process apparently went smoothly (Saturn, going-through scenario), there appeared to be much greater congruence of objectives than in other cases; that is, there was much less need to align conflicting goals by means of corporate governance. In all the other cases, where goal conflict was present to a considerable extent, it was the deficiency of corporate governance, its inability to manage a clash of interests, that made it possible for politicking to emerge, and for strategy to become more and more feeble.

Consequently, *losses are inevitable in most privatisations where goal conflict is present*, which must be the general case. Some players, going for a slice of the pie, may assume they have enough bargaining power to come out of the process as winners. Others may be mistaken in their belief that the size of the pie will not be affected by their action. In any case, if corporate governance is indeed defective, it implies that the total payoff to the actors involved in the privatisation process will probably shrink.

Even if corporate governance were effective in the course of privatisation, the 'pie' is likely to suffer damage. A certain *minimum level of transitional loss* exists regardless of the smoothness of the process. This is because resource replenishment is delayed and even the efficient use of the existing, insufficient, resources is impeded by the fact that managerial decisions are thwarted by the uncertainty that surrounds issues of ownership. It follows that the primary task of a government that attempts to manage the transition process may be less a maximising one in terms of proceeds from privatisation than a minimising one in terms of inevitable transitional losses (provided it has the option of prioritising).

Resource replenishment is an obvious prerequisite for a turnaround, yet it has been neglected in earlier literature; so obvious, it may even seem tautological – certainly, if we put in enough resources, turnaround must occur. However, explicitly including this issue in the framework also suggests an important *trade-off between properties of the privatisation process and the level of resource replenishment* required for a successful post-privatisation turnaround. The privatisation process may exacerbate the firm's difficulties, thus rendering a proportionally higher level of resource replenishment necessary if a turnaround is eventually to be achieved (assuming product market competition). Even if the firm is thus saved and put on a path of sustainable growth, this certainly implies *inefficient resource allocation* at the macro-level. In the worst case, the increment in resource replenishment due to a muddling-through or struggling-through privatisation scenario may push the required level of total resource replenishment higher than the eventual owner is able to provide, resulting in the firm's turnaround failure. Resource replenishment can also be regarded as an indicator of the new owners' intent to turn the acquired target around. Resource replenishment is all too often assumed, but occasionally owners may have other ideas, as Pluto's early experience and fragmented information on some Mars subsidiaries in the Deimos story seem to indicate.

Instead of focusing on long-term effects and implicitly assuming a central, rational decision-maker who plans, then implements, privatisation, the political bargaining framework regards privatisation as an evolutionary process which unfolds in a sequence of numerous little steps as time passes by. Privatisation processes do not necessarily follow predictable routes; despite apparent commitments at a point, the events may often take an unexpected direction. Participation of actors with conflicting interests and who are playing politics makes the flow and final outcome of privatisation processes difficult to predict on the basis of the rational actor model. In the course of privatisation, the interests and motivations of players do change. Preferences should probably not be treated as chiselled in stone. Similarly, supposedly unified interest groups (e.g. state, management, foreign investors) may be internally divided to the extreme. They cannot – as they often are – be viewed as homogeneous. Temporary alliances, probably at the individual level, may cut across these groups.

Managers do not see themselves as having to be passive subjects of privatisation; instead, with the assumption that the firm will eventually be privatised in any case, they use various tactics to influence the process and its final outcome. In this sense, privatisation itself is a strategy variable at management level (as opposed to government or agency levels). Management does have strategic choices to influence privatisation which must be taken into account by other players. Privatisation goals appear central in managerial decision-making. On the one hand, privatisation *per se* is a central issue, requiring much managerial time and attention. On the other hand, possible decisions on almost every aspect of organisational life are filtered through assumptions about their likely effect on the achievement of goals that are related to privatisation. In cases when privatisation goals and business goals seem to be in conflict, the former often take priority over the latter. In the process of privatisation, attempts are often made to resolve internal organisational conflicts by way of politics, which may give rise to extreme strife. Theories of power, and 'power games' in particular, may prove to be useful in analysing privatisation as organisational change (sometimes upheaval). It is also apparent from the case evidence that, at least in the transitional context but perhaps more generally, in every fast-changing environment with weak corporate governance, intense politicking damages company health.

The methodology that we employed suited the dynamic nature of the research question and appears to have brought results undiscovered by previous research. It could also serve an important purpose for any research dealing with complex contemporary phenomena: that of the in-depth description which might enable other researchers to formulate new hypotheses and test them with more robust methods, thus advancing our knowledge in a cumulative way. However, the case study design was not without difficulties. Leaving aside problems of securing access, dealing with complexity, and the labour-intensive nature of the work, the most important limitation of this study is the generalisability of the findings. Our findings are bounded within a specific (even though probably not too limited) context, and it will require further research to see if they hold true in different settings. We single out three contextual constraints upon the generalisability of the theory.

First, the general context of this research was Hungary where the management initially had quasi-ownership entitlements and bargaining was a main mode of operation. In some other countries, where these initial conditions are absent, effective corporate governance during the transition period might be achieved, thus lessening the scope for politicking, preserving the firms' productive capabilities, and eventually making the completion of privatisation less urgent. In addition, privati-sation techniques other than those chiefly used in the Hungarian privatisation may also curtail the possibility for bargaining in the transition period.

Second, politicisation may be less of an important feature in other countries with different macro-economic and political conditions. In particular, domestic resource abundance (as in the reunited Germany) or even a less pressing resource scarcity (for example, lower foreign debt, as in the Czech Republic) may permit the attainment of desired social objectives with less harm than in Hungary, with the additional benefit of likely ongoing social support for the government's privatisation policy.

Third, the selection of firms for this study was confined to those that were hit by shocks and faced challenges at the beginning of the transition period. Thus, the performance positions of these firms were soon deteriorating and called for rapid turnaround strategies, and conse-quently fast completion of privatisations. It may be appropriate to assume that most state-owned enterprises in transitional economies fall into this category.

Our political bargaining approach emphasises evolving processes. However, processes spring from an earlier structure. In the Hungarian privatisation, the legacy of the past and current economic and political conditions certainly impose constraints upon policy choices. One of these choices is to transfer ownership entitlements to those who can pay for them, or to create an opportunity for the wider population to participate in the appropriation of state property. The first option implies privatisation mainly in favour of the old *nomenklatura* and foreign owners. The second option may, although it may be politically more favourable, blur the rules by which privatisation decisions are made and make room for politicisation which, in turn, probably increases the scope for politicking. Since politically favoured social strata are resource-deficient, the eventual owner who gets selected by politically defined criteria may well be unable to provide sufficient resources for the post-privatisation era. In such cases neither will economic rationality be satisfied nor will social and political objectives be met. This presents another dilemma: the government, if it wishes to achieve its socio-political objectives, should grant concessions to favoured groups to acquire such state property as does not call for significant levels of resource replenishment; however, for such property there are likely to be cash-paying bidders whom the government cannot afford to disregard under the pressure of high foreign debt, the need of resource replenishment nationwide, and external monitoring of its conduct towards foreign investment.

This does not necessarily imply that the faster and less politicised the privatisation, the better. As our case studies indicate, one cannot reasonably expect that a suitable match of acquirer and target state-owned enterprise would be ensured by the fastest possible process. In the given context of privatisation, however, politicking is a principal mechanism for preventing an unsuitable match (a premature, hasty deal) from happening. Paradoxically, even in this 'positive' role, politicking appears to bring harm to the total payoff, and the dilemma translates into a choice between different levels of losses.

The above discussion offers a plausible resolution to the last dilemma brought up here, which is the choice between privatisation and facilitating the endogenous development of the emergent private sector. It appears that a government may attempt to execute privatisation of firms facing similar situations to those covered by our case studies, by selling them as soon as possible for cash (also in the hope that at the beginning of the transition period the electorate's support is sufficient enough for such a policy). At least some firms that are believed to need less resource replenishment may be earmarked to be acquired later by emerging domestic entrepreneurs, but only if effective control can be ensured until privatisation is complete. Finally, small entrepreneurship could be facilitated, including the creation of opportunities to acquire *individual assets* of state-owned enterprises, from the resources that are probably only wasted when used to create unsustainable matches of owners and firms.

Even if emphasis is placed on nurturing new private start-ups, governments must carry on with large-scale privatisations. In the light of our findings, a few specific policy recommendations seem timely. These would call for politicians' self-restraint, legislation that would ensure transparency, the establishment of faster procedures *and* far tighter control over state agencies as well as soon-to-be-privatised firms (for fast but at the same time cautious progress with the privatisation agenda), more transparent bidding processes, and other improvements. The logic behind these recommendations is to reduce the scope for politicking, and thereby at least limit the damage to the value of what is still in state ownership. One would be inclined to offer these recommendations – with the additional advice to master political skills, since the question of whether these recommendations are put in place will be sure to be resolved through politics.

Several issues which were raised in this book have not been discussed in detail because of the lack of sufficient case evidence, or have not been followed up because of our deliberate effort to focus only on the most important variables and their relationships. These issues, five of which are listed below, lend themselves to further research.

First, how does information asymmetry affect privatisation? It is evident from the case studies that information asymmetry is a major advantage to insiders, which the state can cope with only somewhat arbitrarily, acting upon beliefs rather than knowledge. We have in effect subsumed information asymmetry under the various tactics of politicking. In further research, a possible way of enhancing the political bargaining approach could be the analysis of this phenomenon on its own in the context of national transition.

Second, what is the role of bureaucratic routines and organisational culture prevailing within state agents such as the State Property Agency or its more recent successor, the State Privatisation and Asset Management Company? How are preferences and expectations transmitted to case officers? Assuming that there is something to be learnt from a sample of one, such a unique organisation should be a prime candidate for research inquiry. For example, our cases hinted that 'covering up' might have been prevalent. In addition, what are the mechanisms of negotiation amongst the various agents of the state and what is the effect of their being divided? An example is the relationship between the State Property Agency and the ministries. Also note that issues which had earlier been discussed by the SPA's Board of Directors were later pre-negotiated at the level of the Privatisation Branch Committee (created only after approximately two years of the privatisation process) between various agents of the state. This also implies the involvement of interests represented by different state agents.

Third, what role do coalitions and networks play in privatisation? Apart from noting alliance-building which seems to justify the relevance of the question, we have not explored it further, although it emerged from the review of the policy context as an important one. Although most authors confine the term to intra-organisational coalitions, the problem exists and is probably more acute if one is interested in coalitions and networks based on personal and social relations across several organisations. This would certainly be a difficult research undertaking. Yet, more targeted research with appropriate methodology might reveal more evidence about this phenomenon and its role in privatisation.

Fourth, when can we say privatisation is complete? It appears that politicking may continue after privatisation (in the sense of the divestment of the majority of the state's shareholding). However, the state's remaining stock, even if in the minority, continues to shape firm behaviour since it is still often the subject of a contest. Neptune is the most pertinent example here. In terms of firm behaviour, privatisation may have to be redefined and be considered to have occurred when this minority state ownership ceases to have a behaviour-shaping effect, that is, when the uncertainty surrounding the eventual future of state minority is eliminated, and the private owner(s) can indeed act at will.

Fifth, if corporate governance in the course of privatisation is defective almost by default, what can prevent the management from abusing its existing power and taking advantage of its privileged position. Is there nothing more than corporate governance to discipline managers? Mainly on the basis of Saturn, it appears that one can also consider another force, namely ethics, that may significantly determine the likely scenario and its outcome – if only in a few cases.

Appendix

Methodology

During the research project the results of which are presented in this book, several 'judgement calls' (McGrath, Martin, and Kulka, 1982) were made regarding research design, case selection, and methods of data collection and analysis.

The replicative, longitudinal case study design was selected in order to develop a middle-range theory (Yin, 1984). This fits the dynamic and causal nature of the issues concerned. Instead of revealing static relationships, it promises to yield an explanation of the dynamics of the relationships. It is applicable to the situation of the small, yet very heterogeneous population of privatised firms in Hungary, and offers depth for generating theory (Walton, 1973), while allowing a focus on change processes within the broad social, economic, and political context (Easterby-Smith, Thorpe, and Lowe, 1991; Gill and Johnson, 1991; Pettigrew, 1990). It relies on theoretical sampling, starting with a partial framework (or, in the case of pure grounded theory-building, with no framework at all) and developing the sample and the emergent theory in tandem (Glaser and Strauss, 1967). In short, it fits Marshall and Rossman's (1989: 21) description of what they call 'real research' which 'is often confusing, messy, intensely frustrating, and fundamentally non-linear'.

This design is certainly not without major problems. Dealing with time, the selection of sites, choices about data collection, confidentiality, handling the inherent complexity of the 'stories', the required labour intensity, the often 'slippery' qualitative data, and generalisability (external validity) are among the most frequently mentioned difficulties (Leonard-Barton, 1990; Pettigrew, 1990; Van de Ven and Huber, 1990; Yin, 1984).

While these problems are acknowledged (and have indeed been experienced in this research too), scholars dealing with change processes have developed some guidelines and procedures for conducting rigorous case study research (Organization Science, vol. 1. nos. 3, 4; Dyer, Wilkins, and Eisenhardt, 1991; Eisenhardt, 1989b; Miles and Huberman, 1994; Yin, 1984). Tactics recommended in methodological literature and carefully used in this research to ensure rigour in case study research included the use of multiple data sources, establishment of chain of evidence, pattern-matching, explanation-building, cross-case pattern search, use of different data collection and analysis methods, deliberate search for counter-evidence, replications in multiple-case studies, and the use of case study protocol.

As far as case selection is concerned, privately established firms and those state-owned enterprises in which significant state ownership was intended to be maintained in the long term were obviously excluded from this study. The target population of firms was confined by using pre-established criteria. In addition, we attempted to define a segmented population in order to control for variables (as in an experimental design) that might have an effect on turnaround success. The criteria used, their definition as a requirement that firms must meet to be selected, and examples of sectors excluded from this study as a result of applying the criteria are given in table 13.

A number of sectors were excluded on more than one criterion. The application of these criteria also defines relatively clearly the target population in terms of firm size and industry, providing a group of middle-size and large (but not giant by Hungarian standards) state-owned firms with numbers of employees in the range of some 300–2000 people, and an asset value of about HUF 0.5–3.0 billion (around US\$ 10–50 million), that operate in the consumer goods sector. Within this sector, known cases provided the variety (for example in terms of final owners) necessary for comparisons. In addition, within this sector there are industries with more than just a few firms.

Before the pilot studies, a list of already or soon to be privatised firms was obtained. On the basis of this list and public information systematically collected from the Hungarian press, a shortlist of about a dozen candidates was prepared. For choosing two firms as subjects of pilot studies from the shortlist, a couple of further special considerations guided us. It was an objective to find a firm that was known to have been subject to a complex or problematic privatisation process, in the hope that an extreme case might reveal unexpected features. We also sought for an exemplary case so as to learn from a comparison of extremes. A natural consideration was the progress of privatisation; that is firms, to be selected for the pilot study, had to belong to sectors where privatisation had proceeded significantly, or could reasonably be expected to

Table 13. *The definition of the target population*

Criteria and definition	Examples of excluded sectors
Criteria related to privatisation	
Ownership commonalities Firms must have common initial ownership arrangements and be subject to a common privatisation legislative framework.	Agriculture (state farms and co-ops); firms initially owned by local municipalities (soviet-type 'councils'); small service; firms involved in 'self-privatisation'.
Lack of specialities in privatisation process There must be no peculiar feature in the privatisation process that might dominate strategy during privatisation and subsequent performance.	Foreign trade firms (they were deprived of their only main asset, their head-quarters building, by the SPA); firms that are known to be scandalous privatisation cases (with the exception of Pluto, chosen for learning from an extreme case).
Criteria related to strategy	
Market conditions Firms must face competition.	Natural monopolies, public utilities (but firms initially in a monopolistic position owing to administrative protection are included).
Organisational status Firms must be independent going concerns with a history of pre-, during, and post-privatisation phase.	Divisions and holding centres (but spin-offs created from legally independent subsidiaries were included).
Criteria related to performance	
Initial market and/or financial position Firms must enter the transition period with poor performance and/or facing serious challenges (needing strategic turnaround).	Firms that are likely to compete successfully without any strategic change in their behaviour.
Strategic viability Firms cannot be expected *ab initio* to be bound to fail owing to an industry effect.	Notoriously loss-making industries such as coal mining.
Lack of state dependency The state must not play a decisive role with respect to firms' business success (or failure).	All firms involved in the so-called consolidation programme (bail-out by the state); a further thirteen large firms bailed out by the state under a special programme.

proceed considerably within the time limits of the study. Finally, selection was also influenced by access. The privatisation deal of a third firm that was also targeted as a possible candidate for a pilot study was subject to litigation by losing bidders. Access to two others, however, could be secured. These are referred to as Pluto and Venus in this book.

The subsequent sampling process followed recommendations on theoretical sampling (Glaser and Strauss, 1967; Parkhe, 1993; Strauss and Corbin, 1990; Yin, 1984). In theoretical sampling, each case must be carefully selected for purposes of either literal replication (predicting results similar to the preceding cases) or theoretical replication (predicting contrary results but for predictable reasons). Note that an *a priori* set of selection criteria is not required by, and in fact is contrary to the logic of, theoretical sampling; yet, for a pilot study, as we have presented above, it seems necessary to erect a few signposts that can guide initial case selection.

In accordance with the exploratory nature of this research, sampling, analysis and theory-building are interwoven processes. Data collection and parallel data analysis feed into an emergent theory which in turn orients further efforts at data collection. This process implies constant comparisons between cases that have already been analysed and those yet to have information collected about them, making sure that variance in the dependent variable, the *sine qua non* of all comparative studies, will be present. The emergent theory controls the process of data collection, hence the name 'theoretical sampling'. Its dominant logic, as in experimental designs, is replication, rather than 'sampling' as in survey work, or variance analysis in general.

In this research, we could only approximate this ideal procedure of selecting cases one by one as the emergent theory suggests. On the basis of the emergent theory derived from the two pilot cases, six further cases were selected. First, possible case subjects were selected from an updated version of the aforementioned list of privatised enterprises. Second, a shortlist of ten firms was prepared on the basis of information gathered from our own vast archive of press-clippings. This information was used to judge if certain firms were acceptable by the criteria presented in table 13. Firms on which cases had already been prepared by or on behalf of the Budapest-based Institute for Privatisation Studies (a semi-independent research organisation often commissioned by the SPA) were also excluded, since we believed that following such an earlier research inquiry our investigation might be unwelcome, if not rejected altogether. Finally, this shortlist was finalised, and reduced to six firms, making use of external advice regarding whether necessary variance between shortlisted cases could be expected.

One of the six firms chosen had to be dropped when, following our choice, the firm became the beneficiary of a state rescue package and its privatisation was postponed. On another firm, we prepared a case study in Hungarian (as in all but two other cases, for the purpose of communicating with the managements), but it then had to be dropped for several reasons, including alleged procedural mistakes in the privatisation process. We believed that a research inquiry could be mistaken by possible informants as a covert element of an investigation, thereby reducing the possibility of preparing a true and fair account of the events. In addition, and more importantly, many of the apparent features of this firm's privatisation process seemed to simply 'imitate' characteristics known from other cases, without adding to the emergent theory, and implying that 'conceptual saturation' (Strauss and Corbin, 1990) may have been reached. The number of case studies was kept relatively low not only because 'conceptual saturation' seemed to emerge but also because an optimal trade-off between width and depth was sought. After the pilot studies revealed a quite different story from what had been expected, a choice was made in favour of depth; we considered it very important to gain as detailed and complete a picture as possible of what was actually going on in the privatisation processes.

In sum, the first two pilot cases were followed by four more cases, selected not one by one but at about the same time. This approach was also made necessary by uncertainties surrounding our access opportunities which had been laboriously built up.

Throughout this research, issues of access, confidentiality, and anonymity required careful attention. Once the cases had been selected, we employed a range of tactics to enlist support from all possible informants, interviewees and document-keepers alike. These tactics, used in combination as some of them opened the way to the use of others, included the following:

- letter of reference from Ph.D. supervisor
- letter of reference from a publisher with an attached copy of the manuscript of the author's paper on privatisation (Antal-Mokos, 1994)
- letter of recommendation from a former SPA executive
- reference to faculty membership in Hungary
- presentation of our research
- letters commissioning research on behalf of a Hungarian research institute
- assurance of confidentiality and anonymity
- contacts with former college friends
- assumed trust based on informant's acquaintance with the author's relative.

Table 14. *Tactics used for disguising case subjects*

Tactic	Used for disguising
Aggregation	Industries
Changing nationality	Foreign organisations and persons
Using expressive pseudonyms	Organisations (firms and institutions)
Combining two real players in one role (e.g. two persons combined in one role of 'a Responsible Politician') Unifying gender (male for all players)	Persons
Rounding, or providing only approximate range of amount Expressing a value in relation to another value Multiplying values by a constant	Quantitative data
Lack of specification	Exact date of occurrence of events

All those involved were aware of, and agreed to, the final utilisation of the cases for the purposes of this research, while requiring due observation of confidentiality and anonymity. Therefore, we followed a protocol to disguise the organisations and persons appearing in the case studies, as summarised in table 14.

Information for the cases were collected from three main types of source: documents, interviews, and press reports. Documents perused were of great variety and quantity. Occasionally, more important parts of documents were not noted but read aloud and recorded for making a transcript in the evenings. This 'repetitive noting technique' helped us increase sensitivity to relevant issues. In order to keep track of the vast number of documents on each case (a 0.5 to 2.5 metre stack of paper per firm), and to organise our notes and transcripts, a simple filing method was developed around subjects, dates, and sources. To indicate the range of documents studied, examples are listed below:

- Documents relating to investment tenders: Information Memorandum, call for bids announcements, bids submitted, minutes taken at meetings of tender evaluation committees
- Documents relating to executive appointments: job tender announcements, applications, appointments, bonus descriptions, evaluations

- Advisors' applications, reports, analyses, and sales recommendations
- Briefs and proposals, internal memoranda, minutes, and resolutions
- Share sale contracts, syndicate agreements
- Company Deed of Foundation, Articles of Association
- Proposals from management to Enterprise Council, minutes of Enterprise Council meetings, documents prepared for, and minutes taken on, company board meetings and shareholders' meetings
- Financial reports, organigrams, plans, budgets, and other company documents
- Correspondence between parties involved in the process of privatisation (state agents, management, union, consultant, potential investor, lawyers, party politicians, ministers and state secretaries, banks, local government, taxation office, etc.).

The documents constituted a very wide range of sources of information. We often had the opportunity to peruse different draft versions of the same document which permitted the tracking of changes in viewpoints and positions. We could also compare representations of the same event by different people. Finally, the marginal notes and remarks made on these documents while they were being circulated proved to be a useful source of information, too, for checking and cross-checking meticulously every piece of evidence before making an inference.

The next main source of information was the interviews conducted with state agents, owners, executives and in some cases other employees of the firms concerned, and other key informants such as consultants involved in privatisation. Interviews were arranged after the author had obtained familiarity with the cases from press reports and documents. Interviews usually started with some initial time spent building trust, communicating interest in the firm and commitment to a thorough and impartial case study for research purposes, and giving interviewees an assurance of confidentiality. The interviews followed a semi-structured format, suitable for interviewing the elite (Marshall and Rossman, 1989: 94). For each interviewee, a contact summary sheet (see Miles and Huberman, 1994: 51–3) was developed. It included a 'tailor-made' list of issues, taken from a general list of questions, and modified according to the interviewee's position, the known or presumed part he or she had played in the privatisation process, and occasionally, what had been said by other interviewees in preceding discussions. This list was used in a free manner as unexpected but interesting details arose.

In the case of some 'critical interviews', conducted with executives who were known to have played an important part in the events, interviewees were asked, after some initial time for building trust, about the use of a tape-recorder, which was purposely kept in sight from the beginning.

The more ambiguous issues were revealed, typically in the course of document analysis, and the more details required further clarification, the more interviews were conducted in relation to a particular case. Furthermore, in the cases that we considered exemplary in the light of the emergent theory ('prototypical' cases in the sense that they appeared to fit neatly to the whole emerging theoretical framework), attempts were made to hold discussions with a diverse range of interviewees. A smaller set of interviews was deemed sufficient in other cases, which served the purpose of concept development, or validating a particular relationship, rather than corroborating the whole framework. In some cases, self-appointed interviewees who wanted to have their opinion heard were also included with the sole purpose of signalling the researcher's genuine commitment to a thorough understanding of local details. Thus, at two firms the number of interviewees reached more than a dozen, including owners, executives, middle managers in headquarters, plant managers, union leaders, ESOP trustees, and a driver (the latter chosen deliberately as the best source of information on the frequency and destination of executives' travel). However, in two other cases that appeared unambiguous on the basis of available documents, only a few key informants were interviewed, mainly for the purpose of validating a draft case study. Finally, interviews were also a matter of personal collaboration with the researcher.

The third source of information was a systematically collected set of press reports on the firms involved and their industries. Some of the cases received considerable attention and publicity. Press reports were also used to become familiar with the firms before conducting the interviews, and to establish issues that would need special attention or clarification during the discussions. This type of source included:

- articles and reports available in English in *The Financial Times* and via *Reuters News Service*
- the complete series of *Privinfo*, a Hungarian bi-weekly specialising in privatisation, officially supported by the SPA
- press-clippings of thousands of articles related to privatisation that had appeared since 1989 in *HVG* and *Figyelő* (two economic weeklies) and in three of the Hungarian dailies with national coverage
- a selection of articles from local newspapers and company newsletters.

Based on these sources of information, detailed chronological case histories were prepared. Subsequent analysis was carried out at two levels: within each case, and across all the cases.

For intra-case analysis, various displays and networks were used (Miles and Huberman, 1994).

For cross-case analysis, we followed the underlying logic of pattern-matching that compares an empirically based pattern with a predicted one on the basis of different aspects of the phenomenon concerned (Campbell, 1966; Parkhe, 1993; Strauss and Corbin, 1990; Yin, 1984). While promising attempts have been made recently to develop a formal protocol for quantitative pattern-matching (Larsson, 1993; Levie, 1995; Vagneur, 1995), this route was not taken in this research. Conclusions were instead corroborated by matching patterns observed in the cases with our theoretical propositions in a qualitative way. In this sense, this research remains a pure qualitative study in that it does not employ quantitative methods of data analysis, although it makes use of quantitative data.

Political events in Hungary, 1987–94

1987

January   Miklós Németh is appointed Head of the Economic Policy Department of the Central Committee of the Hungarian Socialist Workers' Party (HSWP, the communist party).

June   Miklós Németh is elected as a member, and Secretary, of HSWP Central Committee.

Károly Grósz is elected Prime Minister.

July   Financial institutions, the Chamber of Commerce and the Ministry of Finance prepare a joint plan to develop a securities market.

1988

January   Hungarian citizens are allowed to obtain a 'world passport' and to travel freely to any country without further permission.

Personal Income Tax and (a VAT-like) General Tax on Turnover are introduced.

May   The first union that is independent of the HSWP-related National Association of Unions is established.

Károly Grósz, Prime Minister, is elected General Secretary of HSWP; János Kádár takes the newly created position of President; Miklós Németh, Rezső Nyers, and Imre Pozsgay are elected members of the Political Committee.

The Association of Young Democrats is established.

June   A demonstration is held on the anniversary of the execution of Imre Nagy, Prime Minister of Hungary during the revolution in 1956; the police interfere.

July   Imre Pozsgay is appointed Minister of State.

September   After a year of existence as a loosely organised group of intellectuals, the Hungarian Democratic Forum (HDF), as an independent social organisation, is established; later turned into a formal political party.

October A number of large state-owned enterprises are transformed into companies on the basis of loopholes in existing legislation.

Independent representatives (Members of Parliament who do not belong to any party, at this time 24 per cent of all MPs) wish to create a parliamentary faction.

November On 7 November, a paid holiday for the anniversary of the Soviet communist revolution of 1917, about 100,000 Hungarians travel to Austria for one day only and spend 0.5 billion schillings on goods ranging from refrigerators to perfume.

Association of Free Democrats is established.

Miklós Németh replaces Károly Grósz as Prime Minister; Rezső Nyers is appointed Minister of State; the introduction of a 'limited' multi-party system (that would grant 51 per cent of the seats to the HSWP while the rest would be contested) is proposed at a sitting of the House.

1989

January The Company Act comes into force.

Imre Pozsgay openly judges 1956 (until now officially considered a counter-revolution) a 'people's rising'; two weeks later the HSWP's Central Committee deems Pozsgay's public announcement premature and unfortunate.

Withdrawal of some Soviet armed forces is announced (the agreement between Hungary and the Soviet Union on total withdrawal of Soviet troops is to be signed in March 1990).

February The HSWP's Central Committee announces that 'political pluralism can be realised in a multi-party system' (which was earlier accepted only as a 'solution possible in principle').

A wave of resignations, started in autumn 1988 and caused by 'motions of no confidence', reaches its peak with the resignation of the Chairman of the House.

March Eight organisations establish the Opposition Round Table.

April A new HSWP Political Committee is elected, only two of the earlier members remaining.

May On the basis of a decision made by the Political Committee in February, the removal of the so-called Iron Curtain between Austria and Hungary started.

49.65 per cent of the shares in Tungsram Rt. are sold for US$ 100 million to a Western bank consortium led by Girozentrale; the agreement stipulates that the shares can only be resold after three years; Hungarian Credit Bank buys back the shares in November and sells 50 per cent + 1 share to General Electric for US$ 150 million; the price difference was evenly split between the two banks.

János Kádár, Communist leader since 1957, is relieved of his position as President with reference to a report on his health.

The HSWP's 'Reform Circles' demand that the party change its name and introduce substantial reforms.

The Transformation Act is passed.

June   Following two months of discussions behind the scenes, political negotiations start among the HSWP, the Opposition Round Table and seven other social organisations.

Imre Nagy (with many others) is reburied on the day he was executed three decades earlier; some 300,000 people are present.

A four-strong HSWP Presidium, including Grósz, Németh, Pozsgay, and Nyers, is established.

July   János Kádár dies; on the day that the formal legal process of the political rehabilitation of Imre Nagy and his associates ends, the Supreme Court declares their earlier sentences unlawful.

A scandal is prompted by the HSWP's attempt to create companies and transfer properties currently in its use to these companies.

The HDF gets all four seats in Parliament in by-elections.

September   The Hungarian government opens the western border to East Germans; in the following five weeks about 110,000 East Germans move to West Germany via Hungary.

The HSWP and the Opposition (except the Free Democrats and the Young Democrats) sign an agreement on the political transformation.

October   The Hungarian Socialist Party is established as a 'socialist, social democratic' successor of the HSWP; later a new, communist, HSWP is established.

The Hungarian Republic is proclaimed (without 'People's' in its name).

December   The Council of Ministers (Cabinet) approves the bills on the protection of state assets, and on the establishment of a

State Property Fund (later to be established as the State Property Agency).

1990

March   First round of general elections (65 per cent of the electorate vote).

April   Second round of general elections (45 per cent of the electorate vote); of 386 seats in Parliament, Hungarian Democratic Forum has 165, Alliance of Free Democrats 94, Smallholders' Party 44, Hungarian Socialist Party 33, Association of Young Democrats 22, Christian Democrats 21.
            Pact between HDF and Alliance of Free Democrats is signed, allowing smoother operation of the legislature.

May   The Government, led by Miklós Németh, submits its resignation and remains as 'interim'.
            József Antall is elected Prime Minister; presents the Programme of National Renewal; the new Cabinet is introduced.

September   First round of local elections (with the participation of 40 per cent of the electorate).

October   Second round of local elections (33 per cent turnout); independent candidates (many of whom were previous chairpersons of former Soviet-type local councils) achieve overwhelming victory; in larger towns and at the county level, the Alliance of Free Democrats wins most seats.
            Popularity of coalition government (HDF in particular) begins to fall and decreases throughout the Government's term.
            'Taxi blockade': taxi-drivers, supported by the Alliance of Free Democrats, paralyse traffic throughout the country for three days, protesting against an increase in the price of petrol; hospitalised Prime Minister substituted by Minister of Home Affairs.

November   Hungary is first Eastern European member of European Council.

1991

January   Government increases centrally set prices (e.g. milk); by the end of the year, inflation rate approaches 40 per cent.

February   Visegrad Countries sign agreement on co-operation while competing to join 'Europe'.

March	Four year long 'Kupa-programme', named after Finance Minister, on creating conditions of a social market economy.
April	By-elections reduce number of HDF MPs; several MPs change faction, HDF loses seats.
May	New law on accounting passes.
	Law defines division of authority between central government and municipalities; Government is slow to devolve state-owned assets; financial position of several municipalities deteriorates.
June	Last Soviet soldier leaves Hungary; debate between Budapest and Moscow on environmental damage etc.
	First Act on Compensation (as opposed to full in-kind restitution) passes, after one-year parliamentary debate and three resolutions by the Supreme Court; other Acts to follow.
September	Government's new privatisation strategy: state ownership to be reduced to under 50 per cent by 1994; foreign ownership to be raised from 3 per cent to 20–30 per cent, firms to be retained in state ownership in the long run will be managed by new organisation (later to be established as State Asset Management Co.); Government is slow to specify firms to belong to SAMCo.
	'Self-privatisation' (later to be called 'simplified privatisation') starts.
	Debate between President of the Republic and Government on issues of authority becomes tense; Supreme Court is to issue judgements.
October	Government's plan for accelerating 'pre-privatisation'.
November	New party leader of Alliance of Free Democrats; this party's frequently changing political course is criticised; faction leader resigns (to become party leader a year later).
	President of National Bank fired by Prime Minister because of his signing the Democratic Charter (a political declaration).
December	Following referendum, Parliament approves Act on hosting World's Fair in Budapest in 1996, after much debate and Vienna's rejection of joint hosting, and Government's withdrawal.
	National convention of HDF: the 'national' wing seems to gain strength relative to the 'liberal' wing.

1992

January   Tamás Szabó appointed as Minister without Portfolio in charge of privatisation; SPA has new Chairman of Board.
              New Act on bankruptcy.
              The media war intensifies and goes on throughout the Government's term.

February   Authority debate continues: disagreement between President and ministers on certain issues.
              World's Fair, to be hosted in Budapest with full government guarantee, is registered by International Expo Office (BIE). (New government will withdraw from hosting World's Fair in November 1994.)
              Factions do further 'reshuffling': Smallholders' Party leader Torgyán, a member of the coalition, departed from his party's faction with nine supporters and moved to Opposition, while those who remained loyal to Government were to be expelled from the party; others changed faction; by the end of the year, Government has twenty-four seats more than absolute majority.

March   Interest rate on Existence Loan decreased, and ceiling removed.

May   By-elections bring two seats to Opposition, against a minister and a state secretary.

June   Rival smallholders' parties.
              Government approves GAM Programme on economic development, prepared by Economic Strategy Group led by Tamás Szabó, a rival to the Kupa Programme; the second Kupa Programme followed in September.

August   István Csurka's writing is regarded as nationalistic and ultra right-wing, Nazist by some; Prime Minister distances himself from Csurka in early September.

October   With the removal of the statues of Marx and Engels, no more monuments erected under the communist regime remain on public sites in Budapest.
              Some skinheads with fascist symbols disturb anniversary of 1956 revolution; President does not deliver his speech.

November   Association of Young Democrats removes age limit of thirty-five years for prospective party members; they regard the Democratic Charter as a 'Trojan horse' to bring co-operation between Socialists and Free Democrats.

December   Compensation notes are traded on the Stock Exchange.
              Increasing conflicts within HDF; Prime Minister strengthens

his position against Csurka's wing by restructuring party leadership.

1993

January
Presidents of the radio and television, whose dismissal had been requested by the Prime Minister but rejected by the President for eight months, resign.

Prime Minister openly attacked by Csurka at the HDF national convention; Prime Minister manages to resist, Csurka becomes member of Presidium again; he will be expelled from the faction, then from the party, later in 1993.

February
Government reshuffled, six new ministers, including Finance, and Industry and Trade; changes at state secretary level too.

March
Hungary becomes associated member of EFTA.

May
MPs continue changing factions; Csurka's supporters establish independent group within HDF faction, then leave HDF and establish independent faction; the coalition (HDF, Christian Democrats, remaining Smallholders) has only two more seats than an overall majority; in November, three senior MPs leave Young Democrats but return their mandates before choosing their new party, the Free Democrats (one of them later becomes a minister after the 1994 election).

June
Chairman and CEO of SAMCo submits his resignation.

July
Revised state budget approved by Parliament; deficit more than originally planned, reaching 6.5 per cent of GDP.

August
Lower rate of ÁFA (VAT) increased from 6 per cent to 10 per cent, household energy becomes subject to 10 per cent ÁFA, as requested by IMF to adjust Hungarian taxation to Western models, while higher ÁFA rate remains at 25 per cent because its lowering was objected to by the Government.

Preliminary figures show dramatic decrease in exports; foreign trade deficit reaches US$ 2.7 billion.

September
SPA managing director offers his resignation because of payment to Csurka's firm for privatisation propaganda film never prepared; offer rejected by minister.

November
First national convention of Party of Hungarian Justice and Life elects Csurka as co-president.

December
Bank consolidation programme continues, equity of eight

commercial banks raised by some HUF 120 billion (US$ 1.2 billion) altogether.

A well-known economist and public writer is condemned by the court, following Prime Minister's action, after he stated that the Hungarian public administration was corrupt and ministers could be bought.

Prime Minister dies.

1994

January   President and CEO of SAMCo resigns; position is taken over by former SPA managing director (further changes in these positions after the elections in May).

February   Debt consolidation programme for indebted firms with sound business plans launched with slow progress; consolidation of fourteen large firms continues outside of the programme.

Hungary joins NATO's Partnership for Peace.

New leaders of HDF elected; campaign programme anticipates winning the election.

April   Hungary officially requests European Union membership.

Last sitting of Parliament before elections: 219 new Acts, 213 modifications in four years, 23,000 voting procedures.

May   Between two rounds of elections, Alliance of Free Democrats rejects the possibility of a HSP–Alliance of Free Democrats coalition if Hungarian Socialist Party proposes Gyula Horn as Prime Minister.

General election brings Socialist Party's overwhelming victory: 209 seats of 386 total (54 per cent); Young Democrats (20 seats) and HDF (38 seats) are considered greatest losers.

Coalition agreement between HSP and Alliance of Free Democrats signed.

July   New government introduced by Gyula Horn, Prime Minister.

September   Planned date of submission of new privatisation law to Parliament; coalition parties' debate begins.

November   Government submits new privatisation law, placing emphasis on privatisation for cash; passed with several modifications compared to original plans only in May 1995 following debates between senior and junior parties of the coalition; altogether, 1995 is a successful year for privatisation in terms of proceeds to the state due to sale of large utilities. 1996 will witness more sales, scandals, dismissal of the whole board of the State Privatisation and Asset Management Co. (established earlier by merging SPA and SAMCo), and the resignation of the Privatisation Minister.

References

Abbott, A. 1990. A primer on sequence methods. *Organization Science*, 1: 375–92.

Aharoni, Y. 1981. Performance evaluation of state-owned enterprises: a process perspective. *Management Science*, 27: 1340–7.

Allison, G. T. 1971. *Essence of Decision*. Boston, MA: Little, Brown & Co.

Antal, I. (ed.) 1989. *Gazdasagi társaságok gyakorlatából – esettanulmányok, szemelvények 1–2. kötet* [Company practice – cases, excerpts, vols. 1–2]. Course notes, Management Development Centre, Budapest University of Economic Sciences. Mimeo.

Antal, L. 1985. *Gazdaságirányítási és pénzügyi rendszerünk a reform útján* [Our system of economic management and finance on the way of reform]. Budapest: Közgazdasági és Jogi Könyvkiadó.

Antal-Mokos, Z. 1990. A stratégia tartalma, kialakulásának folyamata és a szervezeti struktúra [Strategy content, process, and organisational structure]. *Vezetéstudomány*, 21(2): 5–14.

1994. A privatizáció hatása a vállalati stratégiákra átmeneti gazdaságban – egy folyamat-megközelítés [The effect of privatisation on organisational strategy in a transitional economy – a process-view]. *Vezetéstudomány*, 25(8): 8–21.

Arogyaswamy, K., V. L. Barker III, and M. Yasai-Ardekani 1995. Firm turn-arounds: an integrative two-stage model. *Journal of Management Studies,* 32: 493–525.

Aylen, J. 1988. Privatisation of the British Steel Corporation. *Fiscal Studies*, 9(3):1–25.

Batt, J. 1994. Political dimensions of privatization in Eastern Europe. In S. Estrin (ed.), *Privatization in Central and Eastern Europe*, London: Longman.

Birnbaum, P. H. 1985. Political strategies of regulated organizations as functions of contest and fear. *Strategic Management Journal*, 6: 135–50.

Bishop, M. and J. Kay 1988. *Does Privatization Work? Lessons from the UK.* London: Centre for Business Strategy, London Business School.

Boone, T. S. 1994. Positive and negative aspects of Hungary's privatization programme. In H. Smit and V. Pechota (eds.), *Privatization in Eastern Europe: Legal, Economic and Social Aspects.* Irvington-on-Hudson, NY: Transnational Juris Publications, Inc. and Dordrecht: Martinus Nijhoff.

Bös, D. 1991. *Privatization: A Theoretical Treatment.* Oxford: Clarendon Press.

Bourdieu, P. 1978. *A társadalmi egyenlőtlenségek újratermelődése* [The reproduction of social inequality]. Budapest: Gondolat.

Boycko, M., A. Schleifer, and R. W. Wishny 1994. Voucher privatization. *Journal of Financial Economics*, 35 (2): 249–266.

1996. A theory of privatisation. *Economic Journal*, 106 (435): 309–319.

Brabant, J. M. van 1992. *Privatizing Eastern Europe: The Role of Markets and Ownership in the Transition.* Dordrecht: Kluwer Academic Publishers.

Branyiczki, I., Gy. Bakacsi, and J. L. Pearce 1992. The back door: spontaneous privatization in Hungary. *Annals of Public and Cooperative Economics*, 63: 303–16.

Brunnen, D. J. 1989. Developing an enterprise culture at British Telecom. *Long Range Planning*, 22(2): 27–36.

Burgelman, R. A. 1983a. A model of interaction of strategic behavior, corporate context, and the concept of strategy. *Academy of Management Review*, 8: 61–70.

1983b. Corporate entrepreneurship and strategic management: insights from a process study. *Management Science*, 29: 1349–64.

1991. Interorganizational ecology of strategy making and organizational adaptation: theory and field research. *Organization Science*, 2: 239–62.

Campbell, D. T. 1966. Pattern matching as an essential in distal knowing. In K. R. Hammond (ed.), *The Psychology of Egon Brunswik.* New York: Holt, Rinehart & Winston.

Canning, A. and P. Hare 1994. The privatization process: economic and political aspects of the Hungarian approach. In S. Estrin (ed.), *Privatization in Central and Eastern Europe.* London: Longman.

Carroll, G. R., J. Goodstein, and A. Gyenes 1988. Organizations and the state: effects of the institutional environment on agricultural cooperatives in Hungary. *Administrative Science Quarterly*, 33: 233–56.

Chakravarthy, B. S. 1982. Adaptation: a promising metaphor for strategic management. *Academy of Management Review*, 7: 35–44.

Child, J. 1972. Organizational structure, environment and performance: the role of strategic choice. *Sociology*, 6: 1–22.

Cook, P. and C. Kirkpatrick (eds.) 1988. *Privatisation in Less Developed Countries.* New York: Harvester Wheatsheaf.

Crane, K. 1991. Institutional legacies and the economic, social, and political environment for transition in Hungary and Poland. *American Economic Review* (AEA Proceedings and Papers), 81: 318–33.

Csanádi, M. 1987. A döntési mechanizmus szerkezetéről [On the structure of the decision-making mechanism]. *Társadalomkutatás*, 4(1): 5–27.

1991. *Mely vállalatok és miért?* [Which enterprises and why?]. Budapest: Pénzügykutató Rt.

Csányi, V. 1989. *Evolutionary Systems and Society: A General Theory of Life, Mind, and Culture.* London: Duke University Press.

Csillag, I. 1994. A közel ülők, a közelebb ülők és a mieink [Those who sit close, those who sit closer, and those of our ranks]. *Figyelő*, 21 July, reprinted in Gazdaság, 27(2): 116–19.

Czakó, Á. and E. Sík 1995. A hálózati tőke szerepe Magyarországon a rendszer-váltás előtt és után [The role of network capital in Hungary before and after the system change]. *2000*, 7(2): 3–12.

DiMaggio, P. J. and W. W. Powell 1983. The iron cage revisited: institutional isomorphism and collective rationality in organizational fields. *American Sociological Review*, 48: 147–160.

Dyer, W. G., Jr., A. L. Wilkins, and K. M. Eisenhardt 1991. Better stories, not better constructs, to generate better theory: a rejoinder to Eisenhardt 'Better stories and better constructs: the case for rigor and comparative analysis'. *Academy of Management Review*, 16: 613–27.

Earle, J. S., R. Frydman, and A. Rapaczynski 1993. Introduction. Privatization policies in Eastern Europe: diverse routes to a market economy. In J. S. Earle, R. Frydman, and A. Rapaczynski (eds.), *Privatization in the Transition to a Market Economy: Studies of Preconditions and Policies in Eastern Europe*. London: Pinter, in association with the Central European University.

Earle, J. S., R. Frydman, A. Rapaczynski, and J. Turkewitz (with contributions). 1994. *Small Privatisation: The Transformation of Retail trade and Consumer Services in the Czech Republic, Hungary and Poland*. CEU Privatization Reports, vol. III. Budapest: Central European University Press.

Easterby-Smith, M., R. Thorpe, and A. Lowe 1991. *Management Research: An Introduction*. London: Sage.

Eisenhardt, K. M. 1989a. Agency theory: an assessment and review. *Academy of Management Review*, 14: 57-74.

1989b. Building theories from case study research. *Academy of Management Review*, 14: 532–50.

Eisenhardt, K. M. and L. J. Bourgeois III 1988. Politics of strategic decision making in high-velocity environments: toward a midrange theory. *Academy of Management Journal*, 31: 737–70.

Eisenhardt, K. M. and M. J. Zbaracki 1992. Strategic decision making. *Strategic Management Journal*, 13 (special issue, Winter): 17–37.

Estrin, S. 1991. Privatization in Central and Eastern Europe: What lessons can be learnt for Western experience. *Annals of Public and Cooperative Economics*, 62: 159–82.

1994. Economic transition and privatization: the issues. In S. Estrin (ed.), *Privatization in Central and Eastern Europe*. London: Longman.

Estrin, S., A. Gelb, and I. J. Singh 1991. *Socialist enterprises in transition: a framework for case studies*. Draft manuscript, London Business School, 19 December.

Estrin, S. and V. Pérotin 1991. Does ownership always matter? *International Journal of Industrial Organization*, 9: 55–72.

Fama, E. F. 1980. Agency problems and the theory of the firm. *Journal of Political Economy*, 88: 288–307.

Fama, E. F. and M. C. Jensen 1983. Separation of ownership and control. *Journal of Law and Economics*, 26: 301–26.

Frydman, R., A. Rapaczynski, J. S. Earle *et al.* 1993. *The Privatization Process in Central Europe.* CEU Privatization Reports, vol. I. Budapest: Central European University Press.

Galbraith, C. and D. Schendel 1983. An empirical analysis of strategy types. *Academy of Management Journal*, 26: 153–173.

Gatsios, K. 1992. *Privatization in Hungary: Past, Present and Future.* Discussion Paper no. 642. London: Centre for Economic Policy Research.

Gill, J. and P. Johnson 1991. *Research Methods for Managers.* London: Paul Chapman Publishing.

Glaser, B. G. and A. L. Strauss 1967. *The Discovery of Grounded Theory: Strategies for Qualitative Research.* New York: Aldine de Gruyter.

Glueck, W. F. 1972. *Business Policy: Strategy Formation and Management Action.* New York: McGraw-Hill.

Granovetter, M. 1985. Economic action and social structure: the problem of embeddedness. *American Journal of Sociology*, 91: 481–510.

Hafsi, T. and H. Thomas 1986. Understanding strategic decision process in state-owned enterprises. In J. McGee and H. Thomas (eds.), *Strategic Management Research.* Chichester: Wiley.

Hambrick, D. C. 1983a. An empirical typology of mature industrial product environments. *Academy of Management Journal*, 26: 213–30.

1983b. High profit strategies in mature capital goods industries: a contingency approach. *Academy of Management Journal*, 26: 687–707.

Hambrick, D. C. and S. M. Schecter 1983. Turnaround strategies for mature industrial-product business units. *Academy of Management Journal*, 26: 231–48.

Hammer, R. M., H. H. Hinterhuber, and J. Lorenz 1989. Privatization: a cure for all ills? *Long Range Planning*, 22(6): 19–28.

Hannan, M. T. and J. Freeman 1984. Structural inertia and organizational change. *American Sociological Review*, 49: 149–64.

Hare, P. 1991. Hungary: in transition to a market economy. *Journal of Economic Perspectives*, 5(4): 195–201.

Haskel, J. and S. Szymanski 1990. *A bargaining theory of privatisation.* Working Paper no. 91, Centre for Business Strategy, London Business School.

Hemming, R. and A. M. Mansoor 1988. *Privatization and Public Enterprises.* Occasional Paper no. 56. Washington, DC: International Monetary Fund.

Hirsch, P. M., R. Friedman, and M. P. Koza 1990. Collaboration or paradigm shift?: Caveat emptor and the risk of romance with economic models for strategy and policy research. *Organization Science*, 1: 87–97.

Hofer, C. W. 1975. Toward a contingency theory of business strategy. *Academy of Management Journal*, 18: 784–810.

1980. Turnaround strategies. *Journal of Business Strategy*, 1(1): 19–31.

Hrebiniak, L. G. and W. F. Joyce 1985. Organizational adaptation: strategic choice and environmental determinism. *Administrative Science Quarterly*, 30: 336–49.

Jarrell, G. A., J. A. Brickley, and J. M. Netter 1988. The market for corporate control: the empirical evidence since 1980. *Journal of Economic Perspectives,* 2(1): 49–68.

Jensen, M. C. and W. H. Meckling 1976. Theory of the firm: managerial behavior, agency costs and ownership structure. *Journal of Financial Economics,* 3: 305–60.

Jensen, M. C. and R. S. Ruback 1983. The market for corporate control: the scientific evidence. *Journal of Financial Economics,* 11: 5–50.

King, Lord, of Wartnaby 1987. Lessons of privatization. *Long Range Planning,* 20(6): 18–22.

Kornai, J. 1957. *A gazdasági vezetés túlzott központosítása* [The over-centralisation of economic administration]. Budapest: Közgazdasági és Jogi Könyvkiadó.

　1980. *A hiány.* Budapest: Közgazdasági és Jogi Könyvkiadó. English edition. *Economics of Shortage.* Amsterdam: North-Holland (1980).

　1986. The Hungarian reform process: visions, hopes, and reality. *Journal of Economic Literature,* 24: 1687–737.

　1990a. The affinity between ownership forms and co-ordination mechanisms: the common experience of reform in socialist countries. *Journal of Economic Perspectives,* 4(3): 131–147.

　1990b. *The Road to a Free Economy: Shifting from a Socialist System: The Example of Hungary.* New York: W.W. Norton.

　1992. *The Socialist System: The Political Economy of Communism.* Oxford: Clarendon Press.

Kornai, J. and Á. Matits 1990. The bureaucratic redistribution of the firm's profits. In J. Kornai (ed.) *Vision and Reality, Market and State: New Studies on the Socialist Economy and Society.* Hemel Hempstead: Harvester Wheatsheaf. Hungarian edition of the full study was published in 1987, Budapest: Corvina.

Kovács, S. 1988. Előírni vagy leírni? [To prescribe or to describe?]. *Közgazdasági Szemle,* 35: 1281–92.

Larsson, R. 1993. Case survey methodology: quantitative analysis of patterns across case studies. *Academy of Management Journal,* 36: 1515–46.

Leonard-Barton, D. 1990. A dual methodology for case studies: synergistic use of a longitudinal single site with replicated multiple sites. *Organization Science,* 1: 248–66.

Levie, J. 1993. *The effect of government nurturing policies on early corporate growth: a multi-lensed approach to hypothesis generation.* Working paper presented at the British Academy of Management Annual Conference, Milton Keynes, September.

　1995. *The effect of government nurturing policies on early corporate growth in Denmark, Ireland and Scotland, 1973–1987.* Unpublished Ph.D. thesis, London Business School, University of London.

Levinthal, D. A. 1991. Organizational adaptation and environmental selection: interrelated processes of change. *Organization Science,* 2: 140–5.

Levy, B. 1987. A theory of public enterprise behavior. *Journal of Economic Behavior and Organization,* 8: 75–96.

Mahoney, J. 1984. What makes a business company ethical? *Business Strategy Review*, 5(4): 1–15.

Markóczy, L. 1989. Erőforrás-függőség és vállalati magatartás [Resource dependence and firm behaviour]. *Közgazdasági Szemle*, 36: 820–9.

Máriás, A., S. Kovács, K. Balaton, E. Tari, and M. Dobák 1981. Kísérlet ipari nagyvállalataink összehasonlító szervezetelemzésére [An attempt of comparative organisational analysis of large industrial enterprises]. *Közgazdasági Szemle*, 28: 838–52.

Marsh, D. 1991. Privatization under Mrs. Thatcher: a review of the literature. *Public Administration*, 69: 459–480.

Marshall, C. and G. B. Rossman 1989. *Designing Qualitative Research*. London: Sage.

Matolcsy, Gy. 1990. Defending the cause of the spontaneous reform of ownership. *Acta Oeconomica*, 42: 1–22.

1991. *Lábadozásunk évei: a magyar privatizáció: trendek, tények, privatizációs példák* [Years of our convalescence: the Hungarian privatisation: trends, facts, privatisation examples]. Budapest: Privatizációs Kutató Intézet.

Mayhew, K. and P. Seabright 1992. Incentives and the management of enterprises in economic transition: capital markets are not enough. *Oxford Review of Economic Policy*, 8(1): 105–29.

McGrath, J. E., J. Martin, and R. A. Kulka 1982. *Judgment Calls in Research* (Studying Organizations: Innovations in Methodology, vol. II). London: Sage.

McKelvey, B. and H. E. Aldrich 1983. Populations, natural selection, and applied organizational science. *Administrative Science Quarterly*, 28: 101–28.

Miles, M. B. and A. M. Huberman 1994. *Qualitative Data Analysis: An Expanded Sourcebook*. London: Sage.

Miles, R. E. and C. C. Snow 1978. *Organizational Strategy, Structure, and Process*. New York: McGraw-Hill.

Miller, D. and P. H. Friesen (in collaboration with Henry Mintzberg) 1984. *Organizations: A Quantum View*. Englewood Cliffs, NJ: Prentice-Hall.

Mintzberg, H. 1978. Patterns in strategy formation. *Management Science*, 24: 934–48.

1979. *The Structuring of Organisations: A Synthesis of the Research*. Englewood Cliffs, NJ: Prentice-Hall.

1983. *Power In and Around Organizations*. Englewood Cliffs, NJ: Prentice-Hall.

Mintzberg, H. and J. Waters 1982. Tracking strategy in an entrepreneurial firm. *Academy of Management Journal*, 25: 465–99.

1985. Of strategies, deliberate and emergent. *Strategic Management Journal*, 6: 257–72.

Mizsei, K. 1993. Hungary: gradualism needs a strategy. In R. Portes (ed.), *Economic Transformation in Central Europe: A Progress Report*. London: Centre for Economic Policy Research and Commission of the European Communities.

Mizsei, K., M. Móra, and Gy. Csáki 1994. Experiences with privatization in

Hungary: the early transition period. In D. A. Rondinelli (ed.), *Privatization and Economic Reform in Central Europe: The Changing Business Climate*. Westpoint, CT: Quorum Books.

Monge, P. R. 1990. Theoretical and analytical issues in studying organizational processes. *Organization Science*, 1: 406–30.

Monks, R. A. G. and N. Minow 1995. *Corporate Governance*. Oxford: Blackwell Business.

Morley, W. B. 1986. The privatization of British Telecom: its impact on management. *Long Range Planning*, 19(6): 124–9.

Murrell, P. 1992. Evolution in economics and in the economic reform of the centrally planned economies. In C. Clague and G. C. Rausser (eds.), *The Emergence of Market Economies in Eastern Europe*. Oxford: Basil Blackwell.

Nilakant, V. and H. Rao 1994. Agency theory and uncertainty in organization: an evaluation. *Organization Studies*, 15: 649–72.

Parkhe, A. 1993. 'Messy' research, methodological predispositions, and theory development in international joint ventures. *Academy of Management Review*, 18: 227–68.

Pennings, J. M. 1992. Structural contingency theory: a reappraisal. *Research in Organizational Behavior*, 14: 267–309.

Pettigrew, A. M. 1990. Longitudinal field research on change: theory and practice. *Organization Science*, 1: 267–92.

Pfeffer, J. 1981. *Power in Organizations*. Marshfield, MA: Pitman.

Pfeffer, J. and G. R. Salancik. 1978. *The External Control of Organizations: A Resource Dependence Perspective*. New York: Harper & Row.

Pinkley, R. L., T. L. Griffith, and G. B. Northcraft 1995. 'Fixed Pie' à la mode: information availability, information processing, and the negotiation of suboptimal agreements. *Organizational Behavior and Human Decision Processes*, 62(1): 101–12.

Porter, M. E. 1980. *Competitive Strategy: Techniques for Analyzing Industries and Competitors*. New York: Free Press.

Ramanadham, V. V. 1989. *Privatisation in Developing Countries*. London: Routledge.

Rausser, G. C. and L. K. Simon 1992. The political economy of transition in Eastern Europe: packaging enterprises for privatization. In C. Clague and G. C. Rausser (eds.), *The Emergence of Market Economies in Eastern Europe*. Oxford: Basil Blackwell.

Rees, R. 1988. Inefficiency, public enterprise and privatisation. *European Economic Review*, 32: 422–31.

Rich, P. 1992. The organizational taxonomy: definition and design. *Academy of Management Review*, 17: 758–81.

Robbins, D. K. and J. A. Pearce II 1992. Turnaround: retrenchment and recovery. *Strategic Management Journal*, 13: 287–309.

Sajó, A. 1990. Diffuse rights in search of an agent: a property rights analysis of the firm in the socialist market economy. *International Review of Law and Economics*, 10: 41–59.

Sárközy, T. 1993. *A privatizáció joga Magyarországon (1989–1993).* Budapest: Akadémiai Kiadó. English edition. *The Right of Privatization in Hungary (1989–1993).* Budapest: Akadémiai Kiadó (1994).

Schipke, A. 1994. The political economy of privatization. In A. Schipke and A. M. Taylor (eds.), *The Economics of Transformation: Theory and Practice in the New Market Economies.* Berlin: Springer-Verlag.

Schleifer, A. and R. W. Vishny 1992. *Privatization in Russia: first steps.* Paper presented to conference on *Transition in Eastern Europe,* National Bureau of Economic Research, Cambridge, MA, 26–29 February.

1993. Corruption. *Quarterly Journal of Economics,* 108(3): 599–617.

1994. Politicians and firms. *Quarterly Journal of Economics,* 109(4): 995–1025.

Schoorman, F. D., M. H. Bazerman, and R. S. Atkin 1981. Interlocking directorates: a strategy for reducing environmental uncertainty. *Academy of Management Review,* 6: 243–51.

Slatter, S. S. 1984. *Corporate Recovery: Successful Turnaround Strategies and Their Implementation.* Harmondsworth: Penguin.

Stark, D. 1990. Privatization in Hungary: from plan to market or from plan to clan? *East European Politics and Societies,* 4: 351–92.

Stark, D. 1994a. Új módon összekapcsolódott régi rendszerelemek: Rekombináns tulajdon a kelet-európai kapitalizmusban – I [Old system elements combined in a new way: Recombinant property in East European capitalism, part 1). *Közgazdasági Szemle,* 41: 933–48.

1994b. Új módon összekapcsolódott régi rendszerelemek: Rekombináns tulajdon a kelet-európai kapitalizmusban – II (Old system elements combined in a new way: Recombinant property in East European capitalism, part 2); *Közgazdasági Szemle,* 41: 1053–69.

Stevenson, W. B., J. L. Pearce, and L. W. Porter 1985. The concept of coalition in organization theory and research. *Academy of Management Review,* 10: 256–68.

Stone, R. 1994. *Political aspects of privatisation.* Paper presented at the London Business School CIS-Middle Europe Centre Seminar Series.

Stopford, J. M. and C. Baden-Fuller 1990. Corporate rejuvenation. *Journal of Management Studies,* 27: 399–415.

Strauss, A. and J. Corbin 1990. *Basics of Qualitative Research: Grounded Theory Procedures and Techniques.* London: Sage.

Swann, D. 1988. *The Retreat of the State: Deregulation and Privatisation in the UK and US.* New York: Harvester Wheatsheaf.

Szakadát, L. 1993. Property rights in a socialist economy: the case of Hungary. In J. S. Earle, R. Frydman, and A. Rapaczynski (eds.), *Privatization in the Transition to a Market Economy: Studies of Preconditions and Policies in Eastern Europe.* London: Pinter, in association with the Central European University.

Thiemeyer, T. 1986. Privatization: on the many senses in which this word is used in an international discussion on economic theory. In The privatization of public enterprises: a European debate. *Annals of Public and Cooperative Economics,* Special Issue.

Török, Á. 1992. Egy 'vagyoncsökkentő' vállalat a magyar elektronikai iparban [Asset-stripping firms and their perspectives: a case study from the Hungarian electronics industry]. *Közgazdasági Szemle*, 39: 46–58.

Tsoukas, H. 1994. Socio-economic systems and organizational management: an institutional perspective on the socialist firm. *Organizational Studies*, 15: 21–45.

Urbán, L. 1993. The role and impact of the legislature in Hungary's privatization. In J. S. Earle, R. Frydman, and A. Rapaczynski (eds.), *Privatization in the Transition to a Market Economy: Studies of Preconditions and Policies in Eastern Europe*. London: Pinter, in association with the Central European University.

Vagneur, K. 1995. *Financial performance measurement effects on hierarchical consistency and performance*. Unpublished Ph.D. thesis, London Business School, University of London.

Van de Ven, A. H. and G. P. Huber 1990. Longitudinal field research methods for studying processes of organizational change. *Organization Science*, 1: 213–19.

Vickers, J. and G. Yarrow 1985. *Privatization and the Natural Monopolies*. London: Public Policy Centre.

1988. *Privatization: An Economic Analysis*. Cambridge, MA: MIT Press.

Voszka, É. 1993. Spontaneous privatization in Hungary. In J. S. Earle, R. Frydman, and A. Rapaczynski (eds.). *Privatization in the Transition to a Market Economy: Studies of Preconditions and Policies in Eastern Europe*. London: Pinter, in association with the Central European University.

1995. *Az agyaglábakon álló óriás: Az Állami Vagyonkezelő Részvénytársaság felállítása és működtetése* [Giant on clay legs: The establishment and operations of the State Asset Management Company]. Budapest: Pénzügykutató Rt.

Walsh, J. P. and R. D. Kosnik 1993. Corporate raiders and their disciplinary role in the market for corporate control. *Academy of Management Journal*, 36: 671–700.

Walton, J. 1973. Standardized case comparison: observations on method in comparative sociology. In M. Armer and A. D. Grimshaw (eds.), *Comparative Social Research: Methodological Problems and Strategies*. London: Wiley.

Williamson, O. 1975. *Markets and Hierarchies: Analysis and Antitrust Implications: A Study in the Economics of Internal Organization*. New York: Free Press.

1990. Chester Barnard and the incipient science of organization. In O. Williamson (ed.), *Organization Theory: From Chester Barnard to the Present and Beyond*. Oxford: Oxford University Press.

Winiecki, J. 1992. The political economy of privatization. In H. Siebert (ed.), *Privatization: Symposium in Honor of Herbert Giersch*. Institut für Weltwirtschaft an der Universität Kiel. Tübingen: Mohr.

Yarrow, G. 1989. Does ownership matter? In C. Veljanovski (ed.), *Privatisation and Competition: A Market Prospectus.* London: Institute of Economic Affairs.

Yin, R. K. 1984. *Case Study Research.* Beverly Hills, CA: Sage.

Zajac, E. J. 1988. Interlocking directorates as an organizational strategy: a test of critical assumptions. *Academy of Management Journal*, 31: 428–38.

Zif, J. 1981. Managerial strategic behavior in state-owned enterprises: business and political orientations. *Management Science*, 27: 1326–39.

Press sources in Hungarian:

Privinfo, a bi-weekly published with the support of the State Property Agency.

Heti Világgazdaság and *Figyelő*, economic weeklies.

Magyar Hirlap, *Magyar Nemzet*, and *Népszabadság*, national dailies.

Index

Page ranges in *italics* indicate occurrences in figures or tables.